D0044190

DEFENDING The DECLARATION

DEFENDING *The* DECLARATION

How the Bible and Christianity Influenced
the Writing of the Declaration
of Independence

Gary T. Amos

Wolgemuth & Hyatt, Publishers, Inc.
Brentwood, Tennessee

The mission of Wolgemuth & Hyatt, Publishers, Inc. is to publish and distribute books that lead individuals toward:

- A personal faith in the one true God: Father, Son, and Holy Spirit;

- A lifestyle of practical discipleship; and

- A world view that is consistent with the historic, Christian faith.

Moreover, the company endeavors to accomplish this mission at a reasonable profit and in a manner that glorifies God and serves His Kingdom.

© 1989 by Gary T. Amos

All rights reserved. Published September 1989. First edition.

No part of this publication may be reproduced, stored in a retrieval system, or transmitted in any form by any means, electronic, mechanical, photocopy, recording, or otherwise, without the prior written permission of the publisher, except for brief quotations in critical reviews or articles.

Unless otherwise noted, all Scripture quotations are from the King James Version of the Bible.

Wolgemuth & Hyatt, Publishers, Inc.
1749 Mallory Lane, Suite 110, Brentwood, Tennessee 37027.
Printed in the United States of America.

Library of Congress Cataloging-in-Publication Data

Amos, Gary T.
      Defending the Declaration : how the Bible and Christianity
influenced the writing of the Declaration of Independence / Gary T.
Amos. — 1st ed.
      p. cm.
Includes bibliographical references.
ISBN 0-943497-69-8 : $14.95
      1. United States. Declaration of Independence. 2. United States — Influence. 5. Political science — United States — History — 18th
century. I. Title.
E221.A49 1989
973.3'13 — dc20   89-37599
                                                                                    CIP

To J. Franklin Sexton

Whose teaching awakened me to the Christian world view and to the hand of God in American History.

CONTENTS

ACKNOWLEDGMENTS

THE AUTHOR THANKS Ron Nash, Herbert Schlossberg, Marvin Olasky, Victor Porlier, Wilbert Rosin, Hubert Morkin, Craig Stern, George Grant, Ray Allen, Gary North, and Duggan Flanakin for reading and criticizing the rough draft. Thanks also go to friends and students who encouraged the writing and asked probing questions.

Special thanks go to Joe Kickasola for detailed comments and corrections on the final draft.

Finally, to my wife and children who sacrificed much so that this book could become a reality, I give my deepest love, appreciation, and thanks.

What value this book may have is not due to any genius of my own. I stand on the shoulders of giants. The ideas in it are not mine but those of great men long dead.

INTRODUCTION

HUNDREDS OF BOOKS AND THOUSANDS OF ARTICLES have been written about the Declaration of Independence. Countless people have spent their lives teaching and writing about it. In nearly every book about America's history, the Declaration is conspicuously present. For one person in one lifetime to read all that has been written about it is probably impossible.

One would think that nothing is left to say about the Declaration and how it fits in the grand scheme of American history. It is tied into all we know about the early colonies, the founding fathers, and the birth of the United States as a nation. We learn about it in grammar school, are reminded of it in high school, and celebrate it every year on the Fourth of July.

So why another book? The reason is simply this: much of what we have heard for years about the Declaration of Independence and the American Revolution is wrong. If we were wrong about something that did not matter, I would not have used almost ten years of my life to try to find the answers and four years to do this book. But the meaning of America is at stake. And we all care about that.

Where we take America depends in part on where we think it came from. In a sense we try to live what we believe the American

1

dream to be. It is hard enough to remember the details of your own dream once you awake, but to remember the details of the "American dream" from our forefathers is especially hard. This book is about some of the details of their dream.

Why I Wrote This Book

I care a great deal about America for many reasons. But at one time I did not. A child of the '60s, the drug culture, and the anti-war mood of the nation, I remember being ashamed of America. Converted to Christianity in 1971, I became a pacifist and conscientious objector. But studying the Bible changed my thinking about many things, including pacifism. It soon changed my thinking about America.

I went to college to become a preacher but, after a prayer experience, decided to study both theology and law. I studied Old and New Testament theology, several years of New Testament Greek, Biblical interpretation, and a whole range of other subjects dealing with Christianity and the Bible. I was particularly interested in church history—where the church had obeyed God through the centuries and where it had failed. No longer being anti-American, I was interested as well in the impact of the Bible and Christianity on the history of America.

While I was studying the Bible and theology, I was also studying early American history as part of my prelaw degree. I read book after book in which authors wrote about people, ideas, and events, saying that their ideas were not Christian. Yet, I was learning in my Bible classes and theology studies that some of those very ideas were Christian. By 1977 I was frustrated with the number of Christian ideas that were being traced to non-Christian sources. It was an unsettling experience.

I did not doubt some things then. From numerous history books I learned that John Locke was a deist; that most of the founding fathers were deists; that Jefferson copied Locke when writing the Declaration, so the Declaration was deistic. In short, I learned that America was born a deistic rather than a Christian nation. I knew Perry Miller and certain other historians had misread the Puritans in important ways. But the Puritans came before

1776. I had no reason to doubt that Jefferson and the Revolutionary fathers were deists and that their principles were not Christian.

In 1980 I was asked to do some research that required me to read John Locke (1632–1704). Here was a man who was supposed to be a deist. He was someone who rejected the God of the Bible; who did not believe in Jesus Christ; and who rejected prayer, miracles, and the inspiration and authority of the Scriptures. I found most of Locke's books in the library, sat down, and began to read.

I could not believe my eyes. In page after page, Locke confessed Christ, the Bible, miracles, and many other elements of orthodox Christianity. And it was all very clear. He was not using vague words or hard-to-understand sayings. At first I was angry. I felt like I had been tricked or robbed. I had been told by some of the best and brightest that Locke was a deist who rejected Christianity and the Bible. I had been lied to. And Locke had been lied about.

I had a history degree and had read many books about John Locke. But I had never read Locke's own writings. And everything I had learned about him was wrong. I kept on reading, being careful to note those places where Locke agreed with the Bible, particularly with the writings of the Apostle Paul. I found that as Perry Miller had misread the Puritans because Miller had not read the Apostle Paul in the New Testament, particularly Romans 1 and 2, other historians had misread Locke because they did not know when Locke was following the Apostle Paul, whom Locke often quoted. One cannot understand John Locke without reading Paul, and one cannot understand Paul without a thorough knowledge of the book of Romans in the New Testament.

I made up my mind that I would read the founders for myself to see who else had been misrepresented. That was 1980. By 1984 I had read Jefferson, Madison, Washington, Witherspoon, Adams, Marshall, and a host of others. This was all taking place during an intensive study of the impact of Christianity on the growth and development of European law, particularly the English common law. By 1983 I had found that every key term in the Declaration of Independence had its roots in the Bible, Christian theology, the Western Christian intellectual tradition, medieval Christianity, Christian political theory, and the Christian influence on the six-hundred-year development of the English common law. Knowing it and proving it are two different things. So in 1983, when I made up my mind to do a book on the relationship of the Bible and Christianity to the Declaration of Independence, I began the research leading to this book.

At first, I intended to show how the average person on the street has a seriously wrong view of the American Revolution, the founding fathers, the Declaration of Independence, and how Christianity fit into that whole picture. I also intended to show how historians generally have misunderstood the Declaration in certain ways because most of them are trained historians, not trained theologians or lawyers. Since the Declaration is a legal document of theological significance, one needs to know theology and law as well as history to do justice to the relationship between Christianity and the Declaration.

The Christian Attack on the Declaration

About that time, a group of Christian historians published a book on Christianity and the founding of America called *Search For "Christian" America* (1983). I was hoping that their book would make mine unnecessary. But when I read the book in 1984 I was horrified. Not only did these Christian writers take the same "secular" approach of non-Christian writers, they were almost vindictive in their charge that Christianity had little or nothing to do with the American Revolution.

Of all the books I had read on the subject, theirs was the worst. Even a few "secular" historians had admitted that Christianity and Christian ideas had been important in the American Revolution and the Declaration, though in a limited way. But these Christian historians denied even the most obvious Christian ideas and influences.

It is understandable for a historian to overlook, fail to detect, or mischaracterize Christian ideas or Biblical sources if the historian is inwardly opposed to Christianity, or does not take seriously the impact of the Bible and Christianity on history, or has not spent time mastering Biblical materials. It is ironic—tragic—that Christian writers would have a poorer grasp of the impact of the Bible and Christianity on history than would "secular" historians.

Search For "Christian" America has been widely received by evangelical readers. It has even been used as proof of America's "secular" roots by a leading humanist magazine in its ongoing diatribe against Christian involvement in American public life. So I have found it necessary in some ways to write this book as a direct response, with a major focus on an evangelical audience.

Theirs was not the only "Christian" attack on the Declaration, however. Years earlier, Gregg Singer had written an influential history of early America that trashed the Declaration of Independence as anti-Christian and deistic. Others called it a political propaganda tract of no legal or political significance. For many Christian writers the Declaration became an embarrassment.

That did not stop some of them from longing to be able to say that America had always been a Christian nation. They could see the clear influence of Christianity in the Constitution. And they could see the Christian legacy in the colonies from the early days to independence. But standing between the colonies and the Constitution was the Declaration of Independence, the one shameful blot on America's Christian law tradition.

These Christian intellectuals could not respect the Declaration. But they could not ignore it either, especially since it was *the* document that gave birth to the United States as a nation. In their argument for America's Christian past, the Declaration was the Achilles' heel. For better or for worse, the Declaration of Independence was somehow what America was all about, and it was not about Christianity.

To get Christian intellectuals to agree on anything is rare. But Christian scholars from the left, right, and center all agreed that the Declaration was anti-Christian and deistic. It offended their faith, and more importantly, it offended God. Their duty, then, was to blast the Declaration, to ensure that ordinary Christians would not be deceived into thinking that it had anything good to say. And in this they have been sadly mistaken.

Their view of the Declaration dominates almost every Christian seminary and college in America. It has fueled a growing sense of shame and guilt about America that has spread among Christian young people in the past few years. It gives a reason—a wrong one—for anti-American activism among some Christian political and social organizations.

In other words, the attacks on the Declaration are not only misguided, they are destructive. Hence the title—*Defending The Declaration*. Christians need to know that the Declaration is not against the Bible and Christianity. Rather, its whole structure and its terms have direct historical links to the Bible and Christian theology. The Declaration is not some deep "secular" ditch between the Christianity of the colonies and the Christian ideas in the U.S. Constitution.

My earlier purposes for writing remain: The first is to clear up the wrong views of the Declaration and Revolution generally shared by average Americans. The second is to take issue with how the experts as a whole have viewed the impact of Christianity and the Bible on the American Revolution and the Declaration of Independence.

The Declaration and the Man on the Street

More than ten years have passed since the 200th birthday of the Declaration of Independence. That was 1976: the year Jimmy Carter made religion and politics front-page news with his "born-again" presidency. By 1980 the new "religious right," as it came to be called, rejected Carter for Ronald Reagan. During these years, a verbal war began between those who believed America was born a Christian nation and those who did not. TV news, newspapers, magazines, radio and TV talk shows, and TV preachers kept the debate always in front of the American audience.

The debate got louder when the "religious right" helped Reagan win a second term in 1984, three short years before the 200th birthday of the U.S. Constitution. As if things were not already interesting enough, Pat Robertson left Christian TV to run for the presidency in 1987. Then the fight over how the founding fathers viewed religion and politics turned into a verbal brawl. It was one of *the* media events of the decade.

On one side were the American Civil Liberties Union, the People for the American Way, the National Organization of Women, and a host of other groups who, for the most part, insisted that the founding fathers wanted to keep Christianity out of public life. For them, separation of church and state was meant to protect politics from religious dogmatists, zealots, and crazies. They saw the Declaration of Independence and the Constitution as written by "secular" men with "secular" ideas to give birth to America as a "secular" nation, quite apart from Christian principles.

Christian activists like Robertson, on the other hand, insisted that the American forefathers intended to found the nation on Christianity. They had not intended to kick Christianity out of public life. Robertson was not alone in that claim. Across America a flood of preachers and activists repeated the theme, getting their message out through books, magazines, radio, and even satellite TV. Both sides missed the point in crucial ways.

It did not take an Einstein to figure out how most people thought on the matter. Opinion polls, surveys, letters to editors, and talk show calls were just some of the ways Americans made their views known. During the debate, it became clear that the average person on the street understands America's early history along the following general lines:

- At first, America was settled by religious and Christian people. Pilgrims, Puritans, and other sorts of Christians came here for freedom of religion and freedom to run their own lives. But by the time of the American Revolution, most of the leaders in America were no longer religious. They were deists.

- Deists were people who believed in God but not in a Christian way.[1] They thought that God had made the universe like a clock, wound it up to run on its own tension, and then walked away from it. He does not work miracles, hear and answer prayer, or speak through prophets and inspired books such as the Bible.[2]

- For deists, God was an absentee landlord who never came to check on his property. He was not actively involved in running His universe. He made it to run itself. He had left men alone, and left them to figure out the truth of the universe by the use of their minds alone. So the most important thing for man was to depend on his own reason. Nature became the source of all truth, and by thinking about nature, man could reason his way to the truth. Man did not need God or the Bible.[3]

- Since they were deists, the founding fathers felt great irrita-
  tion or antagonism toward Christianity. After all, Christianity
  had been responsible for political oppression and mixing
  church and state. As deists they were now "secular" or unreligious. They wanted to change America so that it would no
  longer be a religious nation as it had been. So when they
  declared their independence from England, they did it with
  words that made America a deistic, or unreligious nation,
  rather than a Christian one. A little later they separated
  church from state to get Christianity out of the law and political life.

In this view of history, America was never a Christian nation,
and the founding fathers never intended it to be.

The Myth of Deism

Now for the surprise: Hardly anyone in the colonies fit this
description. No one who played a key role in writing the Declaration or approving it thought this way in 1776, not even Thomas
Jefferson.

The "clockmaker God" idea about deism and the founding fathers was invented by teachers in the 1890s and later years to explain the religious ideas of the colonies. A small handful of French
and English philosophers in the mid-1700s had believed this way.
Sloppy interpreters of American history took that obscure European view and pasted it onto the history of the American revolution. As a device to explain the general view of the founding fathers, it is all wet.

For example, John Adams has been called a deist. He helped
write the Declaration of Independence and was a key player in the
American Revolution. Adams once wrote in his diary that a nation
that took the Bible for its law book would be the best of nations.[4]
On another occasion he wrote: "The great and Almighty author of
nature; who at first established the rules which regulate the world,
can as easily suspend those laws whenever his providence sees sufficient reason for such suspension. This can be no objection, then, to
the miracles of Jesus Christ."[5] Adams sometimes strongly criticized
those who had used organized religion as a way to control people

politically. But he was far from critical about the principles of Christianity. He thought Christian principles were the heart and soul of the effort for nationhood and independence:

> Who composed that Army of fine young Fellows that was then before my Eyes? There were among them, Roman Catholics, English Episcopalians, Scotch and American Presbyterians, Methodists, Moravians, Anabaptists, German Lutherans, German Calvinists, Universalists, Arians . . . Deists and Atheists. . . . Never the less all educated in the general principles of Christianity: and the general principles of English and American liberty. . . . The general principles, on which the Fathers achieved independence, were . . . the general principles of Christianity.[6]

But did not John Adams, as president, sign the Tripoli Treaty (1797) that said that the government of the United States was not in any sense founded on the Christian religion? Yes, he did. But what did he mean? He meant simply that "the Christian religion" as a formal institution was not a part of the American government in the same way that the religious structures of Islam are a part of Islamic governments. From many things that Adams and his contemporaries wrote it is clear that they did not use the word *religion* to exclude Christian ideas or principles as some do today. True, the founders did not make institutional religion a part of the government. But they never thought of excluding Christian principles.

Another example is Thomas Jefferson. He doubted the deity of Christ and the inerrancy of Scripture.[7] He even railed against the abuses of organized religion, but not against Christian principles.[8] He believed the moral principles found in the four Gospels should be the guide of every man's life.[9] As President, Jefferson read from a collection of these principles nightly.[10] Because he took Christian principles seriously, he was extremely troubled by the immoral practice of slavery, saying: "I tremble for my country when I reflect that God is just; that his justice cannot sleep forever. . . . The Almighty has no attribute which can take side with us."[11]

Jefferson is a notable example of how a man can be influenced by Biblical ideas and Christian principles even though he never confessed Jesus Christ as Lord in the evangelical sense. Like most of the founders, he was very supportive of Christian principles, even going so far as to call Jesus of Nazareth "our Savior," but he never could bring himself to accept the Christ of Christianity: God in flesh.

Must a political leader confess Jesus Christ as Lord and Savior to be able at all to accept and act on Biblical principles for government? Many people seem to think so. We are told that since Jefferson denied the deity of Christ, he could not have accepted any other truly Biblical ideas. Every legal and political idea he had must, therefore, have been non-Christian.

This sort of thinking breaks a number of rules of logic and is out of step with the Bible itself. Is it not remarkable for us to assume that Christians can easily be influenced by non-Christian ideas, but somehow non-Christians cannot be influenced by Christian ideas? The point is, even if Jefferson had confessed Jesus Christ as Lord and Savior, some would still trace his legal and political ideas to deism. A "born-again" Jefferson would not automatically mean that the Declaration contained Christian ideas.

Another more subtle claim lies just beneath the surface of such thinking. If the Declaration can only contain Christian or Biblical ideas as long as Jefferson and others confessed Jesus Christ as Lord in an evangelical way, then a Christian view of government excludes unbelievers. To have a Christian nation would require all leaders to believe in eternal redemption before they could have the slightest grasp of God's plan for civil justice. Only Christians would be competent to do anything where civil government is concerned.

Ultimately the church would have to be merged with the state, and Christians would be in charge of the state. Rather than seeing that a government is "Biblical" or "Christian" if its laws and structures agree with what God has said about civil justice and social order, a "Christian" nation would be one where "confessing Christ" becomes the test by which a person's political and legal ideas are approved. Such a state would be primarily concerned with salvation rather than justice. It would confuse God's redemption plan with his creation plan.

It is true that many sincerely believe Christianity requires these things. My reading of the Bible and of the teachings of Christianity tells me just the opposite. I believe it is factually wrong and a terrible insult to Christians to say that our religion by its very terms requires government to be totalitarian and despotic. If true Christianity requires a religious test of faith in Jesus Christ, an establishmentarian principle, we are back to using civil power to enforce right belief. Jefferson would howl. So would the Baptists.

After all, for the greater part of western history, and under English law, the state controlled religion. Church and state were not institutionally separated. When Jefferson and others said harsh things about institutional Christianity, it was to object to the political alliance between government and the organized church, because some powerful religious people had used religion as a pretext to oppress others. What Jefferson opposed were the institutional abuses in the name of Christianity, not Christian principles themselves. Interestingly enough, when Jefferson as president renegotiated the Tripoli Treaty, he took out the words which said America was not founded on the Christian religion.

The fact is most of the founders were religious. They were not committed "secularists." They believed that God answered prayer. And they believed that He took an active part in the everyday affairs of men. Most of them believed that God had spoken to man in a special way through the Bible. More importantly, most of them believed that the future of the nation largely depended on whether the country hearkened to the Bible or not. Even Jefferson feared that God would judge America. So the facts of history do not support our modern consensus about the founding fathers as anti-Christian secularists. When Americans today think that all the founders were deists who consciously rejected the Bible and Christian principles, they are basing their opinions on a myth.

The Myth of an American Enlightenment

If the typical person's view is so clearly wrong, why have the experts in colleges and universities not spoken out? It is because the view from academia is distorted, too. The experts feel no need to correct the popular view because it is close enough to their own, even if it is wildly inaccurate on some of the details. Were the man on the street to go to a library to find what the experts say about Christianity and the American Revolution, he would come away with an understanding that goes something like this:

- True Christianity, from its earliest days, was always a "faith." Neither Christ nor his apostles gave "reason," in the sense of inferential logic, any important part to play in Christianity. Indeed, the Bible condemns human reason as corrupted by sin and hostile to God. It was the Greeks and Stoics for whom "reason" was philosophically important. To attach any importance to "reason," or to give it any significant role in Christianity, is to mix Christianity with paganism, and undermine faith with rationalism, making it no longer true or authentic Christianity. Faith and reason are mutually exclusive terms in Christianity.[12]

- In the 1200s, Thomas Aquinas introduced rationalism into Christianity by merging Aristotle's thought with the Bible.[13] From then on, medieval Christianity was scholastic and very rationalistic, meaning that it was somehow not authentically Christian. Aquinas' rationalism, a perversion of faith, sowed the seeds of secularism into the so-called "Christian" culture of western Europe.

- When the Church of England split from Rome, rationalism remained a part of Anglican theology. So church leaders like Richard Hooker in the 1500s, who was widely read, were partly Christian, but were infected with rationalism which is un-Christian. This means that anyone who followed Hooker's way of thinking was also tainted with rationalism.[14] The stage was set for faith to be rejected completely if science ever made faith unnecessary.

- John Calvin, on the other hand, tried to restore Christianity to pure "faith" during the 1500s in a way that gave reason no important role in theology and religion. He made God a great mystery, totally inscrutable, and made God's will unknowable. Calvin made the physical universe a mystery too, an unsolvable riddle. Calvinism required that what one believed about God or the world must be taken on sheer faith alone, apart from any thought or reason. This is because God is unpredictable and so is His universe. Calvin's followers over the next century tried to stay true to his teaching. For a while Puritans, Presbyterians, Huguenots, and other "Calvinist" groups were satisfied simply to believe in the mysterious Deity preached by Calvin.[15]

- Puritans in the 1600s did not stay true to the pure Calvinist faith, however. William Ames in the early 1600s relied on a Stoic notion of *synteresis* to explain how nature, reason, the law of God, and the law of nature are linked.[16] Ames also made a crucial concession to rationalism by admitting that cosmology, or the design of the universe, can be discovered by reason. Ames went so far as to adopt a natural rights theory of government, as did John Owen in the mid-1600s.[17]

- During this time the Puritan divines often defended reason against the heresy of fideism. They saw no contradiction between reason and faith, but used reason as a handmaid and support for faith.[18] At the same time, they based Puritan education in the schools and universities on the Greek and Roman classics, mixing huge doses of pagan philosophy as well as rationalism into their Christianity.[19] Finally, in 1676, Richard Baxter made a strong defense of the importance of reason for Christianity. He and the other Puritans of the 1600s did not realize that they were lessening the importance of the words of the Bible.[20] They were also bringing into the citadel of Calvinist theology the Trojan horse of rationalism.[21] Like Aquinas before them, they were paving the way for deism, secularism, and a rejection of the Bible.

- The whole edifice of Christian faith came crashing to the ground because of the discoveries of Isaac Newton, published in 1687.[22] Newton found a way to explain the universe by physical laws, making the universe no longer a mystery. Other scientific advances meant that man could understand his world without simply accepting what goes on in it by "faith." This struck at the heart of Calvinism. And it gave religious rationalists an opportunity to drop religion.

- John Locke jumped at the opportunity. Building on the earlier religious rationalism of Hooker, Locke took the fatal, anti-Christian step.[23] In 1690 he wrote *An Essay On Human Understanding*, denying innate ideas, a concept that was popular in religious philosophy at the time. In the process he argued in a profoundly convincing way that all revelation should be subjected to reason. Even the Bible was acceptable only if it agreed with reason. Thus, at the turn of the eighteenth century, Newton's science and Locke's extreme rationalism became the two cornerstones of a whole new way of thinking.[24]

- Soon a movement began wherein some Europeans started saying that they no longer needed faith. Reason was enough. To know the truth, all one had to do was study the created universe and learn its secrets. This movement was called the "Enlightenment." It meant that to one degree or another, the physical universe was now the chief object of study and veneration. Nature itself became the source of truth, while God became more and more irrelevant. Reason replaced faith.[25]

- The men of the Enlightenment who made reason the final test of all truth were called "deists." Even if they believed in God, miracles, prayer, the deity of Jesus Christ, His ascension, His resurrection, and the inspiration of the Bible, but would do so only if such faith agreed with their reason; they were deists. They had placed the authority of the mind over the authority of the Bible. They had exalted reason over faith.

- Calvinism was in serious trouble. Thanks to Newton, the Calvinists could now begin understanding and explaining the universe. It was no longer a dark riddle. Such knowledge was heady stuff. Thanks to Locke, pursuing such knowledge became intellectually fashionable. So the Calvinists of the late 1600s and early 1700s could no longer be satisfied with an unexplainable God. They needed reasons to justify their theology, and they too fell into full-blown rationalism.

- In America the turning point came when two Puritans stepped away from the older Calvinism, hoping to adapt it to Newton's view of the world. The first was John Wise, a previously little-known preacher from Ipswich. The second was the famous Puritan father, Cotton Mather.

- In 1717 John Wise wrote his *Vindication of the Government of the New England Churches* to argue for keeping the Puritan style of church government in Massachusetts and against changing to a

Presbyterian form. In it he made human reason equal to revealed truth in the Bible.[26] In 1721 Cotton Mather wrote his *Christian Philosopher*, which called nature a second revelation from God.[27] Wise paved the way for political deism. And Mather's book was the first consistent expression of deistic thought in America.[28] Mather's innovations on reason introduced the rationalistic cancer of Enlightenment thought into the weakening body of American Puritan religion.[29]

- Jonathan Edwards, one of the leading lights of the First Great Awakening in the 1740s, went further to embrace parts of John Locke's way of explaining epistemology.[30] At the same time, the Presbyterians from Scotland were surrendering to the Enlightenment by adopting a philosophy of common sense, which made man's reason independent from the Bible. As the First Great Awakening progressed through the colonies, it gained converts to Christianity but also to rationalism. As the number of Presbyterian immigrants increased, their type of religious rationalism spread with them as well.[31] By the middle 1700s "Christians" were everywhere in the colonies. But almost all of them had at least one foot in the Enlightenment, and were welcoming with open arms the deistic and Enlightenment-based ideas coming in from France and England.

- Outside of Puritanism, Presbyterianism, and the other denominations of Christianity, a new religion of nature arose. The Bible of this religion was Matthew Tindal's *Christianity As Old As the Creation* (1730).[32] Man's reason is enough to know all that man needs to know to please God, Tindal insisted. To be a good "Christian" and find true religion, one need only to study creation by using one's reason. Across the colonies, interest in the old-time religion was beginning to droop anyway. But good manners still required a man to give polite lip service to religion. Natural theology, therefore, became the deists' religion, and gave basically unreligious men a way to sound pious without demanding much spirituality from them.

- So when the 1770s arrived, the colonies were completely awash in Enlightenment rationalism and deism.[33] There was no true Christianity in the American colonies. The soul of the

Church had been completely possessed by the demon of false epistemology. It did not matter if Washington, Adams, Franklin, and others prayed or not. Even if they believed in the Bible, Jesus Christ, prayer, miracles, or salvation by faith, they were still deists.[34] And it did not matter that preachers such as Roger Sherman and John Witherspoon supported independence; they were men of the Enlightenment. They were Christian rationalists.

• The fact that preachers throughout the colonies helped start the Revolution with their preaching is irrelevant. Even if one could find in their sermons before 1776 every idea found later in the Declaration, this would not mean that the Declaration was Christian. Christians in the colonies had years before been captured by the subtle deception of the Enlightenment and were full partners in the deistic heresy on which the United States was born.[35] That is why they could sign or support the Declaration of Independence. "Liberty" became their new religion, while the Declaration and the Constitution became the "twin sacraments" for their new found idolatry.[36]

Demythologizing the Myth

What you have just read about the American Enlightenment may sound convincing, parts of it may even be familiar. In general, it captures the overall view of early America as is taught in American colleges and universities.[37] Keep in mind that it is a composite sketch. There are many variations on the theme, and not all historians agree with every part of the above summary. But it does fairly represent what most historians think and the understanding a typical reader would gain on the matter by spending hours in the library. Like the popular view discussed earlier, this more technical view from the experts is also severely flawed. What follows is a brief synopsis of the problems with this interpretation. More detailed treatment of these different points appear at various places later in the book.

First, the most basic flaw is this: Writers who hold this view have almost universally ignored the Bible itself, particularly the writings of the Apostle Paul, when building their case for rationalism and the Enlightenment. They have not asked whether Aquinas, Hooker, Ames, Owen, Baxter, Locke, Wise, Mather, or Tindal tried to follow the Bible in their views of the relationships among God, man, nature, and law. Neither have they admitted that most of these men openly claimed to be following the Bible. Nor have they shown that any of them failed to follow the Bible when trying to do so. References to Romans 1 and 2 and to other passages of Scripture abound in the original sources but go unnoticed by these historians. To my knowledge, every historian of the period who takes this view has committed the error of question-begging, guaranteeing a particular conclusion by assuming a wrong definition of Christianity.

Second, the error of question-begging takes several different forms. Writers assume that ideas are deistic by definition. They do not start by explaining the differences between Christianity and deism nor show into which category an idea fits. Also, since they routinely ignore what the Bible and Christianity teach, they are unaware when an idea is Christian. Thus, they call many Christian and Biblical ideas deistic, capturing Christianity for paganism. Also, they assume that Christians can be influenced by non-Christian ideas, but for the most part do not admit that non-Christians can be influenced by Christian ideas. So a double standard exists.

Third, I have yet to find anyone with this view of history who does not wrongly assume that the New Testament and true Christianity separate faith and reason in the way set forth above. The "faith versus reason" dichotomy is a straw-man argument. It does not accurately represent the Bible's teaching on the human mind and its role in human life and service to God.

The New Testament uses nearly forty different Greek words to describe reason, mind, and intellect. These occur in more than 1,500 different places in the New Testament. A number of these are used in highly technical ways in the Scriptures. In Romans 12:1-3, for example, the Apostle Paul uses seven different Greek words for the mind and intellect to explain how Christians are to live and serve God. He also links reason and faith in verse 3. If Paul and the New Testament were measured by the standards used against Hooker, Wise, and Mather, the Apostle and his writings would have to be dismissed as rationalistic and tending toward deism.

Now for the real shock. Roger L. Emerson, writing in the *Dictionary of the History of Ideas*, attributes deistic tendencies even to the Apostle Paul, saying: "Elements of the deistic position are as ancient as critical religious thought itself. . . . Saint Paul's statements concerning the law of the Gentiles (Romans 2:13-15) yield the base for a natural religion."[38] If even Paul had deistic tendencies, the historians are right to find Mather and Wise to be deistic, since they accepted implicitly the writings of Paul as divinely inspired. The same is true of Jonathan Edwards and John Witherspoon, the great colonial preachers whom historians have dismissed as Enlightenment men. If the colonial preachers and even Paul are to be considered deistic, no wonder historians think that the founders in general were deists. How could they conclude otherwise?

Fourth, besides failing to understand the Bible and Biblical epistemology, these writers often misrepresent what certain people believed or said. Catholics such as Aquinas are routinely misrepresented, as are many later Protestants. For example, John Calvin did not try to make God or the universe a mystery so as to make Christianity a riddle. There was no dichotomy between Calvin and William Ames. Saying Ames revised Calvin to make Calvinism rational, setting up the Puritans as targets for the Enlightenment, is simply false.

Fifth, this history also makes the Puritans humanistic syncretists for studying the classics of the Greeks and Romans. One gets the impression that true Christianity requires Christians to be uneducated morons. Such a view fails to account for what the Bible and Christian theology have to say about the image of God in man. Although men are fallen and corrupted by sin, they still retain something of the image of God. To the extent that their words and works reflect that image, Christians are to use and benefit from them. It is wrong to say that Puritan education was unchristian because it respected the value of classical learning.

Sixth, this history greatly misstates the impact of Newtonian cosmology and its relationship to the Bible and Christianity. We are given the impression that before Newton published the *Principia* in 1687, Christians did not really believe that the universe worked according to fixed laws. Rather, Christians viewed the universe as a magical or mystical organism, miraculously vitalized by angelic powers according to the unpredictable whim of its Creator. Thus, anyone who lived after the time of Newton and who believed in a reasonably ordered universe according to fixed law would not be thinking in Biblical or Christian terms.

Much of this writing attributes to pre-Newtonian Christians a view of God and the universe they did not hold. The Bible talks repeatedly about fixed natural laws in the *cosmos*. The importance of fixed natural laws was a part of Christianity long before Newton ever wrote. By misrepresenting the impact of Newton, these writers have set up a false dichotomy between those Christians who lived later than Newton and those who came earlier. By the same token, all the talk about the impact of Newton on Wise and Mather to turn them into Enlightenment men is meaningless drivel. Both Wise and Mather held the same view of the laws of nature and of the relationship of reason and revelation, as had most of the pre-Newtonian Puritans.[39] And their views were consistent with the Apostle Paul in the New Testament.

Finally, I will mention a number of other problems here and address them later. One is the misreading of John Locke. I am convinced that Locke's *Essay On Human Understanding* has been greatly misunderstood by writers of our day. I am not at all convinced that the links between Locke's epistemology and the New Testament have been adequately traced. Another is that most writers, in calling certain religious language deistic, fail to understand the Biblical Creator/Redeemer distinction or the religious error called the nature/grace dichotomy and often are mistaken in imputing "deistic tendencies" to anyone who uses creation language.[40] Because of the kinds of errors noted above, I suspect that a great deal of the writing about Scottish common-sense philosophy as a form of Enlightenment thought is also defective.

I must admit here that in 1980 I did not know about Merwyn Johnson's excellent book on Locke, published in 1978.[41] Distrustful of secondary sources, I bypassed modern writers and read Locke directly. Once satisfied that I had understood Locke, I went on to study the other matters that occur in these chapters.

Only during work on the final draft did I get around to reading Johnson. He shows that, without question, Locke was indeed a Christian who was Trinitarian in doctrine and who believed in the divinity of Christ.[42] I think Johnson is being polite when, speaking of various charges made against Locke, he says: "In the light of the evidence . . . such charges are, in a word, incredible."[43]

The research of many others, like Johnson, on these matters is right on target. I regret that I have probably failed to find some of the best sources. But they are in the minority, sometimes hard to find, and often difficult to read. The average person is more likely to discover the wrong view because most of the popular writing goes that way. The bulk of modern writing on the American Enlightenment and the American revolution makes a Pauline view of the world—God, man, law, nature, epistemology, and so forth—a Newtonian concoction brewed and served up by Puritan compromisers. It turns Biblical and Christian ideas into raw material of the Enlightenment.

By the alchemy of history and the wave of the historian's pen, Biblical and Christian ideas are changed into Enlightenment paganism. This makes it impossible for a Christian who takes Romans 1 and 2 seriously not to be called a child of the Enlightenment. And it causes the Christianity of early America to be described in such a way that no Christian influence on the founding could be possible. I am convinced, therefore, that a serious new look at the founding of America should be taken. The chapters that follow are my meager and insignificant contribution to such a look.

The Theme of This Book

My theme is simple. The Declaration of Independence was not the bastard offspring of anti-Christian deism or Enlightenment rationalism. The ideas in the Declaration are Christian despite the fact that some of the men who wrote them down were not. Those ideas are not opposed to the teachings of the Bible or of mainstream Christianity. The popular notion that the intellectual heritage of the Declaration traces solely to deism, the Enlightenment, the Renaissance, and from there to pagan Rome and Greece is seriously flawed. Indeed, much of what we have been told for years about the Declaration's intellectual heritage and the meaning of its terms is largely a series of myths.

This book will show that most of the key terms and ideas in the Declaration of Independence arose from the Judeo-Christian intellectual tradition. It does not deny that there was such a thing as the Enlightenment or deists. But many of the ideas used by deists were borrowed from the Bible and Christianity. Where the Declaration is concerned, its legal and political theories are consistent with Biblical principles and with historical mainstream Christianity, both Catholic and Protestant.

It is a mistake to read the Declaration of Independence as an ingenious "secularized" assault on the Bible, Christianity, or the western Christian tradition. The Declaration stands squarely inside that tradition, reflecting how profoundly Biblical principles had influenced the world in which the framers lived and worked.

I strongly disagree with my Christian brothers who have set out to prove that the founders rejected Christian principles and consciously built the American government on an anti-Christian base. For example, Mark Noll, Nathan Hatch, and George Marsden have written that the "principles of the American revolution" were "basically secular," and that the founders' "political ideals" were "naturalistic."[44] They insist that Christians in the colonies failed to influence the way America was founded because they were too busy mimicking deists, "baptizing political philosophies," and making an idol of nationalism.[45] They deny that the country was founded on "Christian principles."[46] They say that the founders relied on "Whig" ideology instead of Christian Biblical principles.[47] And "Whigs . . . often transformed the defense of political freedom into a nearly idolatrous worship. . . . 'Radical' Whigs were often also full partners in the Enlightenment."[48] This is close to saying that Christians in the colonies were really idolaters and heretics.

I disagree with Noll, Hatch, and Marsden that all the founders, including John Witherspoon, were infected with anti-Biblical rationalism. When they wrote that Witherspoon "explicitly excluded the Bible" in thinking about Revolutionary politics, they were mistaken.[49] Had they read two sentences beyond the quote they chose, they would have found Witherspoon saying that any human wisdom opposed to the Bible is "false and dangerous."[50] Indeed, Witherspoon often referred to the necessity of the Bible, but they somehow missed that fact and thought he rejected the Bible.

They have concluded that the "War for Independence was not a just war," "(T)he American revolution was not Christian," "It was not Biblical," and "It did not establish the United States on a Christian foundation."[51] And even though "religion" abounded in the colonies, "theology of every stripe was something on the fringe of American society."[52] They admit that Christianity influenced culture in the colonies, but they deny that Christianity had any impact on how the founding documents were drafted. In the words of Mark Noll, "(A)lthough the Bible had worked itself into the foundation of national consciousness, it contributed little to the structures built upon that foundation."[53]

Noll's last point is the key for this book. He believes that the ideas in the Declaration were not Christian even if many of the colonists were. I maintain that the ideas themselves were Christian even if some of the founders were not. The Bible did more than work itself into the foundations of national consciousness. It did indeed influence the structures on which America was built, even to the extent of affecting how the Declaration of Independence was drafted.

I also strongly differ with the widely known view of Christian writer C. Gregg Singer, who insisted that the framers rejected Christian principles:

> Behind the political philosophy of the American Revolution . . . lay a view of God and of human nature which was not Christian but deist, which was not orthodox and conservative but radical. It thus follows that the American Revolution in its basic philosophy was not Christian, and the democratic way of life which arose from it was not, and is not, Christian, but was, and is, a deistic and secularized caricature of the evangelical point of view. . . . The fact that John Witherspoon and other evangelicals of the day were willing to sign the Declaration should not blind us to the essentially anti-Christian character of Jeffersonian democracy.[54]

This bleak view of the founding fathers is not only wrong, it is causing devastating results in the Christian community. Many wrestle with guilt or embarrassment over America's "anti-Christian" heritage. Others become infected with negativism from reading these cynical and jaundiced accounts of America's past.

When Christians accept these mistaken views they begin to feel vulnerable. They become defensive and think that they must continually apologize for America's past. Many feel alienated, as though it is wrong or useless to participate in the public process.

After all, Christians have always been on the outside looking in when it comes to American politics, and maybe that is where they really belong. Others, such as members of Witness for Peace and those associated with *Sojourners* magazine stay in the political process but feel compelled always to take an anti-American stand. Either way, the wrong view causes Christians to be a negative political force, instead of a positive one.

More is at stake, of course, than effective Christian political involvement. Christians need to know that when they oppose the principles of the Declaration of Independence, they are opposing many of the very principles to which the Bible and the church gave birth. By accepting a flawed version of America's founding, they have been misled into giving away part of the heritage of the church. They need to know that they do not have to feel ashamed of America's founding heritage or feel spiritually obligated to be anti-American. They do not have to be politically irrelevant, on the outside looking in.

This book seeks to set the record straight about Christianity and the American Revolution. The church did directly influence the legal and political theory of the Declaration of Independence. The church was not on the fringe of culture.

How the Book Is Organized

First, due to the controversial nature of this book, I have found it necessary to depart from the ordinary practice of using short footnotes and have used many substantive and explanatory footnotes. In early drafts when I used standard footnotes to support my points, my readers were not convinced that I really had my facts right. They needed more proof. Since this book may become something of a debater's manual for defending the influence of Christianity on the Declaration, I wanted to make available the source materials on which the arguments are based.

Second, there is some repetition of sources and notes in the book. The reader will discover that the repetition is necessary because one source may serve as evidence for more than one argument dealing with the substance and ideas of the Declaration. Overlap is inevitable. And I have not expected the reader to memorize difficult material in one chapter so as to keep it in mind when reading a later chapter.

Also, any book has limits. This one is no exception. Many arguments and debates about the Declaration and the Revolution exist; I simply did not have time or space to address them all. For example, I have been asked to include a treatment of the influence of Masonic thought on the founding fathers. Although such a survey would certainly be pertinent, it could not be fit within length limitations and time deadlines. Furthermore, my research into Masonry several years ago did not convince me that it merited treatment here. At the time of this writing, I remain unconvinced that Masonry was philosophically important to the Declaration or the Revolution.

The book is organized to respond to what I feel are key criticisms of the Declaration and the Revolution, particularly for a Christian audience. The first is that the founders had no real reason to take up arms against the king, meaning the revolution was unjustified. Chapter 1 tells what was happening in the colonies and how bad the situation really was. Giving a brief summary of events leading up to the Declaration helps to set the stage for the more technical discussions that follow.

Chapter 2 and those following answer the charge from Noll and others that Christianity had little to do with the ideas and terms that went into the text of the Declaration. Chapter 2, then, deals with "laws of nature and of nature's God," words expressing the legal theory of the Declaration. Chapter 3 analyzes "self-evident truths," a term embodying the epistemology or knowledge theory of the Declaration. Chapter 4 discusses "unalienable rights endowed by the Creator," the phrase that carries the rights theory of the Declaration. Chapter 5 chronicles "government by the consent of the governed," words linked to a Christian theory of revolution. Chapter 6 discusses "Divine Providence" and "Supreme Judge," terms dealing with the founders' concept of God.

These chapters give a new look at the history of ideas. Ordinarily, the ideas about law, rights, knowledge, civil authority, God's governance, and self-government found in the Declaration have been traced to deism, the Enlightenment, the Renaissance, and from there to ancient Rome and pagan Greece.[55] Meanwhile, the Bible and Christianity have been overlooked and underestimated as innovative and creative influences on western thought.[56] Although I do not deny the non-Christian influences outright, I think there is good reason to believe that the major ideas in the Declaration trace more clearly to the Bible and the church than most writers have thought.

A major thrust of each chapter is to examine a phrase or idea from the Declaration to find whether it stands inside or outside of the Judeo-Christian intellectual tradition. Can the ideas embodied in the Declaration of Independence be traced to the church and the Bible? Or must they be traced to deism, the Enlightenment, the Renaissance, and ultimately to pagan Rome and Greece? Are early American notions about law, rights, liberty, and resisting tyrants anti-Biblical at the core? In short, is it true that the Bible and Christianity had little or nothing to do with developing the great legal and political ideas of western liberty and constitutionalism?

The following chapters show that the Declaration's ideas are firmly rooted in the Bible and the Judeo-Christian tradition. Without the Bible and Christianity, the Declaration of Independence could never have been written.

O N E

FOUNDING AMERICA

BY MAY OF 1775, THE AMERICAN COLONIES had their backs to the wall. For ten years relations between England and its American colonies had been deteriorating. Now the cords were about to snap. Earlier, in August, King George III decreed that the colonies were in rebellion and must be crushed militarily. By April he had ordered General Gage to march on Concord and Lexington. The King refused to be pacified.

It had not always been this way. From the time of the first permanent settlement in Jamestown in 1607, the English kings had prized the American colonies. They nurtured and protected them. The colonies were strategically important to England. They were crucial to England's economy and made England a key player among the dominant European powers.[1]

But by the close of the French and Indian War in 1760, some in England began to see America as a threat. Why? The population of the colonies was growing rapidly. Soon more people would be living in America than in England itself. Also, England was fast becoming dependent on American raw materials, meaning that in the future, the colonies might use their growing economic clout to affect British policy.[2]

When America was but a wilderness, it seemed right for the king to let the colonies govern themselves. But now they were going too far. The freedom enjoyed in the American colonies was making some Englishmen jealous. England's internal politics were at stake. Neither the king nor Parliament wanted England to become like America. They wanted America to become more like England. The colonies had to be put in their place.

England had its own problems too. The King had a history of fits of insanity, and his mind had been weakened by medicines for gout. He had never fully recovered to be completely in charge of the government. This gave Parliament a chance to try to take some of the king's power for themselves. Parliament had no authority to govern the colonies because the charters were between the colonies and the king.[3] By flexing its muscle over the colonies, Parliament could take some power from the king, thus increasing Parliament's power and decreasing the king's. And it could establish regulatory control over the colonies before they awoke to the fact of their own economic strength and before they could develop the capacity to resist militarily. It was now or never.

The plan was set. If the colonies submitted to Parliament's control—fine. If not, they would be forced to surrender their charters. And they would have to give up most of the ability of self-government, which they had already come to take for granted.

Between 1760 and 1765, Parliament placed a series of tight restrictions on colonial trade and disallowed an unusual number of colonial laws. In 1765, for the first time, it placed a direct tax on all kinds of printed matter. Knowing that the "Stamp Act" would cause a furor, Parliament had already passed the "Quartering Act." That act meant that British soldiers would live in the colonists' homes—to spy on them, and by their very presence scare the colonists into complying with the Stamp Act.

The plan backfired, leading to the "Stamp Act Crisis." The colonists knew immediately that to buy a single stamp was to surrender all claim to self-government. A colonywide boycott of English goods was declared. British merchants soon appealed to Parliament, and in 1766 the Stamp Act was repealed.

The colonists had refused the bait. They had not been tricked into gradually giving up self-government. Parliament knew it could not allow itself to lose the battle. Stronger measures must be used, and the king was compliant. The same day Parliament repealed the

Stamp Act, it passed the "Declaratory Act," which claimed that the colonies were subordinate and that Parliament could pass any law it wished to bind the colonies and people of America.

The Declaratory Act struck directly at the charters. Nothing in the charters gave Parliament such control over the colonies. The charters made the king and the Americans themselves the only rulers of the colonies. Parliament's weaseling in would be nothing less than unconstitutional.[4] To the colonists, the Parliament was usurping the sovereignty that the charters divided between the king and the people in their colonial representatives. Parliament had no more right to govern the colonies than did the ruling bodies of France or Spain.

In 1767 a series of direct taxes was levied by Lord Townshend, the chancellor of the exchequer. The taxes, bad enough in their own right, were enforced out of Boston by the Board of Customs Commissioners, who were little more than bureaucratic racketeers.[5] Honest merchants were convicted without jury trial, so that the members of the board could themselves confiscate one-third of all seizures. England turned a deaf ear to the colonists' complaints of injustice.

Massachusetts responded by sending a "Circular Letter" throughout the colonies to determine what joint action should be taken. Lawyers in the colonies, whether loyalist or not, agreed that Parliament had no authority to tax the colonies or to legislate for the colonies.

The British secretary over the colonies answered the "Circular Letter" by ordering the governor of Massachusetts to dissolve the legislature. British troops were moved to Boston as a show of force. Tensions and agitations grew. Then in March 1770, British soldiers fired into a crowd of townspeople, and news of the "Boston Massacre" raced across the colonies.

The Townshend Acts failed, and most were repealed in April 1770. But again Parliament, refusing to allow the colonists to win, kept one small tax—a tea tax—as a token of control.

In 1773 Parliament opened another round in the sovereignty contest by sending 1,700 chests of tea to colonial ports. The colonists had already refused to buy any tea. But according to Parliament's law, the colonists could be taxed for the tea merely if the tea were unloaded and set on the docks. Lord Townshend could not have cared less if the colonies actually bought and used the tea. More than tea was at stake—it was a matter of power and control.

When the tea ships arrived, the colonists were furious. The first ships went back to England without unloading. But when the ship *Dartmouth* arrived in Boston in November 1773, Governor Hutchinson would not let it leave. The ship sat at anchor in the harbor for days as Hutchinson planned for the unloading of the tea. Other ships also arrived in the meantime. Since the tax could only be levied when the tea was unloaded, someone decided that the tea would never reach the dock. On the night of December 16, a group of colonists disguised as Indians boarded the vessels and threw the chests of tea overboard while cheering crowds watched.

London was filled with talk of leveling Boston with heavy artillery. Instead, a few months after the incident, Parliament passed the "Intolerable Acts." These included the "Boston Port Act," which closed the harbor until the tea tax should be paid; the "Administration of Justice Act," which allowed the governor to suspend the court system; and the "Massachusetts Government Act," which revised the colony's charter, giving the British more extensive and direct control of all internal affairs.

The other colonies could not stand by while Parliament starved Massachusetts into submission. In September of 1774 the First Continental Congress met at Philadelphia. The Congress passed a declaration condemning the actions of the British since 1763. It went further to form the "Continental Association," an organization to promote and enforce a boycott of all British goods and to stop all exports to Britain.

The king and Parliament responded with force, placing the colonies under martial law. By April 1775, British soldiers were already killing Americans. Also, the king began paying Shawnee Indians to raid frontier settlements and take scalps so that colonial militia would be moved away from the coast, making a British military invasion easier.

So in May of 1775, when the Second Continental Congress met at Philadelphia, the cheers of the tea party onlookers were gone. Now the mood was somber. The life-and-death crisis upon them was obvious to everyone. A grave pall settled over the city of Philadelphia, the mood of seriousness reflected in the drawn faces, creased brows, and low, deliberate tones in the delegates' voices. Men accustomed to laughter and lighthearted humor now exchanged customary jests only with great effort. Their ordinarily amicable greetings were now hurried and anxious, their tense smiles quickly fading as their attention turned to the brooding disaster.

Immediately, they placed George Washington in charge of the defenders of Boston. But before he could leave Philadelphia to assume command, the British attacked. Britain was a world power with the men, the guns, the finances, and the developed economy to carry on an offensive war and crush the colonies. To the men of the Second Continental Congress in 1775, a full-scale defensive war against England seemed impossible. They drafted the "Olive Branch Petition," begging Britain for an end to the use of force.

But the delegates knew from experience that they should not expect the king to restrain his troops. Assuming the worst, they drafted the "Declaration of the Causes and Necessity of Taking Up Arms," explaining the right of the colonists to act in self-defense if the British continued with their plan to crush the colonies. As 1775 drew to a close, the only message from England was more force.

With the new year came the British answer. On January 1, 1776, the city of Norfolk was bombed and burned to the ground. The colonists had not misjudged the king. He did not tell his troops to draw back. Instead he had hired German mercenaries to act as assault troops against the farmers in the colonies. The German mercenaries would arrive soon.

Meanwhile, imperial control of the colonial governments tightened. Soon the colonists lost any voice in the ordinary government of their colonies. In May of 1776, the Congress advised all the colonies to set up new governments because the ones already in place were firmly in the king's hands. Virginia was first, passing its new constitution on June 12, 1776, a month before the colonies together declared independence.

Acting on prior instructions from the government at Williamsburg, on June 7, Delegate Richard Henry Lee of Virginia introduced a resolution into Congress calling for a declaration of independence. Virginia wanted the colonies to declare themselves sovereign states. Under the rules of international law, other states could then extend formal recognition and offer military support. Without such aid from the outside, the colonies would be doomed.

While the colonies drafted new constitutions as states, the Congress elected five men to prepare a document claiming nationhood and independence under international law. The five were John Adams, Benjamin Franklin, Roger Sherman, Robert Livingston, and Thomas Jefferson. After discussing what form the declaration would take, the committee appointed Jefferson to write the first draft. The committee made a few revisions to Jefferson's draft before sending it to Congress for more revisions. Congress approved the final draft and voted independence on July 2, 1776.

Jefferson's Declaration bore no hint of fear or dread, only intense resolve. Jefferson spoke simply, directly, like a lawyer laying out the points of a criminal indictment. His Declaration reflected the soul as well as the mind of America. It breathed a manly passion; it looked upward to lofty goals. And, point by deliberate point, it marked out the colonists' case.

The Declaration was about what everyone in America knew. New states can be formed; some should be, if before the court of heaven and world opinion the cause is just. Man's law cannot be arbitrary, without insulting the laws of nature and of nature's God. Truth can be known, sometimes so clearly as to be self-evident. God created men, and created them equal, endowing them with inalienable rights—rights that they could not give away and that no one could take from them.

Because God made men and gave them their rights, men create governments under God's law to protect those rights. A government that destroys inalienable rights deserts its purpose and forfeits its right to rule. Men must endure bad government but not a tyrannical one. And this king, George III, is a tyrant. He is not simply a bad ruler, he is a despot and a destroyer.

What makes him a tyrant? He is bent on destruction; the record is clear. He has done everything the political theorists have called tyranny at least since the Puritan revolution of the 1640s. Jefferson listed over thirty reasons, showing that the king was more than a bad or incompetent ruler. He was a tyrant. He had lost his right to rule.

The final paragraph declared the colonies free and independent. The deed was done. The representatives had acted. Now it was up to the people of America and Divine Providence to make the Declaration more than mere words.

Jefferson's Declaration was a masterpiece of law, government, and rights. He tied together with few words hundreds of years of English political theory. The long shadows of the Magna Carta, the common law, Catholic and Calvinist resistance theories, the English Bill of Rights, and the Petition of Right are cast within its lines.

The ideas were not Jefferson's, but the writing was. And it was magnificent. With the king's English, Jefferson parted the king from his colonies. Through the Declaration, America became the direct heir of the best of the British liberal tradition.

T W O

THE LAWS OF NATURE
AND OF NATURE'S GOD

LAW IS A KEY IDEA in the Declaration of Independence for a very important reason. The Declaration was about being free from England, meaning a war would be fought. Some would call the colonists traitors and rebels and say the revolution was a lawless act. When Jefferson sat down to pen the Declaration, he knew these accusations would come, so his first thought was of law. He wanted the world to know that Americans were not lawless rebels. Instead, England was the lawbreaker. If war must come, it would be England's fault, because Americans had a right to be free — a right flowing from the laws of nature and of nature's God.

The words *laws of nature and of nature's God*[1] in the Declaration of Independence may be the most misunderstood words in American legal history.[2] It was a legal phrase for God's law revealed through nature and His moral law revealed in the Bible.[3] Yet, many people think that the phrase is unchristian or even anti-Christian.[4] They think that by using the phrase, Jefferson and the founders rejected a Christian approach to law and founded America on an anti-Christian idea.[5]

Five reasons are usually given to prove that the phrase "laws of nature and of nature's God" is against the Bible and Christian teaching. First, some say that Jefferson invented the phrase "laws of nature and of nature's God" as a way to reject the Christian law heritage in the colonies. This means that the Declaration represented not only a break with England but a break with America's Christian past. By using the phrase, the founders in 1776 intended to give birth to America as a secular, non-Christian nation.

Second, some say that the phrase is the product of deism and eighteenth-century Enlightenment rationalism, intellectual movements in Europe and America that rejected the Bible and Christianity.[6]

Third, many writers charge that Jefferson took his ideas about the "laws of nature" from John Locke and that Locke was a deist. By copying Locke, Jefferson formed the Declaration around deistic beliefs.[7]

Fourth, some claim that the "laws of nature" idea, though not new with Jefferson, was still a reaction against Calvinism and the Puritan colonial legal tradition.

Fifth, some admit that Christians used the idea of the "laws of nature" long before Jefferson wrote, but insist that Christians borrowed it from the Greeks and Stoics. Even if the founders thought they were using Christian ideas, they were not. Today's Christians, then, must reject any use of the "laws of nature" either by Christianity or by Jefferson because we know better.

The common core of all these arguments is that Jefferson and the founders rejected a Christian view of law and intentionally embraced a pagan view of law.[8] This chapter will show that all five reasons are flawed. The founders did not "invent" the idea of "laws of nature and of nature's God." They did not borrow it from deists or Enlightenment rationalists as a way to make America a secular, non-Christian nation. Instead, they relied on a Christian theory of law that had been part of the common law centuries before the Enlightenment and deism arose. It is true that Jefferson and the colonists were influenced by the writings of John Locke. But Locke was not a deist in his view of God nor in his views of politics and law. To say that Jefferson argued from the "laws of nature" as a way to reject a Calvinist view of law is laughable since the term was always central to Calvinist legal theory. Finally, the intellectual heritage of the Declaration of Independence cannot be traced to a pagan source, because it is impossible to equate the use of "nature" in the Declaration with the way "nature" was used by the Greeks or Romans.

As a whole, this chapter will demonstrate that much of the conventional wisdom is wrong about the legal theory of the Declaration of Independence. It is a mistake to trace that legal theory to deism, the rationalistic Enlightenment, the Renaissance, and ancient Rome and Greece while excluding the direct influence of the Bible and the Judeo-Christian intellectual tradition. Indeed, the legal theory of the Declaration could not have come about without the Bible and the western Christian tradition. The legal theory of the Declaration stands squarely inside the mainstream Christian tradition of law and legal theory.

The "Laws of Nature": An Invention?

Did the drafters depart from the Christian tradition of law in the colonies by using the phrase "laws of nature" in the Declaration? Was this something new and different? Some say yes, meaning that framers consciously rejected a Christian approach to law and government.[9] The claim is historically false.[10]

For example, in 1764, twelve years before the Declaration of Independence, James Otis relied upon the law of nature in his famous protest against the legality of the Stamp and Sugar Acts. In 1765, Massachusetts declared: "1. Resolved, That there are certain essential rights of the British constitution and government which are founded in the law of God and nature, and are the common rights of mankind; Therefore, 2. Resolved, That the inhabitants of this province are unalienably entitled to those essential rights, in common with all men; and that no law of society can, consistent with the law of God and nature, divest them of those rights."[11] In 1774, the First Continental Congress cited the "immutable laws of nature" in their "Declarations and Resolves." And in the years leading up to 1776, the phrase "laws of nature" was frequently used and widely understood by the colonists.

The practice of appealing to the "law of nature" was more than a hundred years old in the colonies. It was firmly established by Puritans coming to New England in the early 1600s. This rugged but highly literate people carved a civilization out of a rough wilderness. They prided themselves on having personal libraries with the works of leading Puritan and Calvinist writers. The books of Puritan theologians became the settlers' textbooks.

Some of the most widely read authors were William Ames (1576-1633),[12] John Preston (1587-1628), Thomas Hooker (1586?-1647), and Thomas Shepard (1604-1649). Perry Miller has shown that these men repeatedly wrote about the "Law of Nature" as part of the foundation of their federal, or covenant, theology. Ames said, for example, that "the Law of Nature" was the same as "that Law of God, which is naturally written in the heart of all men."[13] The starting point of Puritan theology was God's covenant of works with Adam, the first man. According to Miller, "The original covenant of works, therefore, is the law of nature, that which uncorrupted man would naturally know and by which he would naturally regulate his life."[14]

From the very first, the "law of nature" idea was central to Puritan thinking. It was integrated into the whole scheme of Christian theology. It was a cornerstone of colonial jurisprudence. It was also a central theme in Anglican common-law jurisprudence. To say that the founders invented the idea as a way to depart from the earlier Christian legal tradition in the colonies before 1776 is nonsense.

However, it is true that in the ten years before the American revolution, the founders did not rely on the "laws of nature" as the first line of argument against King George III and for good reason. They were still relying on the British constitution. They were focusing on the "rights of Englishmen" secured to them by the colonial charters.

For example, as early as 1606, the first Charter of Virginia promised to Virginians and their descendants "all Liberties, Franchises, and Immunities . . . as if they had been abiding and born, within this our Realm of England."[15] The same guarantee was given in the charters of New England (1620), Massachusetts (1629), Maryland (1632), Maine (1639), Connecticut (1662), Rhode Island (1663), Carolina (1663), and Georgia (1732).[16] As long as the dispute was over English rights and laws, and the king and Parliament were trusted to decide the dispute, the colonists presented their grievances in those terms.

The "rights of Englishmen" were drawn from the various documents that made up England's constitution. England had no single written constitution or comprehensive statement of rights. Instead, the English constitution was an assortment of various documents spanning at least a six-hundred-year period from the Magna Carta of 1215 through the Bill of Rights of 1689 and beyond.[17]

These documents, along with common-law judicial opinions, contained a vast and widely discussed body of rights. By claiming the "rights of Englishmen" promised in the colonial charters, the colonists were standing on a centuries-old tradition they believed to be unshakeable.

The tradition had only recently been strengthened in the British struggle with the Stuart kings in the 1600s, who claimed to rule by "divine right," ignoring such documents as the Magna Carta. Most colonial libraries had the commentaries of Sir Edward Coke, who led the fight against Stuart tyranny and was largely responsible for the "Petition of Right" of 1628. The Petition of Right spelled out in detail many of the "rights of Englishmen" upon which the colonists were relying. More were added by the "Bill of Rights" of 1689. And colonists everywhere were familiar with the writings of William Blackstone, the famous common-law expert whose commentaries on English law contained whole chapters about the rights of Englishmen.

From the time of Patrick Henry's famous House of Burgesses speech in 1765, through the spring of 1774, the claim to the "rights of Englishmen" led the day. Then, the unthinkable happened. Certain powerful members of Parliament began insisting that the colonists were no longer Englishmen or citizens. Word came to the colonists that the majority party considered them to be outside the British constitution and that their charters were meaningless. Some British leaders were saying that the colonists no longer had any rights and could be treated merely as slaves. In the eyes of these leaders, the king and Parliament owned the colonists.[18]

The colonists were horrified. It took them some months to believe what had happened. They were finally convinced that their appeals were falling upon deaf ears when in August of 1775, the king refused to see Richard Penn and receive the "Olive Branch Petition" from the colonists. That same day, the king declared the colonies were in rebellion and must be crushed—so much for the rights of Englishmen.

They were in a position of last resort. They could no longer rely on the constitution of England or on English law, nor could they stand on their rights as Englishmen. There was no English judge to hear their case. So they appealed to a greater constitution, a greater law, a greater judge, and a greater system of rights.

The colonists knew that God had written his laws into the constitution of the universe: the laws of nature and of nature's God. He had created men in his own image, endowing them with "unalienable rights." He is the "Supreme Judge" who rules the earth by His Divine Providence. He judges men and nations. He is higher than the king of England, and His law is higher than Parliament's. His courthouse never closes to men's justice and rights. Since the British had closed the doors of earthly justice, putting an end to law and rights, the colonists appealed to God. That is why the legal language is different.[19]

So it is wrong to say that appealing to the "laws of nature" is a departure from the Christian common law.[20] For centuries English jurists had claimed that God the Supreme Judge was over all human judges and that His law was over all human law. The Declaration marked a change in venue, from human courts to a heavenly one. And it marked a shift in emphasis from human law to divine law. But it was not a change in "the law" because the "laws of nature and of God" had always been the foundation of English law.[21]

The Term "Laws of Nature": Coined by Deists?

Some say that the phrase "laws of nature and of nature's God" is deistic and anti-Christian. By using it, the founding fathers supposedly rejected the Judeo-Christian intellectual tradition. For example, evangelical historian C. Gregg Singer has said: "Indeed, it is not too much to say that many, if not most, of the leaders of the Continental Congress of 1776, who drafted and signed the Declaration of Independence, were greatly influenced by the Enlightenment and were, to varying degrees, self-conscious deists. It must also be observed that this document was grounded in this appeal to natural law and to deism."[22] He goes on to say:

(B)ehind the political philosophy of the American Revolution, as it found its expression in . . . the Declaration, there lay a view of God and of human nature which was not Christian but deist, which was not orthodox and conservative but radical. It thus follows that the American Revolution in its basic philosophy was not Christian, and the democratic way of life which arose from it was not, and is not, Christian, but was, and is, a deistic and secularized caricature of the evangelical point of view. . . . The fact that John Witherspoon and other evangelicals of the day were willing to sign the Declaration should not blind us to its essentially anti-Christian character. . . .[23]

Singer objects mainly to the phrase "laws of nature." He thinks the phrase represents an idea that is opposed to the Bible, and that it was coined by eighteenth-century deists. But the phrase has been used for many centuries to represent the teaching of the Apostle Paul in the book of Romans and still is. For example, in *The New International Commentary on the New Testament*, John Murray shows how the law of nature is a Christian concept based on the teachings of the Apostle Paul.[24]

Nor was the term coined by deists in the seventeenth or eighteenth centuries. The longer phrase "law of nature or God" was used as early as the first decade of the 1300s in a debate between rival Catholic monastic orders.[25] The simple phrase "law of nature" was already part of Catholic theology and canon law at least as early as the eleventh century. Thomas Aquinas used it repeatedly in his *Summa Theologica* in the thirteenth century. So the term "law of nature" was part of Christian legal language at least five hundred years before the rise of deism as a movement.

The "Law of Nature" and the Common Law

From the canon law of the Catholic Church, the term "law of nature" made its way into the common law of England. In the Christian common-law tradition of England from Bracton (d. 1268) to Blackstone (c. 1760s) the term "law of nature" meant the eternal moral law God the Creator established over His created universe. It was a technical term for "creation law"—the original scheme of things purposed or willed by the Almighty.[26]

Sir William Blackstone was a contemporary of the framers. His *Commentaries on the Laws of England* (1765) was one of the primary sources for the colonists' understanding of the English common-law tradition. Blackstone was so popular in the colonies that as many copies of his *Commentaries* were sold in the colonies in the ten years prior to the revolution as in England itself. Blackstone was required reading at almost all colonial universities. Here is how he defined the "law of nature."

> (W)hen the Supreme Being formed the universe, and created matter out of nothing, he impressed certain principles upon that matter. . . . When he put that matter into motion, he established certain laws of motion. . . . If we farther advance to vegetable and animal life, we shall find them still governed by laws; . . . [The operations of inanimate and organic processes] are not left to chance, or the will of the creature itself, but are performed in a wondrous involuntary manner, and guided by unerring rules laid down by the Great Creator. . . . Man, considered as a creature, must necessarily be subject to the laws of his creator, for he is an entirely dependent being. . . . And consequently as man depends absolutely upon his maker for every thing, it is necessary that he should in all points conform to his maker's will. This will of his maker is called the law of nature.[27]

Blackstone's ideas about God and law stand in the mainstream of Christian teaching when viewed in terms of Church history and systematic theology. His view of *ex nihilo* creation and creation law comes directly from the teachings of the Bible and mainstream Christianity. It reflects the influence of Genesis 1, Hebrews 11, and Romans 1 and 2. In the section of the *Commentaries* from which the above quote is taken, Blackstone used seven pages to define the "law of nature." In those pages he covered all the components of an orthodox, Christian view of law.[28]

For him the "law of nature" was the "will of God," which God decreed from the very creation of the world. It binds all men, everywhere, in all circumstances, and in every age.[29] The "law of nature," imposed on men by God Himself, is an immutable law of good and evil to which all men are accountable. Men must have the Bible, special revelation, to know it completely. But they know it also through nature, God's general revelation. However, man cannot know the law adequately through general revelation alone because his intellect is corrupted by sin.[30] The "law of nature" for Blackstone was Christian, not deistic. And Blackstone was a major source of the founders' legal terminology and concepts.

Blackstone's view was not new. One hundred and fifty years before Blackstone, Sir Edward Coke (pronounced Cook) gave a similar definition in *Calvin's Case*, (circa 1610).

> The law of nature is that which God at the time of creation of the nature of man infused into his heart, for his preservation and direction; and this is *lex aeterna*, the moral law, called also the law of nature. And by the law, written with the finger of God in the heart of man, were the people of God a long time governed, before the law was written by Moses, who was the first reporter or writer of law in the world. The Apostle in the Second Chapter to the Romans saith, *Cum enim gentes quae legem non habent naturaliter ea quae legis sunt faciunt* [While the nations who do not have the law do naturally the things of the law]. And this is within the command of that moral law, *honora patrem*, which doubtless doth extend to him that is *pater patriae*. And that the Apostle saith, *Omnis anima potestatibus subdita sit* [Let every person be subject to authorities]. And these be the words of the Great Divine, *Hoc Deus in Sacris Scripturis jubet, hoc lex naturae dictari, ut quilibet subditus obediat superio*. . . . [This God commands in Sacred Scripture, this the law of nature dictates, in order that anyone who is a subject might render obedience to the superior.] (T)herefore the law of God and nature is one to all. . . . This law of nature, which indeed is the eternal law of the Creator, infused into the heart of the creature at the time of his creation, was two thousand years before any laws written, and before any judicial or municipal laws.[31]

Here Coke traces his understanding of the phrase "law of nature" to the Christian Scriptures and to mainstream Christian theology. His words indicate that he took the Bible seriously. Coke intended to stand inside the Christian faith and Christian legal tradition.

The "Law of Nature" and the "Law of God"

Part of the Christian tradition was to speak of the "law of nature" and the "law of God" as two sides of the same coin. Here we find Coke speaking of the law of nature and of God as one and the same thing, simply two different aspects of one law. The "law of nature" is God's eternal moral law inscribed in nature and on men's hearts. The "law of God" is the same eternal moral law revealed in Scripture.

Like Coke, Blackstone equated the "law of nature" and the "law of God":

> The doctrines thus delivered we call the revealed or divine law, and they are to be found only in the holy scriptures. . . . These precepts . . . are found upon comparison to be really a part of the original law of nature, . . . As then the moral precepts of this law are indeed of the same original with those of the law of nature . . . the revealed law . . . is the law of nature expressly declared to be so by God himself; . . . Upon these two foundations, the law of nature and the law of revelation, depend all human laws . . . the law of nature and the law of God. . . .[32]

Both Coke and Blackstone were following the mainstream Christian theological tradition that had been in place for centuries. As noted earlier, by the first decade of the 1300's, Christian theologians were already discussing the doctrine of the "law of nature or God" as a single law.[33]

The Bible and the "Law of Nature and of God"

The Christian practice of speaking of the "law of nature" and the "law of God" as a single law grew out of the church's reading of the New Testament in Romans 1 and 2. There the Apostle Paul denounced a mistake of certain legalists who claimed that the only valid "law of God" was the Mosaic legislation in the Pentateuch. They denied God's general revelation in nature. They did not believe that God had written His moral law on the hearts of unbelievers. They tried to honor God's law by making Biblical law the only law of God. The Apostle pointed out that to say this was not to protect God's law, but to deny God's law, because God Himself gives general revelation in nature and in men's hearts. In the name of honoring the law of God, the legalists were in fact repudiating the law of God and consequently attacking God's sovereignty and omnipotence.

Some writers say that the Apostle Paul took his ideas in Romans 1 and 2 from the Greeks and Stoics.[34] This would mean that the church's views about the "law of nature" were borrowed from the Stoics. However, Paul was relying on the teachings of the ancient Hebrew Scriptures in the Old Testament.

Centuries before the Stoic tradition had arisen in Greece, the Hebrew Scriptures had affirmed God's creation laws over all things.[35] The general revelation of God's moral law to all men in common was one of the primary themes of the book of Job, one of the oldest books in the Bible.[36] Psalm 19 and similar passages taught that God uses creation itself as a teaching tool for mankind, to communicate through nature God's laws and preceptual ordinances.[37] In numerous places, the Old Testament gave specific examples of the fact that God spoke supernaturally even to non-Jews.[38] The nature of that revelation was moral and general only, and was not on the same par with the specific oracles that God revealed to Hebrew prophets uniquely.[39] Nevertheless, it was abundantly clear from the Old Testament that before God gave the revealed law through Moses and later prophets, God had already given a general revelation of moral law to the whole of mankind in common.

In Romans 1 and 2, the Apostle Paul explained the implications of this Old Testament view of the twofold nature of God's law for the gospel age. According to the Apostle, God's creation law is not in conflict with His Scriptural law. God's law is not at odds with itself, nor inconsistent. Following Paul, the early church sought to speak of law in such a way as to affirm the validity of both sides of the law of God, without misrepresenting either side. The phrase "laws of nature and of God," which was in settled use by the time of the rise of medieval Christianity, grew out of this desire to affirm the validity both of the natural, pre-Mosaic law as well as the written law of Scripture.

The "Law of Nature" and Trinitarian Theology

The theology of the early church was trinitarian. This meant that although the Son is subject to the Father, the Father and the Son are one and, as God, are coequal and coeternal. Likewise, although the general revelation of God's law is subject to special revelation, the two are nonetheless a unity and equally valid as a statement of God's law. R.J. Rushdoony explains how trinitarianism was at the base of the legal theory of the early church:

> True law, it was held, came from the triune God, and its claims were universal. All men know the law, because at creation it was inscribed on the tables of man's heart, and thus all men are subjects of the law and rebel in terms of it. Irenaeus declared that the Ten Commandments simply restated what creation had originally implanted: "They (the Jews) had therefore a law, a course of discipline, and a prophecy of future things. For God at the first, indeed, warning them by means of natural precepts, which from the beginning He had implanted in mankind, that is by means of the Decalogue (which, if anyone does not observe, he has no salvation), did then demand nothing more of them."[40]

With the rise of the canon law, the phrase "laws of nature and of God" was devised by Catholic law scholars as a shorthand way to affirm the validity of God's law, both natural and written. It addressed God's law in the same order of timing that God had revealed it historically — first, the general; then, the special. The phrase was trinitarian in the sense that it did not try to subordinate any part of God's law to any other part.[41] Following Paul, the church viewed denigrating any part of God's law as a heresy. Since God's law is a unity, to deny any part of God's law is to deny the whole law of God. This is why Puritans such as John Wise were right to speak of general revelation and Scriptural revelation as equally from God.

The Common Law and Jefferson

Blackstone's use of the phrase carried forward a custom that was at least five hundred years old, which itself grew out of the orthodox Christian practice to speak of God's one law from two different perspectives. It was the "law of nature" and "of God." This long-established symmetry was continued in Jefferson's phrase "the laws of nature and of nature's God." By using the distributive plural "laws," Jefferson distinguishes between two laws: the law of nature, and the law of God who is over nature. At the same time, the distributive plural links the two together to show that they really signify the same thing.[42] Jefferson was not coining a new term or concocting a new idea.

Historian Richard Perry, in *Sources of Our Liberties*, says that Jefferson was not creating new ideas. Perry traces the development of western liberty from the Magna Carta in 1215 through the Constitution of the United States. Of Jefferson's political philosophy in the Declaration, Perry says: "There was nothing in that philosophy that was new. It was not Jefferson's task to create a new system of politics or government but rather to apply accepted principles to the situation at hand."[43]

We can also confidently assume that Coke's Christian view of the laws of nature had an impact on the thinking of those who drafted and ratified the Declaration of Independence. Louis Wright, tracing the impact of the Magna Carta on the American founding fathers, thought it significant that "The writings of the founding fathers and their speeches frequently cite Magna Carta and Coke's commentary. Many of them of course had Coke's *Institutes* as well as his *Reports* in their libraries. John Adams . . . had studied his Coke diligently. . . ."[44] Jefferson studied Coke diligently as well.[45] He and Adams served together on the Declaration's drafting committee.

Coke was not the only common law scholar of the early 1600s to use the term "law of nature." John Selden, a contemporary of Coke and a famous common law scholar, once said, "I cannot fancy to myself what the law of nature means, but the law of God."[46] Selden wrote *De Jure Naturali et Gentium Iuxta Disciplinam Ebraeorum* (1640), [*The Law of Nature and of Nations According to the Hebrews*]. In it he traced the idea of the law of nature to the ancient Hebrews living just after the time of Noah's flood. Selden's analysis makes the idea of the "law of nature" of Hebrew origin, and pre-Greek.[47]

Before the time of Coke and Selden, the term "law of nature" was used by the great English law scholar John Fortescue (1396-1486). Before Fortescue, it was used by Henri De Bracton (d. 1268), a Catholic archdeacon who is called the "Father of the Common Law." Neither Coke nor Blackstone was speaking in a vacuum. They represented the mainstream use of the legal idea of law of nature tracing back to the very birth of the common law. That the common-law tradition was rooted squarely and explicitly in mainstream orthodox Christian legal thinking is evidenced by the words of many English jurists from Bracton to Blackstone.

Once we understand from this clear historical record that the phrase "law of nature and of God" had been for centuries an ordinary term in the Christian common law and in Christian legal philosophy, to say that Jefferson took the idea from deism and the Enlightenment is absurd. Coke used the term "law of nature"— supported by Scriptural citations—at least fifty years before the start of the Enlightenment, and one hundred years before the spread of deism.[48] For someone to claim that the phrase was born of deism or the Enlightenment as an attack on Christianity is indefensible.[49]

A Single Standard of Ethics: Aquinas and Natural Law

It is also crucial that we recognize that the common-law tradition was not fostering two standards of ethics, making the moral precepts of Scripture the rule only of religious ethics, and man's reason the foundation of natural ethics. To do so would have made a part of ethics and some ethical decisions independent of the Word of God. The common law was not humanistic. The phrase "law of nature and of God" expressed a unity, so that the phrase affirmed the validity of God's law. At the same time, the phrase stood for the proposition that the government does not enforce the "entire" law of God in Scripture, but only the moral law, not the ceremonial or political law. The phrase was calculated to reflect the unity between God's creation law and revealed law, with the revealed law dispositive for man.[50]

Singer's criticism of the natural law tradition is based on the erroneous belief that the medieval church and the English common law made nature and the Bible two independent sources of ethics. This error is usually traced to Thomas Aquinas (1225-1274), who supposedly made human reason a source of law and truth equal to Scripture. Aquinas was a key figure in the Catholic "natural law" tradition leading up to Coke and Blackstone and finally the Declaration of Independence. Francis Schaeffer best explains this supposed mistake of Aquinas.

Aquinas had an incomplete view of the Fall. He thought that the Fall did not affect man as a whole but only in part. In his view the will was fallen or corrupted but the intellect was not affected. Thus people could rely on their own human wisdom, and this meant that people were free to mix the teachings of the Bible with the teachings of the non-Christian philosophers.[51]

Supposedly, Aquinas made the mind of man equal to Scripture, opening the door for natural law to be based on man's reason alone without subjecting reason to the law of the Bible. There are three problems with this view about Aquinas. First, Aquinas believed that man's intellect was corrupted and not merely weakened by sin. According to Aquinas, the mind is part of the soul and the entire soul is corrupted by sin.[52] Second, when dealing with man's reason in relationship to law, Aquinas said that natural law in man's mind must be submitted to the overruling control of the written law in Scripture.

The written law is . . . given for the correction of the natural law, either because it supplies what was lacking in the natural law, or because the natural law was perverted in the hearts of different men, as to different matters, so that they thought those things good which are naturally evil, which perversion stood in need of correction.[53]

Aquinas did not believe that any ethical decision could be based on the natural law alone. Even the most mundane matters of life are under the rule of Scripture.

(I)t was necessary for the directing of human conduct to have a Divine law . . . because, on account of the uncertainty of human judgment, especially on contingent and particular matters, different people form different judgments on human acts; and from this also different and contrary laws result. In order, therefore, that man may know without any doubt what he ought to do and what he ought to avoid, it was necessary for man to be directed in his proper acts by a law given by God, for it is certain such a law cannot err.[54]

Third, this view fails to account for two of the different ways in which Aquinas used the term *reason*. In one context, reason meant inferential logic or the process of thinking and understanding. As a function of the human soul and personality, reason is inevitably corrupted and flawed by sin. In another context, reason denoted God's perfect wisdom and knowledge, which God communicates to man by the divine activity of His own Spirit directly upon man's soul and through man's environment, causing man to know it intuitively.

According to Aquinas, God's wisdom is true reason and the only "right reason." This kind of reason, coming from God, is unfallen in terms of its source, though man's perception of it is inevitably corrupt. Man seeks to suppress and deny this witness coming from God but can never escape it entirely. Nevertheless, if we are to understand Aquinas correctly, reason as a light shined in man by God must always be distinguished from reason as man's inferential logic and understanding.

Someone might object that Aquinas was concerned here only with the intellect, not with ethics. This would mean that Aquinas was following the old neo-Platonic idea that man's problem was not rebellion but incorrect knowledge. But Aquinas had earlier insisted that "all of the parts of the soul" including the intellect are "corrupted by original sin."[55] "Mortal sin," he says, is in "man's reason," which must be restored by "justifying grace," not merely by the addition of faith as some have suggested of Aquinas.[56] The Fall was not simply metaphysical, but moral, according to Aquinas. And the Fall affected even man's knowledge of the cosmos, because man's intellect "is dazzled by the clearest objects of nature; as the owl is dazzled by the sun."[57]

A careful reading of Thomas Aquinas's views of law show him anticipating Blackstone by five hundred years, saying that natural law in man's reason must be submitted to the overruling control of Scripture. It is incorrect, at least where Aquinas and Blackstone are concerned, to say that the "law of nature" tradition made "natural law" independent from the control of Scripture.[58]

Was John Locke a Deist?

John Locke was not a deist—not in his views of God, nor in his views of law and politics.[59] When he used the phrase "law of nature" to describe the natural part of God's revealed law and how it relates to the Bible, he was squarely within the mainstream Christian tradition. Yet most believe that Locke was a deist, or at least tended toward deism, by rejecting the Christian view of God and the Bible.[60]

Locke was widely read in the American colonies.[61] Without question, he influenced the way Jefferson wrote the Declaration of Independence.[62] If Jefferson borrowed Locke's view of the law of nature, and Locke was a deist, America was born a deistic nation, not a Christian nation. This idea is the essence of what might be called the "deistic America" thesis.

Carl Becker, more than anyone else, is the Aesop behind the "deistic America" fable. In 1922, Becker wrote a book about the Declaration of Independence, which, though not really creating any new ideas, brought together various ideas about the Declaration in a new and novel way. Because Becker was a master stylist and a great popularizer, his book caused quite a sensation. It was revised and reissued in 1942.[63] His book set the standard by which the Declaration has been interpreted by a generation of historians that followed him.

Becker explained the Declaration this way. When Jefferson wrote the phrase "laws of nature and of nature's God" he had in mind John Locke's *Second Treatise on Government* (1690). Jefferson followed Locke because Locke was a deist who had purposely rejected the Catholic and Puritan compact theory of government. Locke instead had based his writings on naturalism and rationalism, deifying nature and denaturing God.[64]

According to Becker, Catholics and Protestants had worked out a Biblical argument, "which Locke might have used to justify the Revolution of 1688."[65] But Locke

> had lost that sense of intimate intercourse and familiar conversation with God which religious men of the sixteenth- and seventeenth-centuries enjoyed. Since the later seventeenth century, God had been withdrawing from immediate contact with men, and had become, in proportion as he receded into the dim distance, no more than the final Cause, or Great Contriver, or Prime Mover of the universe.[66]

Here Becker attributes to Locke a belief in the "watchmaker God/absentee God" kind of deism. Whereas true Christianity viewed God as actively involved in running His world and revealing Himself to men, in deism God is "conceived as exerting his power and revealing his will indirectly through his creation rather than directly by miraculous manifestation or through inspired books."[67] Becker concludes, "In the eighteenth century as never before, 'Nature' had stepped in between man and God; so that there was no longer any way to know God's will except by discovering the 'laws' of Nature, which would doubtless be the laws of 'nature's' god as Jefferson said."[68] Deism, then, gave birth to Locke's ideas about revolution and, through Jefferson, gave birth to the American Revolution.

Becker did not deny that Locke quoted the Bible. But according to Becker, nature, not God, became the source of law and rights for Locke. Nature had stepped in between man and God, the age of miracles was past, and God no longer spoke through inspired books, namely, the Bible. So for Locke, the Bible was not a divine word from God.

I find it baffling that Becker would make such a claim. Locke had cited the Old Testament example of Jephthah who led the Israelite army in defense against the Ammonites. They were in a state of war, Locke explained, because there was no earthly authority to whom the Israelites could appeal to hear their case against the Ammonites.[69] There was no earthly deliverer for the Jews, thus Jephthah

> was forced to appeal to heaven: "The Lord the Judge," says he, "be judge this day between the children of Israel and the children of Ammon" (Judges xi. 27.), and then prosecuting and relying on this appeal, he leads out his army to battle. . . . Where there is no judge on earth, the appeal lies to God in heaven.[70]

In explaining what Locke meant by this passage, Becker wrote:

> We see, he says, that in the dispute between Jephthah and the Ammonites, "he [Jephthah] was forced to appeal to Heaven: 'The Lord the Judge (says he) be judge this day.'" Well, of course, says Locke, 'everyone knows what Jephthah here tells us, that the Lord the Judge shall judge.' But the trouble is the Lord does not do it now; he reserves his decision till the Day of Judgment. Jephthah appealed to the Lord, but the Lord did not speak, did not decide

the dispute between Jephthah and the Ammonites; the result of which was that Jephthah had to decide it himself by leading out his armies.[71]

One wonders how Becker could think the words "this day" meant some "future day." Nothing Locke said in using Jephthah as Biblical authority for the way to carry out a just war in self-defense matches Becker's interpretation. Furthermore, God did act that day; He did not reserve judgment to some future day. The "Spirit of the Lord came upon Jephthah" (Judges 11:29), and when Jephthah met the Ammonites "the Lord gave them into his hand" (Judges 11:32). Becker misread Locke badly, so badly, in fact, that he turned Locke's meaning completely backwards.

Two things are important here. First, Becker has misrepresented Locke's view of the Bible. Second, he has accused Locke of holding deistic views of God and nature when Locke did not.[72] He has, in effect, ascribed to Locke the equivalent of the modern dictionary definition of deism, which is "The belief claiming foundation solely upon the evidence of reason, in the existence of God as the creator of the universe who after setting it in motion abandoned it, assumed no control over life, exerted no influence on natural phenomena, and gave no supernatural revelation."[73] If we examine each part of this definition we find that none of them describes Locke's views.

First, Locke relied on Scripture — supernatural revelation — as authority for his political principles. Both the first and second treatises overflow with direct Scriptural citations as authority. Second, Locke relied upon Scripture in Judges 11 and elsewhere, which said that God intervened and governed in the daily affairs of men and nations, meaning that Locke believed that God influences natural phenomena. Third, Locke obviously believed that God exerts control over life, since he agreed that God gives men victory in battle in response to prayer. Fourth, he did not believe God abandoned the universe; otherwise, why would Locke use as an example the fact that God answered the prayers of Jephthah, a mere man? Fifth, since Locke relied on Scripture we cannot say that he relied on the evidence of reason alone. Sixth, Locke did not put nature in opposition to Scripture since he believed that the law of war was the same in Judges 11 as in the law of nature from creation. Locke even explicitly stated that both nature and Scripture are declarations of God's eternal law.

How Becker could claim that Locke had rejected inspired books and relied on reason alone defies logic, when it is so abundantly clear that Locke repeatedly relied on the authority of Scripture throughout the *Second Treatise*. Locke's use of Scripture sometimes consumes whole pages. He repeated the Jephthah example at least three more times in other parts of the *Second Treatise*.[74] From these it is clear that Locke meant that God judged now and not at some future date. God was not an absentee God to Locke.[75] It also defies logic for Becker to claim that Locke believed God was disinterested and uninvolved in the affairs of men since Locke said that God Himself had transferred Saul's kingdom to David.[76]

Other of Locke's writings show how wrong Becker was. Locke's *Reasonableness of Christianity* (1695), his *Discourse on Miracles* (1706), and his *Letters Concerning Toleration* all rely heavily on the Bible.[77] Even Locke's *Essay Concerning Human Understanding*, which Becker also mentions, openly asserts that the Bible is a special divine revelation of the highest authority from God to man. There Locke says that everything in the text of the Old and New Testaments is "infallibly true" since it is the "will of God . . . clothed in words."[78] Later he says that the "Christian religion" was not devised by the minds of men but received "from revelation."[79] For "(w)hen God declares any truth to us, this is a revelation to us by the voice of his Spirit."[80]

In Book 4, chapter 10 of the *Essay*, Locke quotes in its entirety Romans 1:20 from the Apostle Paul as an example of "as certain and clear a truth as can anywhere be delivered."[81] In chapter 16 he discusses the miracles in the Bible, which are a "testimony . . . of God himself."[82] When God speaks supernaturally or confirms His word with miracles "(t)his carries with it an assurance beyond doubt . . . evidence beyond exception. This is called . . . 'revelation,' and our assent to it, 'faith' . . . (W)e may as well doubt of our own being, as we can whether any revelation from God be true."[83]

Finally, Locke says: "Whatever God hath revealed is certainly true; no doubt can be made of it."[84] He cautions that men must be careful not to be deceived by the Prince of Darkness, who tries to make delusions and lies sound like divine truth from God.[85] But once a man has tested the spirits or proved whether a claimed revelation is divine as the Bible requires, he may accept the revelation as from God.[86] Thus, Scripture and God's spiritual witness to man's soul are

> unerring rules to know whether it be from God or no. Where the truth embraced is consonant to the revelation in the written word of God, or the action conformable to the dictates of right reason or holy writ, we may be assured that we run no risk in entertaining it as such.[87]

Locke Was Not a Deist

Locke clearly believed that the Bible was supernatural revelation, and should not be subordinated to man's finite understanding.

> The holy Scripture is to me, and always will be, the constant guide of my belief; and I shall always hearken to it, as containing infallible truth relating to things of the highest concernment. And I wish I could say there are no mysteries in it: I acknowledge there are to me, and I fear always will be. But where I lack the evidence of things, there yet is ground enough for me to believe, because God has said it: and I shall immediately condemn and quit any opinion of mine, as soon as I am shown that it is contrary to any revelation in the holy scripture.[88]

Locke believed that men could be saved only by believing in Jesus Christ.

> Not that any to whom the gospel hath been preached shall be saved, without believing Jesus to be the Messiah; for all being sinners, and transgressors of the law, and so unjust, are all liable to condemnation, unless they believe, and so through grace are justified by God for this faith, which shall be accounted to them for righteousness.[89]

In numerous places Locke said that men had to be justified by faith in Jesus Christ, and must repent and believe that Jesus Christ is the Messiah and Son of God.[90] He spoke of man's baseness and the corruption of human nature.[91] He even called man "degenerate."[92] He believed in miracles, special providence, and the resurrection of Christ.[93] He was not orthodox in all of his beliefs, but he was far from being a deist.[94]

Locke, Jephthah, and Jefferson

If Becker was wrong about Locke's use of Jephthah and Judges 11:27, this has important implications for the Declaration of Independence. Jephthah had called on God as Judge, or, in Locke's words, "Supreme Judge," in the war with the Ammonites. God was asked to weigh in on the side of the innocent party and give victory to its army. If Jefferson, in the last paragraph of the Declaration, was following Locke by calling upon God as "Supreme Judge" who gives military victory to those whose defense is just, then we have a direct link between the Bible and the Declaration of Independence. Locke's language was consciously drawn from Scripture and was explained in terms of Scripture. If the drafters of the Declaration were aware of that passage in Locke and meant to follow it, this means they were asking God to miraculously deliver the Continental Army from the British if the British were in the wrong. Such a position is hardly deistic.

Locke and the "Law of Nature"

Becker also charged that Locke was a deist for using the term "law of nature" in a way that departed from traditional Christian understanding. Locke used the term but in the same way that mainstream Catholics and Protestants did. He did not make natural law in man's mind the source of the law of nature as Becker mistakenly tries to show.[95] Rather, Locke explained the law of nature and natural law much in the same way as had John Calvin and the Westminster Reformers.[96]

Locke wrote his *First Treatise on Government* to refute Sir Robert Filmer's *Patriarchia*, a defense of divine-right monarchy based on the notion that Adam was the first king and that the king of England was a direct heir of Adam. In the *First Treatise*, Locke attempted to show that when God created Adam, God did not provide for any of Adam's descendants to be superior to any others simply by inheritance or royal succession. Locke refuted divine-right monarchy not by rejecting the Bible but by arguing from the Bible.

In the *First Treatise*, Locke used two crucial terms about law: the "law of nature" and "positive law of God." Locke used the term "law of nature" to mean God's general revelation of moral law in nature. He used the term "positive law of God" to describe how God had specially revealed and published that eternal moral law in the Holy Scriptures.[97] Locke rejected divine-right monarchy because "no law of nature" or "positive law of God" existed to make one man inherently superior to another man.[98] No creation law and no command of Scripture prefers one man over another. Divine-right monarchy finds no support in general or special revelation.

In other places, Locke explained that the "law of nature" is God's general revelation of law in creation, which God also supernaturally writes on the hearts of men. Locke drew the idea from the New Testament in Romans 1 and 2.[99] In contrast, he spoke of the "law of God" or the "positive law of God" as God's eternal moral law specially revealed and published in Scripture.[100] Thus, in Locke's writings we find the same twofold distinction about law that has always been part of Christian law theory. God ordained the law of nature at creation as a general revelation, and specially revealed it as the law of God in the written Scriptures.[101]

Locke repeatedly linked these two ideas together with the phrases "the law of God and nature" and "the laws of nature and of God," which he used interchangeably. Both represented ideas learned from Richard Hooker (1554?-1600), the Anglican clergyman who wrote *The Laws of Ecclesiastical Polity* (1593), and whom Locke often cited.[102] Hooker said that general revelation and special revelation are the two means of knowing God's moral law. All human law must agree with these to be valid. The "rules are two, the law of God, and the law of nature; so that laws human must be made according to the general laws of nature, and without contradiction to any positive law of Scripture."[103]

In all his writings, Locke held to Hooker's definition of law. In his *Essay Concerning Human Understanding*, for example, Locke explained "divine law" as "that law which God has set to the actions of men—whether promulgated to them by the light of nature, or the voice of revelation."[104] For Locke, divine law was foundational to any serious thinking about human society:

That God has given a rule whereby men should govern themselves, I think there is nobody so brutish as to deny. He has a right to do it; we are his creatures; he has goodness and wisdom to direct our actions to that which is best; and he has power to enforce it by rewards and punishments of infinite weight and duration in another life; for nobody can take us out of his hands.[105]

God's divine law, revealed both through nature and Scripture, is "the only true touchstone of moral rectitude; and, by comparing (human actions) to this law, it is that men judge of the most considerable moral good or evil of their actions; that is, whether, as duties or sins, they are likely to procure them happiness or misery from the hands of the ALMIGHTY."[106]

Thomas Peardon, in his edition of Locke's *Second Treatise*, correctly points out that Locke was widely read "not because Locke was original in his political ideas, but rather because he gave clear and reasonable expression to beliefs that were the product of centuries of political experience . . ."[107] Merwyn Johnson convincingly shows that Locke's use of the ideas of laws of nature and of God were not new and novel or deistic.[108]

W. von Leyden makes this clear in his introduction to Locke's *Essays on the Law of Nature*.[109] Von Leyden also notes that besides being influenced by Hooker, Locke was strongly influenced in his understanding of the law of nature by Robert Sanderson (d. 1663), professor of divinity at Oxford, Bishop of Lincoln, and moderator of the Savoy conference with the Presbyterian divines.[110] From these two men, Locke learned a very old and widely received concept of the "laws of nature and of God." To use the phrase was equivalent to saying God's moral decree in creation which God writes on men's hearts, and His positive decrees in Scripture.[111]

Locke's Views of Law Were Not Deistic

To say that Locke made nature the "source" of law, and rejected the mainstream Christian doctrine of law is manifestly wrong. Locke explicitly said that the source of the law of nature was God Himself.[112] Locke is also very much in the mainstream of Christian theology in the way in which he spoke of the law of the Bible. Following earlier Catholic and Protestant practice, Locke separated Biblical law into three categories: moral, ceremonial, and political.

(W)hen St. Paul says, that the gospel establishes the law, he means the moral part of the law of Moses; for that he could not mean the ceremonial, or the political part of it, is evident by what I quoted out of him just now, where he says, that the Gentiles do, by nature, the things contained in the law, their consciences bearing witness. For the Gentiles neither did, nor thought of the judicial (sic) and ceremonial institutions of Moses; 'twas only the moral part, their consciences were concerned in.[113]

By dividing the law of the Bible into moral, ceremonial, and judicial (political) law, Locke was in agreement with the Westminster Confession of Faith,[114] the Westminster Larger Catechism,[115] John Calvin,[116] and even Thomas Aquinas.[117]

Locke was also an heir of Puritan thought by emphasizing that the law of nature is the "moral law," first legislated by God at creation and then specially revealed in the Scriptures.[118] Locke says that God's moral law, decreed in creation, is carried forward in the specific decrees of Scripture, but must not be confused with the ceremonial and political decrees that were given only to the Jews: "But the moral part of Moses's law, or the moral law (which is everywhere the same, the eternal rule of right), obliges Christians and all men everywhere, and is to all men the standing law of works."[119] Indeed, says Locke, the "law of nature" requires men to obey the moral law revealed in Scripture. *In other words, the law of nature requires us to follow the Bible!* "It being a part of the law of nature that man ought to obey every positive law of God."[120]

In a typically undeistic way, Locke declares that once God establishes a law of nature, or moral law, in creation and Scripture, it is not subject to change by man. This moral law—law of nature—is the "eternal law of right, which is holy, just, and good; of which not one precept or rule is abrogated or repealed; nor indeed can be, whilst God is an holy, just, and righteous God."[121] The law of nature belongs to God and only He can change it.[122]

The Declaration of Independence and John Locke

For Locke, the "law of nature" and the "law of God" were two expressions of the same law.[123] Each is a declaration of the will of God. The "law of nature" is the eternal moral law that God legislated in creation and inscribes in men's consciences. The "law of God" is the same eternal moral law as the law of nature, only it is revealed as God's positive law in Scripture.[124] According to Locke, both phrases refer to the Bible. The phrase "law of nature" refers to the Bible because the law of nature requires us "to obey every positive law of God" in Scripture.[125] The phrase "law of God," or to use Jefferson's stylism, the "law of nature's God," directly refers to the moral law of the Bible.[126]

Locke's understanding of the phrase "laws of nature and of God" has enormous implications for what the Declaration of Independence says. If the founders of America were intentionally following Locke by using the phrase "laws of nature and of nature's God," then we must logically conclude that they founded America upon God's creation law revealed in nature and in the express moral commands of Scripture. *In other words, the Declaration of Independence makes the Bible a fundamental part of the legal foundation of America. By referring to the Bible in two distinct ways, the phrase "laws of nature and of nature's God" incorporates by reference the moral law of the Bible into the founding document of our country!* [127]

The long and well-known history of the idea "laws of nature and of God"—that God had revealed His law first through nature and subsequently through Scripture—was what made this concept the logical foundation for the legal theory of the Declaration of Independence. The framers knew that there was no firmer, more respected, legal ground upon which to stand. Educated men in the colonies knew that both sides of the term had a settled place in mainstream Christian orthodoxy. It was a shorthand way to express a very broad and expansive set of ideas and principles.

Christians like John Witherspoon knew that the phrase belonged to the church, and that is why he had no reservations about signing the Declaration of Independence. To support the Declaration did not at all compromise the principles of his orthodox Christian faith. The same is true of the other evangelicals of his day. Whatever Jefferson may secretly have meant by "laws of nature and of nature's God," nothing in the phrase suggested to the ordinary colonist that it was somehow deistic or anti-Christian. The term had been used in various forms for centuries before the rise of the Enlightenment or of deism with virtually no change in meaning.

That is why Morton White is correct in *The Philosophy of the American Revolution* when he says:

Yet Jefferson's moral laws of nature and of nature's God were still viewed at the end of the eighteenth century very much as Hooker had viewed them. They were thought to be decreed by God; they were regarded as precepts for the direction of the voluntary actions of reasonable agents; and some of them were thought to be discoverable by intuitive reason. That is why Jefferson called moral laws "Laws of Nature and of Nature's God."[128]

"Laws of Nature": A Reaction Against Calvinism?

Some have claimed that the founders used the term "law of nature" because they wanted to renounce the Puritan heritage of the colonies.[129] Supposedly, the Declaration made a conscious break with the Calvinism of the New England settlers by relying on "the laws of nature and of nature's God."

To say that the term "law of nature" is contrary to Calvinism and Reformed thinking is strange indeed, since it was always part of Calvinist legal theory. The idea is prominent in the most famous of all Reformed Creeds, the Westminster Confession (1646): "As it is of the law of nature . . . so, in his Word, by a positive, moral, and perpetual commandment, binding all men in all ages."[130]

Furthermore, chapter 19 of the Westminster Confession, "Of the Law of God," explains the Reformed view of natural law and the law of nature in terms almost identical to those previously cited from Coke, Blackstone, and Locke:

> God gave to Adam a law, as a covenant of works, by which he bound him and all his posterity to personal, entire, exact, and perpetual obedience; . . . This law, after his fall, continued to be a perfect rule of righteousness; and, as such, was delivered by God upon mount Sinai in ten commandments, . . . Beside this law, commonly called moral, God was pleased to give to the people of Israel, as a Church under age, ceremonial laws, . . . To them also, as a body politic, he gave sundry judicial laws, which expired together with the state of that people, not obliging any other, now, further than the general equity thereof may require. . . . The moral law doth forever bind all.[131]

The Westminster Larger Catechism continued this theme, with question two referring to the "light of nature in man, and the works of God" declaring God's existence and law.[132] The Catechism, like the Confession, assumes that God's moral law, which He established at creation, is a "rule of obedience" binding all mankind since the time of Adam.[133] The precepts of the moral law, ordained by God at creation as an eternal rule of right, binding all men everywhere by general revelation, are further revealed in the Decalogue by special revelation.[134] Each moral law is also a "law of nature."[135]

John Calvin himself did not see the proper use of "law of nature" and "natural law" as un-Biblical or non-Christian.

> The moral law . . . is the true and eternal rule of righteousness prescribed to the men of all nations and of all times, who would frame their life agreeably to the will of God. . . . Now it is evident that the law of God which we call moral, is nothing else than the testimony of the natural law, and of that conscience which God has engraven on the minds of men, the whole of this equity of which we now speak is prescribed in it.[136]

Calvin and his later followers believed that God ordained His law of nature first as a covenant of works with Adam, that God wrote this law on man's heart and mind as the natural law, and that the law of nature is an eternal rule of right conduct, a moral law, which binds all men, everywhere, in all ages. The precepts of the law of nature were later delivered to the Jews in the Ten Commandments, whose principles bind all nations. Those precepts are distinct from the ceremonial ordinances and judicial regulations given to the Jews as a special people with a special purpose. Nevertheless, at the root of Calvinist theology is a belief in the law of nature as a divine law ordained by God.[137]

Calvinist Political Theory and the "Law of Nature"

When we examine Calvinist political theory we find that Calvinists, Presbyterians, and Puritans were some of the most frequent users of the phrase "law of nature."[138] To speak of the law of nature was the rule rather than the exception. A prime example is Samuel Rutherford, the Scottish Presbyterian theologian who wrote the book *Lex Rex* (*The Law and the Prince*, 1644). Rutherford published *Lex Rex* while in London helping to write the Westminster Confession. His book was released at Westminster just two years before John Locke came there as a high school student. More importantly, *Lex Rex* was in large part the political tract upon which the Puritan revolution of the 1640s was based.

In the very first chapter, Rutherford, this great and fiery Presbyterian divine, asks: "Who can deny the law of nature to be a divine law?"[139] He did not think that the "law of nature" was unchristian or anti-Calvinistic. Rutherford spoke of the "laws of nature" and "of God" in the same way in which Locke, Blackstone, Hooker, and Coke did. To Rutherford the two halves of the phrase stood for the difference, yet unity, between "general revelation" and "special revelation."

Rutherford wrote *Lex Rex* to refute John Maxwell, an Anglican clergyman trained in Renaissance humanism, who defended divine right monarchy and statism. Maxwell claimed that God alone appoints kings. Kings do not answer to their subjects, even for tyranny. The king rules by God's grace and appointment only. He is above the law of nature and is not bound by any law of nature.

The humanists generally believed that the law of nature existed only in the unknown past. Nature was a state of complete license. The only law of nature was self-preservation. When men formed societies, the law of nature ceased to be. The only law in society is positive law, law enacted and enforced by rulers. All that matters is the law of the state and the will of the ruler. That is why most of the humanists were advocates of statism.[140]

Rutherford recoiled at the humanist way of separating nature and grace because it was bad theology and led to slavery rather than freedom. He insisted that there is no nature-grace dichotomy in true Biblical religion.[141] For Rutherford, nature is the realm of God's grace, and God's grace is coordinate with nature. Nature and grace cannot be put in competition with each other.

The law of nature must bind the king, the king's acts, and the king's laws, Rutherford insisted. A king is only truly ruling in grace when he is ruling according to nature, and not against nature. Thus, according to Rutherford, the authority of government rests on two foundations, divine law and the law of nature, and the two laws are one.[142]

Rutherford is important for another reason. Rutherford insisted that one must base his political theory on the law of nature and the law of God for it to be truly Biblical. This idea became the legacy of the Puritan revolution bequeathed through Whig political theory to the American colonies. Rutherford wrote: "Because the estates of the kingdom, who gave him the crown, are above him (the king), and they may take away what they gave him; as the law of nature and God saith, If they had known he would turn tyrant, they would never have given him the sword; . . ."[143] So, Jefferson did not deny Calvinism by starting with the laws of nature and of nature's God. Instead, he began precisely where Rutherford and the Reformed political writers insisted he must. To say that the Declaration is against Calvinism is the reverse of the truth.

Rutherford's statements are surprising, since such language is supposedly deistic. Rutherford, one of eleven commissioners of the General Assembly of the Church of Scotland, could hardly be called a deist. He anticipated both Locke and Jefferson by saying, "God and nature intendeth the policy and peace of mankind, then must God and nature have given to mankind a power to compass this end; and this must be a power of government."[144]

"The power of making laws is given by God as a property flowing from nature. . . . There is no law of nature (which makes one man inherently superior to another). . . . This also the Scripture proveth."[145]

Rutherford argued that the divine-right apologists were wrong to claim that God by direct decree had given the throne to the English kings—that the kings ruled by grace, above the control of nature. They were trying to deny the natural foundations of civil government. According to Rutherford, the "divine-right" theologians were misrepresenting divine law by divorcing it from nature. Certainly, says Rutherford, government is by divine law, but not a divine law of direct appointment, but by nature's law ordained by God: "(T)here is no reason why we may not defend by good reasons that political societies, rulers, cities, and incorporations, have their rise, and spring from the secondary law of nature."[146]

Rutherford knew that to claim that the king ruled by grace and not by nature would in practice place the king above the law. The fine-sounding religious justification for divine right kings was in fact a mere pretense for despotism and tyranny. Thus, the king must be bound by God's laws of nature. "God hath immediately by the law of nature appointed that there should be government, and mediately defined by the dictate of natural light in a community . . . the Scripture's arguments may well be drawn out of the school of nature.[147]

More will be said in a later chapter about Rutherford's defense of the law of nature as a necessary ground for discussing civil government because the law of nature is God's law. It is sufficient for present purposes simply to point out that even the pre-Enlightenment, predeism Calvinists believed, based on Scriptures such as Romans 1 and Psalm 19, that God gave us two books: the book of nature and the book of divine revelation, the Bible. One is a general revelation to all men, the other the specific oracles of Almighty God.

The Rise of Natural Theology

In the early 1600s, the concept of the laws of nature and of God was seen by Calvinists as clearly orthodox and Christian. It did not come as an invention by John Wise or Cotton Mather to alter Calvinist thinking to agree with Newton's physics. The supposed deistic shift worked by Wise and Mather is sheer nonsense. The twofold understanding of God's law was a part of the American colonial mind and experience before Wise and Mather, even before Locke and Newton. Since Catholics, Anglicans, Presbyterians, and Puritans all had used the term over the span of numerous centuries, there is no logical reason why the framers of the Declaration should have suspected that someone might think the term was not a Christian term.

Yet one might object by saying that the rise of "natural theology" between the era of Rutherford and Jefferson provides a basis for suspicion. Natural theology was the belief that man does not need a Bible or a Savior. God has naturally revealed to all men everything that they must do to earn a place in heaven after they die. Since a man can save himself through good works, he does not need forgiveness through the blood of Christ. Natural theology was a deistic religion.

But the "natural theology" movement has been widely misunderstood as well. For example, Matthew Tindal, who wrote *Christianity as Old as the Creation* (1730), has been regarded as "by far the most important writer of the deistic school" and his book called "'the deist Bible.'"[148] He supposedly tried to elevate natural religion or a theology of reason above the revelation of Scripture. What Tindal really tried to do was to make the same claim about organized religion that Rutherford had made about civil government. Statist theologians of his day, working from a premise of a nature-grace dichotomy, claimed that the church and religious leaders were not bound by the laws of nature. They supposedly were under grace alone.

This nature-grace dichotomy led to all sorts of religious abuses, excesses, and horrible injustices, as well as heresies such as antinomianism. Tindal retorted, "how is it possible that the Law of Nature and Grace can differ? How can it be conceiv'd, that God's Laws, whether internally, or externally reveal'd, are not at all times the same, when the Author of them is, and has been immutably the same for ever."[149] Tindal, in essence, wanted to show that religious tyrants are as much bound by the laws of nature as political tyrants.

Tindal was widely read in the American colonies as well. He had much to say about the laws of nature and the laws of God. Tindal's book was based on Christ's reply to a lawyer in Matthew 22. There the lawyer asked Christ what was the greatest commandment of the law. Christ answered with two points from the law, Deuteronomy 6:5 and Leviticus 19:18. Christ said the greatest commandment is to love God perfectly, and the second is to love one's neighbor as oneself. Tindal thought it important that Christ and the apostles placed the moral law and all religion under these two headings.[150]

This approach was hardly deistic. John Calvin had made much of these two requirements in his *Institutes*. Calvin says:

> The moral law, then (to begin with), being contained under two heads, the one of which simply enjoins us to worship God with pure faith and piety, the other to embrace men with sincere affection, is the true and eternal rule of righteousness prescribed to the men of all nations and of all times, who would frame their life

agreeably to the will of God. For his eternal and immutable will is, that we are all to worship him and mutually love one another.[151]

In terms almost identical to Calvin's, Tindal explains how these two requirements are revealed in nature and the Bible.

We have an easy, and a true Notion of that Religion which is from God, and we can never be at a Loss to find out in what it doth consist; it is not a Thing to be alter'd at Pleasure; both the Law of Nature, and the Law of God; both the natural Dispensation under which all Men are born, and the reveal'd Dispensation as we have either in the Old or New Testament; do sufficiently instruct us in the main Heads of it. Nay, I dare be bold to say, so long as Mankind do retain their nature, and are not transform'd into another Sort of Creatures than what God made them at first; it is impossible that there should be any true Religion, but what may be summed up in these two Things; To love God, and our Neighbour.[152]

Tindal's thought is supposed to be deistic. Yet, he follows Rutherford in the argument against the nature-grace dichotomy. And he follows Calvin in making the love of God and of one's neighbor the "two heads" of the law. He clearly says that the law is not subject to the whim of man. Man cannot alter it at pleasure because it is ordained by God.

But the key for this chapter is that this so-called deist said something crucial about the law of nature and the law of God. The law of nature is the natural revelation of God's law. The law of God is the written revelation of God's law in Scripture. The laws of nature and of God for Tindal are the same as for earlier Calvinists and Catholics. It is the law of God in nature and the Bible. If Jefferson were following Tindal, the "laws of nature and of nature's God" would mean the "law of God in creation" and the "law of God in Scripture." The two are a unity, two sides of the same coin.

John Adams, who was on the draft committee with Jefferson, explicitly linked the law of nature with Galatians 5:14 and Matthew 7:12 in the New Testament:

One great Advantage of the Christian Religion is that it brings the great principle of the Law of Nature and Nations, Love your Neighbor as yourself, and do to others as you would that others should do to you,—to the Knowledge, Belief, and Veneration of the whole People.[153]

By the time of the writing of the Declaration of Independence, the twofold idea of the laws of nature and of God had a clear and widely received meaning in the American colonies. The law of nature is God's eternal moral law inscribed in nature and in the hearts of all men. The law of God is the same eternal moral law inscribed in the Old and New Testaments. One is a natural, general revelation. The other is a supernatural, special revelation. The content of both is the same, and the natural revelation is subject to the special. In light of this centuries-old tradition in English law, to say that the founders used the phrase "laws of nature and of nature's God" to repudiate the Christian tradition is really quite far-fetched. As Locke said, the law of nature requires us to obey the moral law of the Bible.[154] Bravo, if the founders were following Locke!

"Laws of Nature": Borrowed from the Greeks?

The last common objection to the "laws of nature" is that the idea was a product of Greek and Stoic thought. Even if Christians had used the idea for centuries, so the argument goes, its intellectual heritage was from Athens rather than Jerusalem. Whether Calvin, Rutherford, the Westminster Confession, or colonial Puritans used the term is irrelevant. To use the term makes the Declaration of Independence a product of Greek philosophy rather than of Christian theology.[155]

The founder's use of the phrase "laws of nature and of nature's God" cannot be traced to Greek and Stoic thought for the following reasons. First, the Greeks could never speak of the laws of nature as such, because they always held law and nature to be antithetical.[156] According to Antiphon, for example, the Sophists held nature to be in opposition to law, custom, and convention.[157] The same can be said of Plato.

Philemon Comicus, in the fourth-century B.C., said that all men are free by nature and are under no laws at all naturally but come under law, custom, and convention by necessity.[158] In the typical Greek approach, all law, properly speaking, is positive law—formally adopted, enacted, and promulgated by some governing authority. In Greek thought, no link between nature and positive law, such as we find in the Declaration of Independence, existed. Furthermore, Stoics never really succeeded in reconciling the two concepts. Although they wished to resolve the earlier contradictions between law and nature, they succeeded only in making "nature" itself a cosmic principle.

Second, Greek philosophy held no place for "nature's God," the belief that God was separate from nature and over nature. The Greek and Stoic worldview equated nature with deity. All that exists emanates from a divine, impersonal force.[159] Greek polytheism meant more than just "many gods," it meant that the universe was a "world of gods," an "ordered totality" forming an integrated nexus.[160] Thus in Greek thought, God became the world, and the world was divine. In Aristotle, for example, the "ideal form" that is the origin and goal of movement shares an indissoluble union both with the "divine essence" of the universe and with the "phenomena of nature."[161]

By the time the Golden Age of Greece had given way to the age of Hellenism, nature was almost always equated with deity. This is especially true of Stoic thought. The Stoics came to see "nature" as the cosmic divine reason that permeated the entire universe and all of existence. This meant that particular things and particular men were simply manifestations of the "stuff" of the universe. Individual men and "God"—the impersonal yet intelligent divine force behind the visible universe—are a unity.[162] As a universal principle nature became infinite, primal matter. Matter was divine and "God" was matter, establishing a chain of being between universal nature and individual nature.

There could be no "nature's God" since deity and nature were ontologically inseparable. The practical effect of such thinking was to make man's so-called "divine reason" the source of law, since man himself was "nature."[163] Cicero, for example, said that the nature of law must be founded on the nature of man: "*A natura hominis discenda est natura jura.*" The Declaration of Independence, on the other hand, maintains that the nature of law must be founded on the nature of God.

There is a limited strand of Stoic thought where *phusis* (nature) is separate from "god." According to this line of thought, the universe was created by a god. He, as the father of creation, spoke the word of creation—a female deity named *phusis* who plays a decisive role in the event of creation. But *phusis* is the real creator here, because she receives the "spirit" and brings forth bodies.[164] There can be no possible relation of this idea to the idea of "nature's God" found in the Declaration.

Third, the Declaration of Independence uses these two concepts, both of which were lacking in Greek thought, to signify one divine law. It follows that the phrase cannot be traced to the Greeks since they had neither concept, much less the ability to combine the two in a coherent unity.

Fourth, in Stoic thought, that which is "according to nature" related only to individual ethics.[165] But the Declaration's "laws of nature and of nature's God" deals with transcendent, immutable norms binding whole societies and nations, as well as individuals. This point is crucial when we consider the words of the Frenchman, Michel Villey, one the foremost twentieth-century experts on natural law.

Villey maintains that the Stoics did not give us a "natural law" but a natural morality: "I am convinced that the true meaning of the expression 'natural law' . . . is set forth in the doctrine of *dikaion phusikon* of Aristotle. . . . Most of our contemporaries have allowed themselves to be led astray by subsequent and inadequate applications of this term, used inappropriately by 'moralists' such as the ancient Stoics. . . ."[166] According to Villey, "natural law" in the classical sense is a "jurisprudence."[167] And "Jurisprudence is completely distinct from other spheres of morality; it is not at all synonymous with 'law' or 'rules'; it is not fixed or already given."[168]

If Villey is right about natural law, the Greek natural law tradition is entirely distinct from what we find in the Declaration of Independence. The Declaration speaks of laws and rules that are fixed and already given. So it is not in the authentic Greek stream as described by Villey.

But can it be Stoic, then, since Villey called them moralist innovators? The key is in the Declaration itself. In the Declaration, the "law of nature and of nature's God" is a law that is decreed and posited by God. This stress on God's positing the law is not at all Stoic.[169] The older Stoics did not speak of "law of nature" at all.

Indeed, the Stoics could not speak of the law of nature to mean a posited law, instead it was a cosmic "force" that propels existence in a certain direction. For both the Greeks and, later, Stoics, the basic fact of nature is not law, but impulse.

For some Greeks, law of nature meant that "whatever is, is right." For example, Callacles said that the "right of the stronger" is according to the "law of nature."[170] If Jefferson were following Callacles, then the law of nature would have entitled the British to crush the colonies.[171] Such a view of nature would have meant the Declaration would never have been written.

Fifth, the earliest place in history where we find the term "law of nature" in common use is not from the Greek Stoics at all, but from Cicero (106-43 B.C.). Here the phrase *lex naturae* or *lex naturalis* is written not in Greek, but in Latin. According to Cicero:

> There is a true law, right reason, agreeable to nature, known to all men, constant and eternal, which calls to duty by its precepts, deters from evil by its prohibitions. . . . This law cannot be departed from without guilt; it is not allowable to abolish any part of it, nor is it possible entirely to abrogate it. Neither can the Senate or the people loose us from this law. . . . Nor is there one law at Rome and another at Athens, one thing now and another afterwards; but the same law, unchanging and eternal, binds all races of men and all times; and there is one common, as it were, master and ruler — God, the author, promulgator and mover of this law. Whoever does not obey it departs from (his true) self, contemns the nature of man and inflicts upon himself the greatest penalties even though he escapes other things which are considered punishments.[172]

The earliest record we have of Cicero's quote is from the Christian writer, Lactantius in the third century A.D.[173] Volume 3 of Cicero's *Republic* from which the quote supposedly was taken, has been lost. Some experts have suggested that even if the quote from Cicero is authentic, Cicero may have created the "Stoic" tradition rather than the Stoics themselves.

Other experts go even further by arguing that Cicero's "quote" is apocryphal rather than authentic, meaning that some later redactor did a little creative work on Cicero as well.[174] In other words, it is altogether possible that the so-called "Stoic" tradition is *not* a Stoic tradition. It could well be that first-century or later Jewish and Christian thinking about the laws of nature was read back into earlier Stoic lore.

The first real occurrence of *nomos phuseos*, law of nature, in common Greek use is in the writings of Philo, the first-century Hellenistic Jew from Alexandria. Even in Philo a mixture of Hebrew thought with Greek terminology is present to come up with the notion of the "law of nature." It appears then that the notion of "law of nature" as a divinely posited law, more than just a rule of individual social conduct, came either just prior to the first century, or simultaneously with the gospel and the New Testament. To attribute it directly to the Stoics has serious problems.

Even in the limited body of Stoic literature, where talk of "laws of nature" is found, the ordinary word for "law" is not used. A study of the ideas represented in these passages shows that it was impossible for the Stoics themselves to be responsible for the Christian natural law tradition that arose with first-century Christianity. Helmut Koster brilliantly summarizes the insuperable obstacles in Stoic thinking that disqualify the Stoics as originators of the western Christian natural-law tradition.

> The whole problem of the Greek concept of nature comes to light in the idea of natural law. To be sure, *phusis* is always a final court and never a created thing. On the one side, however, it can be grasped only rationally, so that knowledge of it, including the norms derived from nature, will always be open to discussion. On the other hand it rules out the power of human decision, since the knowledge of nature leads to a close-knit causal nexus from which man cannot escape to the degree that he is himself nature. Freedom is thus possible only in the inwardness of spirituality in which man is either ready for concurrence in virtue of his freedom of soul (as in Middle and Later Stoicism under the obvious influence of Plato and the Academy) or he turns away from the natural world altogether (as in Gnosticism). Only the Jewish and Christian belief in nature as the creation of God was able to solve these problems. And only here did the concept of natural law become significant, since man could relate himself to the Creator and Lawgiver as the ultimate critical court.[175]

So even where we find later Christians and earlier Stoics supposedly using the same words—"laws of nature"—the ideas represented by the use of the words are radically different in the Christian context. To insist that the Apostle Paul or later Christians "borrowed" Stoic ideas when speaking of the law of nature is not only mistaken, but at once opens the door to undermining the entire New Testament.[176] Heraclitus, for example, used the word *logos* to represent his philosophy of the divine reason ordering the universe. We find the same word in John 1:1. Obviously John's description of the divine *logos* is materially different and goes much farther than that of Heraclitus.[177] In literally dozens of other instances in the Greek New Testament, Greek technical terms are taken over by the writers of Scripture and "Christianized"; that is, filled with a new and specifically Christian meaning.[178]

On the relation of Greek and Stoic thought to the later Christian natural law tradition, natural law expert Michael Bertram Crowe makes an important point:

> The relevance of "universal and divine reason" (*koinos kai theios logos*) governing the universe to the history of the natural law is clear. It is also clear that this conception should not be pressed too far in a Christian-Latin sense of natural law, which would certainly be foreign to a Greek in the age of Heraclitus. It is probably something much more in the nature of a world-order.[179]

To trace the Christian tradition of the "law of nature" to the Greeks and Stoics for no other reason than that the Greeks had conquered Palestine and the writers of the New Testament had used Greek words ignores the essential nature of language and human thought. (The Apostles had much to say about justice, but by using the Greek word *dike* were they pledging allegiance to the Greek goddess of the same name?)[180] It is both a mistake of logic and of linguistics to assume that the Christian tradition of "laws of nature" is the same as found in the Stoics on the mere ground that the phrase occurs in some Stoic writings. It is equally as absurd for sensitive Christians to reject any legitimate use of the word "nature" simply because the Greeks had used the word.

Finally, a careful comparison of the major points of the Stoic "natural justice" concept with the points of the Declaration shows that the Declaration comes down on the side of the Christian tradition.[181] Jefferson and the founders do not stand where Koster describes the Stoics. The Stoic elements are glaringly absent from the Declaration.

Summary

The prevailing myth that says the phrase "laws of nature and of nature's God" proves that the founding fathers rejected the Christian view of law and politics and based America's independence on deism and Enlightenment rationalism is wrong. First, there is no discontinuity in the legal theory between the Declaration of Independence and the earlier documents issued by the Continental Congress. Second, the phrase "laws of nature and nature's God" cannot be a product of deism or the Enlightenment because the term and the ideas embodied in it were in common use in the Christian common law and in Catholic and Protestant theology for centuries before 1776. Third, the term cannot be deistic if Jefferson were following Locke, because Locke was not a deist and Locke's own use of the term was squarely inside the Christian common law and mainstream Catholic/Protestant theological tradition.[182] Fourth, the term cannot be traced to the Greeks or Stoics because it conflicts with Greek and Stoic thought on every fundamental point. Finally, only in the Judeo-Christian theological tradition, including both mainstream Catholicism and Calvinist Protestantism, and in the Christian common law do we find all the factors necessary to give rise to the concepts reflected in the phrase "laws of nature and of nature's God."

T H R E E

SELF-EVIDENT TRUTHS

ANOTHER KEY IDEA IN THE DECLARATION OF INDEPENDENCE is that of "self-evident truths," truths so clear and obvious to the ordinary person that they require no proof. By writing "we hold these truths to be self-evident," the drafters based the Declaration on a particular theory of knowledge, or what the professional philosophers call "epistemology."

Ironically, the term *self-evident*, more than all the others discussed in this book, is the one that most clearly shows the impact of Christianity on the Declaration. But in our time, the term and its history are so widely misunderstood that they have been turned into some of the strongest proofs against the influence of Christianity on the Declaration.[1] Most writers argue that by using this term, the drafters of the Declaration rejected Christian teaching about the human intellect.[2] Supposedly, Jefferson used the term "self-evident" as just one more element of Enlightenment-styled philosophy, one that was rationalistic and un-Biblical.[3] The term, we are told, marked a clear departure from earlier Christian philosophy and Biblical thinking.

Again the culprit was John Locke. The term "self-evident" had been one of the main ingredients of John Locke's philosophy in his *Essay on Human Understanding* (1690), where Locke supposedly exalted human reason over the Bible and God's divine revelation.

The impact of Locke's *Essay* was phenomenal. Historians today generally credit the *Essay* with being one of the two major influences that gave rise to the Enlightenment and deism in England and America. By following Locke, the writers of the Declaration made their own intellects the only infallible source of truth and rejected a Christian view of knowledge. One gets the impression from the more popular writers that the term "self-evident" was invented by the Enlightenment.

Those who say this fail to tell us that the term "self-evident" had been in use for centuries in mainstream Christian philosophy.[4] It grew out of Christian teaching that traced at least to the eighth century A.D. Catholic theologians of the twelfth and thirteenth centuries insisted that things are "self-evident to us when we are innately, or naturally, aware of them."[5] They based their theology of self-evident knowledge on the text of Romans 1 and 2 in the Greek New Testament.[6]

This was the case with Thomas Aquinas (1225-1274). Contrary to popular belief, Aquinas basically agreed with Romans 1 and 2 when he discussed self-evident knowledge in the *Summa*. And while some later than Aquinas sought to secularize the idea, John Locke's use of "self-evident" for the most part follows Aquinas.[7] This means, of course, that Locke's use of "self-evident" may not at all be uniquely a product of the Enlightenment.

If Locke's concept of self-evident knowledge was Biblically sound and in the Christian tradition, serious problems immediately arise with our entire understanding of the Enlightenment in America. This is especially true when we look at such important figures as Matthew Tindal. Tindal agreed with Locke about self-evident knowledge. Tindal reportedly had an incredible impact on the development of deism. Historians have dubbed his book the "Deist Bible." If Tindal turns out to be consistent with the Bible on this point, and he quotes Scripture frequently, we may have to completely revise our interpretation of Tindal's influence on the colonies and ultimately on the Declaration.

It is my belief that the word *self-evident* in the Declaration of Independence does not reflect a view of the human mind that is uniquely a product of the Enlightenment. Rather, it expresses a view of the mind that grew out of a debate in Christian philosophy that was centuries old. That debate traced particularly to the impact on Christian philosophy of Romans 1 and 2 and other writings of the Apostle Paul. From Paul through Aquinas and Hooker to Locke runs a clear thread of understanding representing a Biblically based view of knowledge or epistemology.[8] Because we have misunderstood certain elements of that debate, we have not correctly interpreted John Locke's meaning in his *Essay on Human Understanding* (1690). And we have misunderstood Matthew Tindal in *Christianity as Old as the Creation* (1730). These sorts of errors, of course, finally lead us to misread the Declaration of Independence and its affirmation of "self-evident truths."

This chapter examines the links between the phrase "self-evident truths" in the Declaration and the teachings of the Apostle Paul in Romans 1 and 2. It analyzes the Christian teaching about the human intellect, comparing the theory of rationality in the Declaration with that of the Bible. It also treats Locke's *Essay on Human Understanding*, arguing that Locke did not change the meaning of "self-evident" to give it an Enlightenment twist. Rather, Locke's use is consistent with the Bible. Misunderstanding Locke's use of "self-evident" has caused us to misunderstand his epistemology and how he relates the Bible and human reason.[9] He is much closer to a Biblical view of the mind than we have previously thought. Finally, this chapter argues that the drafters of the Declaration did not reject the Christian view of the mind and human rationality by using the term "self-evident truths."[10]

Christianity and "Self-Evident" Truths

The English term "self-evident" came into common use in the late 1500s as a translation of the Latin term *per se notum*,[11] or "known through the instrumentality of oneself." *Per* is a Latin preposition, which, when used with the reflexive pronoun *se*, for "self," signifies "through the instrumentality or agency of . . . one's own efforts, or oneself."[12] *Notum* is Latin for "known." Our modern English slang "per se" is related to this Latin figure of speech.[13]

Seventeenth-century Enlightenment rationalists did not coin the term "self-evident." Medieval theologians used the term centuries earlier, tracing their views of "self-evident" to the teachings of St. John of Damascus (d. 749), author of *De Fide Orthodoxa*.[14] John was the last of the Greek fathers and the first theological encyclope-dist.[15] "Self-evident" knowledge for the medievalists was that which was "naturally implanted" in men, such as "first principles."[16] It was truth known intuitively, as a direct revelation from God, without the need of proofs. The term presumed that man was created in the image of God, and presumed certain beliefs about man's ratio-nality which traced as far back as Augustine in the early fifth cen-tury.[17] For example, four hundred years before John Locke, Thomas Aquinas wrote:

> The precepts, therefore, contained in the Decalogue are those the knowledge of which man has in himself from God. They are such as can be known straightway from first general principles . . . and those which are known immediately from divinely infused faith. . . . (T)wo kinds of precepts, the primary and general, which being inscribed in natural reason as self-evident, need no further promulgation. . . . These two precepts are primary and general precepts of the law of nature, self-evident to human nature.[18]

In Aquinas, man is not the source of self-evident knowledge, God is. Certain things become self-evident to man because God has created man in His own image and inscribes the requirements of His law on man's heart in spite of man's sin. Certain truths are evident in men's selves, because God makes it evident by promulgating it to them. Aquinas's view is drawn directly from the Apostle Paul.[19]

The Bible and "Self-Evident" Truths

The writings of the Apostle Paul in Romans 1 and 2 are the Biblical source for the Christian belief about self-evident truth.[20] Paul uses two Greek phrases that correspond first to the words and then to the meaning of the Latin concept *per se notum*, or self-evi-dent.[21] The words *phaneros en autois* (evident in themselves) in Ro-mans 1:19 are the Biblical counterpart of the Latin term *per se notum* and the English "self-evident."[22] In Romans 1:20 the words *tois poiemasin nooumena kathoratai* (by means of things that are made, are understood, being clearly seen) give the equivalent of the philo-sophical meaning of *per se notum*.[23]

Paul uses both phrases in the context of what men know naturally by natural revelation, apart from the special revelation of Scripture. According to the Apostle Paul, "what can be known about God" (*to gnoston tou theou*) apart from the gospel of salvation is known by all men, because God causes them to know it. They know the "truth" (*aletheia*), although they suppress that truth with their unrighteousness. Nevertheless, this elemental and fundamental truth is "evident in themselves" because "God revealed it to them" (*theos' autois ephanerosen*). He makes "invisible" truths to be "clearly seen." God has made enough of His truth known to all men this way so that all are without excuse. In a very real sense, all men "know 'the' God" (*gnontes ton theon*).

The rest of Romans 1 and 2 discusses the nature and extent of God's natural revelation to men.[24] The apostle makes it clear that this is a general revelation through nature and through man's conscience. It is a revelation only of the first principles of truth and morality. This revelation comes upon men from God despite man's darkness and sinfulness. Its knowledge does not originate with man, but is a gracious endowment from man's Maker. All men know it naturally, both through conscience and through observing the natural order. It teaches men only of God's justice and wrath at sin, but tells them nothing about the way of salvation which can be known only by hearing and believing the gospel.[25]

So for the Apostle Paul, some truths are *phaneros en autois*, or what the medieval scholars later called *per se notum* and the English "self-evident." They are made known to men by the direct action of God on man's conscience or intuition, and also by God's use of nature as a teaching tool to communicate primary truths to man.[26] It is a divine revelation, but of a different sort than the special revelation of Scripture. Traditionally, some have described this action of God as "common grace," the grace that God gives to all men, believers and unbelievers.[27] It causes all men, no matter how reprobate, to fully know the righteous ordinance of God (*epignontes dikaioma*).[28]

The Christian View of "the Mind"

To demonstrate further that the idea of "self-evident" truths is consistent with Biblical Christianity, we must first determine what the Bible and Christianity have to say about human understanding. Many people seem to think that the Bible and Christianity are unconcerned with the human mind, reason, and rationality. Or they think that the Bible's message about the human mind is totally negative, so that a Christian must be anti-intellectual.[29] However, the Bible has much to say about God's purposes for man's mind. Mainstream Christian theology, especially in the doctrine of man created in God's image, includes is a high regard for the human mind and its proper use in service to God.

According to Christian teaching, the fall of man into sin perverted his capacity to be what God had originally designed him to be. Man's inner nature changed (Ephesians 2:3), his intellect became darkened (Ephesians 4:18), his mind became an enemy to God (Colossians 1:21), and his heart was darkened and became undiscerning (Romans 1:21). Man became a vagabond (Ephesians 2:19), estranged from God as though through a hate-inciting divorce (Colossians 1:21). By nature man became God's active and resolute enemy, hating everything God willed or set about to do (Romans 8:7). Man became the moral offspring of Satan, the father of lies (John 8:44). He became depraved (Romans 1:18-32), the image of God being spoiled and marred (1 Corinthians 15:22; Romans 7:14-24).

This bleak survey of the tragic impact of sin on man is not all that Scripture has to say about the mind of man. According to Scripture, the image of God in man is not obliterated by sin (James 3:9). That image still exists to some extent in man's reason. Therefore, the mind has a very important role to play in God's plan for the human race. Once we take sin into account, we are taught in Scripture to have a high view of the intellect.

The New Testament uses about forty different Greek words to convey its message about the mind.[30] Words dealing with the reason, mind, and intellect occur more than 1,500 times in the New Testament.[31] A thorough study of these words as they are used in the New Testament reveals that Christianity is not supposed to be anti-rational or anti-intellectual. Indeed the Christian "faith," Biblically speaking, has a profoundly rational component. So it would not be incorrect to speak of Christianity as a "reasonable faith."

For example, the first three verses of Romans 12 use seven different Greek words about the mind to convey their message of how to serve God with the intellect. Christianity is called a "reasonable service" (*logiken latreian*) out of a "renewed mind" (*anakainosei noos*), whereby we become equipped to "prove what the will of God is" (*dokimadzein to thelema tou theou*). Verse 3 explicitly links faith and reason as inseparable, saying that we are to think according to the measure of faith.[32] Unlike much of modern philosophy, this verse does not juxtapose or dichotomize faith and reason, but makes them complement each other. Other verses command the development of the mind and reason (1 Peter 1:13; 2 Peter 1:5; Romans 12:2-3) and declare that the Christian is to make careful distinctions about all things (1 Corinthians 2:15).

Throughout history, many great Christian leaders have understood this part of the Bible's message. From its earliest days, the church has had leaders who were well-educated and who had a healthy view of reason. Christian scholars are largely responsible for saving for the West the records of Roman civilization, which came close to total destruction when the Empire fell. The early church had its scholars from Antioch and Alexandria. The medieval church had its scholastics. The Reformed church had Luther, Melancthon, Calvin and the Puritans, to name a few.

Throughout this time, the church has maintained a high view of the human intellect while preaching man's depravity. This is why John Owen was following the Bible rather than "Enlightenment influences" when he wrote *The Reason of Faith* (1677), and *The Causes, Ways, and Means of Understanding the Mind of God as Revealed in his Word* (1678). The same is true of William Ames and a host of other early Puritans who wrote about the role of reason in Christianity.

The Puritan emphasis on intellectual excellence had much to do with the shaping of early American thought leading up to independence. Today they are accused by some of having corrupted Christianity by bringing in a foreign anti-Biblical element of rationalism which, we are told, paved the way for deism.[33]

Others maintain that the very fact that John Locke wrote a book entitled *Reasonableness of Christianity* (1695) indicates that he was trying to corrupt Christianity by exalting rationalism. But the Puritans and Locke were all in their own way attempting to show that the Christian faith is not "blind faith" or mere pietism. They were seeking to be faithful to the Biblical message concerning the proper role of the human intellect in a person's life.[34] However, since many modern interpreters of the Puritans and Locke appear unaware that such a message is in the Bible, they assume that the Puritans and Locke were simply following "the rationalistic spirit of their age," and were precursors of deism.

Such claims distort the message of the Bible and misrepresent the teachings of Christianity. Many Christian leaders throughout the centuries are now being wrongly labeled "humanist" simply for obeying the Biblical command to be good stewards of their minds. Biblical Christianity does not seek to do away with human reason. To claim that it does is a theological heresy. The gospel is not the enemy of reason, sin is. According to Christianity, in certain crucial respects, sin has devastated the human mind, but through the gospel, the Holy Spirit comes to renew and rehabilitate the mind to redeem man's reason from the corrupting effects of sin. God wants to restore and redeem man to true reason and rationality, so that the mind is strengthened in logic and wisdom to serve God.

The *Imago Dei*: Man Created in God's Image

When speaking of the corrupting effect of sin in the minds of all men, we must not overlook the fact that all men, including unbelievers, are still created in the image of God.[35] Sin has marred that image, but according to historic mainstream Christianity, both Catholic and Protestant, sin has not effaced or destroyed that image. The Christian doctrine of the "image of God" has far-reaching implications for a proper view of the human intellect.

The church's teaching that man is created in the image of God comes from Genesis 1:27-31. There we find that in the very beginning, God made man a special kind of creature distinct from all others. Then, Scripture says, man fell through sin and was corrupted. James 3:9 and related New Testament passages reveal, that even though man fell into sin, he retained the image of God.

The doctrine of the image of God in man is a fundamental and indispensable part of Biblical Christianity. An excellent summary of the historic Christian doctrine of the "image of God" in man is found in the writings of J.I. Packer, a renowned theologian and

Bible scholar. In his essay entitled "A Christian View of Man," Packer divides the "image of God" doctrine into four component parts. Interestingly enough, part one emphasizes the fact that man is a rational being.

> First, God, whom Genesis 1 and all Scripture presents as rational, made us rational, able to form concepts, think thoughts, carry through trains of reasoning, make and execute plans, live for goals, distinguish right from wrong and beautiful from ugly, and relate to other intelligent beings. This rationality is what makes us moral beings, and it is the basis for all other dimensions of godlikeness, whether those given in our creation or those achieved through our redemption.[36]

As Packer correctly points out, the starting point of the Christian doctrine of the image of God in man is a belief about man's rationality. Rationality is not denied, dismissed, or minimized, but affirmed. Because man is still in the image of God rationally, he is, therefore, morally accountable.

Christianity teaches that man's rationality is the first dimension of Godlikeness and the basis for all other dimensions of Godlikeness. One of those dimensions of Godlikeness is man's exercise of rationality through creativity.

> Second, God the Creator made us sub-creators under Him, able and needing to find fulfillment in the creativity of art, science, technology, construction, scholarship, and the bringing of order out of various sorts of chaos.[37]

If Packer is correct that God ordained from the very beginning that man exercise his reason creatively in the sorts of activities mentioned above, how wrong it is to say that Christians are humanists when they seek to serve God as a subcreator through "science, technology . . . and scholarship."

The third part of the doctrine of the image of God in man links man's reason to his stewardship.

> Third, God as Lord made us his stewards, that is, deputy managers . . . to have dominion over the estate which is his world.

This role, which presupposes our rationality and creativity, is the special theme of Psalm 8. Man's unique privilege is to harness, develop and use the resources of God's world, not only making animate creatures and vegetation his food, but tapping the resources of raw materials and energy, in order to create culture for two ends which God has inseparably linked — his honor, and our joy. Such cultural activity is natural and instinctive to us.[38]

Part three of the doctrine of the image of God in man means that Christians cannot see themselves as spiritual misfits, or merely devotional creatures who have no part to play in the building of society and culture.

The last element of the doctrine of the image of God in man deals with the moral part of that image.

Finally, God who Himself is good (truthful, faithful, wise, generous, loving, patient, just, valuing whatever has moral, intellectual or aesthetic worth and hating all that negates such worth) originally made man good in the sense of naturally and spontaneously righteous. Righteousness in man means active response to God by doing what He loves and commands and avoiding what he hates and forbids. Human nature as created has a teleological structure such that its fulfillment . . . only occurs as we consciously do, and limit ourselves to doing, what we know that God approves. Unhappily, no one lives this way; in terms of our Maker's design we all malfunction on the moral level, and need both His forgiveness and His inward renewing (new creation).[39]

The most important part of Packer's survey of the image of God in man is his explanation of how much of that image is retained by man outside of Christ. It is important for us to know that if all men are created in God's image, but sin has marred that image, the degree to which that image is retained. Packer says:

What Christians say about the image of God in mankind, therefore, with some variety of vocabulary but substantial unity of sentiment, is that while we retain the image formally and structurally, and in terms of actual dominion over the created order, we have lost it materially and morally, and in terms of personal righteousness before our Creator.[40]

The Christian view of the mind, then, has both a positive and a negative side. Both the Bible and the historic doctrines of the church teach that God created man to be rational and to exercise his rationality in creative ways. It is not God's intention that men cease being primarily rational creatures. Although sin has taken away man's ability to be naturally and spontaneously righteous and corrupted the moral image of God in man, sin has not destroyed the intellect of man structurally or formally.

Redemption does not mean that God goes further by destroying the formal and structural image, making man irrational or antirational. True Christianity is not antirational. God's purpose in redemption is to restore to man the material and moral image (Romans 8:29; Colossians 3:10; Ephesians 4:24). Christians, as redeemed men, should, therefore, be the most excellently rational of all men, since God is restoring that image in them.

This is why it is such a scandal for historians today to say that the Puritans in the colonies had no business studying science, law, art, philosophy, or the classics if they wanted to remain true Christians. The Puritans understood the doctrine of the image of God in man and what it meant for their role in culture. Will Herberg probably said it worst when he wrote: "Nothing is more striking than the fact that, whereas the purpose of Puritan education was Christian, its philosophy and psychology were humanistic, harking back to Athens rather than to Jerusalem."[41]

Christians should not be called humanists, deists, or "Enlightenment men" simply for having as high a view of man's reason and intellect as do the Scriptures. Rationality in religion should not always be suspect. Indeed, antirational Christianity should be suspect since it falls short of God's plan. Likewise, we should not demand that unbelievers be antirational, for to do so would be to deny God's image and purpose for creating man.

Epistemology and the Apostle Paul

So far, I have shown that the Bible indeed teaches that God has two revelations by which He speaks to men. He speaks through nature and through mankind itself, and He speaks in a special way through the Bible. I have also shown that the Bible teaches about the proper role of reason in the life of the Christian and how man is created in God's image to be rational.

These beliefs were not some Newtonian Enlightenment concoction of John Wise or Cotton Mather as a first step toward deism. Nor were they invented by early Puritans such as William Ames in the 1600s. These ideas from the Bible had been taught and believed by Augustine, Aquinas, Calvin, and Hooker. To attribute them to deism and the Enlightenment is absurd.

The fact is that the Bible itself, both in the Old and New Testaments, makes the distinction between God's natural revelation and His special revelation in Scripture, and teaches a proper view of reason and intellect. In the world of Biblical scholarship today, hardly anyone disputes that the Bible teaches a twofold revelation of God's law and that man is a rational creature in the image of God.

All these ideas are brought together in the epistemology of the Apostle Paul. I take it as a given that no one has assailed the effect of sin on the mind and being of man more than Paul. He says that man is alienated and hostile in mind toward God (Colossians 1:21). Man is God's enemy, in complete rebellion to God's law (Romans 8:7). Man is under the direction and control of Satan, the Prince of Darkness (Ephesians 2:2; 6:12), the god of this world who blinds men's minds (2 Corinthians 4:4). Satan's grip on men's minds is like a trapper's snare, which holds men captive to deception and lies because men have lost their senses (2 Timothy 2:26; 3:7-8; 2 Thessalonians 2:9-12). Sin has darkened man's understanding, hardened his heart, and made him callous (Ephesians 4:18). It has made man's reasoning futile, since man is actively morally opposed to God's truth (Ephesians 4:17-18). Indeed, man's mind is depraved (Romans 1:28; 2:1).

This is the same apostle who tells us that all men clearly know what can be known about God (Romans 1:19) because God makes it evident to them in spite of their sin (Romans 1:32). They have a firm grasp on God's truth (Romans 1:18), but suppress and resist it in their minds (Romans 1:18).[42] Sometimes they instinctively do what God's law requires (Romans 2:14), because God writes the requirement of the law on their hearts (Romans 2:15) and affirms it through the voice of their conscience (Romans 2:15).[43]

Paul was not contradicting himself when he wrote these things. Rather, his view of reason was based on his understanding of the psychology of man. The details of that psychology are too complex to discuss at length here. The differences between Hebrew and Greek expressions for mind and intellect also complicate the matter. For our purposes a brief summary is sufficient.

Although Paul was a Hebrew, he wrote and preached using Greek words. By the way he used them, it is clear that Paul believed there is such a thing as "reason" in man, or a cognitive, intellectual function. This is consistent with the Hebrew Old Testament and does not make Paul a Platonist or a Stoic.

For Paul, reason meant two things—first is the intuitive reason or knowledge that comes on man from God (Romans 1:19, 32; 2:15). God, not man, is its source. God speaks supernaturally to man's spirit and conscience to instill into man certain fundamental truths and principles without which man cannot function in God's world (Romans 2:15). Also, God speaks to man through man's sense perception to cause man to be aware of certain elemental moral truths (Romans 1:20). Man cannot escape being influenced and being made aware of this knowledge or reason that comes upon him from without.[44]

Second, reason meant the process of thinking. Here it refers to inferential logic, discursive reasoning, or demonstrative thought. Discursive reasoning is the process of carrying on a rational train of abstract thought based on earlier principles and observations.

According to Paul, the intuitive knowledge and reason instilled into man's spirit by God are to be the moral foundations upon which man does all of his abstract thinking.[45] Once man's mind perceives or becomes aware of the intuitive reason from God, man is supposed to base all of his discursive, demonstrative, and inferential reasoning on the intuitive moral base. Man is to turn his intellect toward the truth revealed to him by God, willfully agreeing with it, and then do his thinking in agreement with it.[46] Thus, the psychology of the Apostle Paul includes two kinds of reason—intuitive reason from God and discursive reason in man's intellect.

But in a fundamental way, says Paul, sin has damaged the link between intuitive reason and discursive reason, particularly where man's duties and relationship to God are concerned. Man is bound by sin. He is in willful opposition to God and to God's truth, especially at the moral level. Thus, when God makes man aware of the truth of man's duties to God and of God's lordship over man, man's fallen will so resists God's truth that man is utterly unable to correctly respond to it.

Where only man's role in human society and civil justice is concerned, God's grace makes it possible for man to respond in certain limited ways to intuitive reason and the knowledge of moral law (Romans 2:15). But at every point where the intuitive witness requires man to obey and worship the living and true God, he refuses to respond (Romans 1:21, 25).

Paul calls this the "futility of their minds" (Ephesians 4:17). Because men morally resist God, they reject his witness about man's relation to God and end up in false philosophy and empty deception (Colossians 2:8). Except in only a very limited way in areas of ordinary civil justice, their discursive reason is completely overcome and perverted by their willful moral opposition to God (Romans 1:21; 10:17-18; 1 Corinthians 3:20).[47] Only by God's grace do they even instinctively carry out some of God's requirements for everyday societal relations. Only by God's grace can they ever reason correctly about mundane matters.

Paul tells Christians, therefore, to "be renewed in the spirit of their minds" (Ephesians 4:23). They must continually work to renew their minds (Romans 12:2), thinking as with the mind of Christ (1 Corinthians 2:16; Philippians 2:5). Only then can they bring their discursive reason into line with the intuitive reason instilled in them by their Creator. Only then are they positioned to begin reasoning soundly, meaning that the human intellect functions in harmony with the truth which God naturally instills into man's heart and mind. To exercise the reasoning powers in a morally sound way, man's moral rebellion must first be substantially overcome.

In terms of the mysteries of the Christian faith—divine truths which were hidden from the wisdom of ages (Colossians 1:26)—man's discursive reason is especially impotent and corrupt. God's natural revelation tells men nothing about the way of salvation (Romans 1:16). The intuitive witness, what older theologians called the "light of nature," only tells men about God's justice and moral law

(Romans 1:18 et seq.). Even when men become aware of general revelation, they do not have a clue about how to be right with God through faith. Knowledge of the way of salvation can only come to men by hearing the gospel message (Romans 10:14-17).

But here, too, Paul does not contradict himself when bringing reason to bear on correctly understanding the Christian faith. Reason plays an important role. Divine truths must be presented in words which ordinary men can understand. As his fellow apostle, Simon Peter, said, Christians must be ready to give to men a reason for the hope that is in them (1 Peter 3:15). To do this well, the Christian must focus a renewed mind on the true revelations of Scripture and submit his will to God before using discursive reasoning to explain or interpret the teachings of Christianity. Otherwise sin will distort and corrupt his understanding of the Bible as well.

Since God is the author of both sorts of divine revelation, they complement each other. Although the natural light of reason in general revelation does not contain the light of the gospel, when the preaching of the gospel shines the light of Christ on men, the natural light of general revelation agrees with it and serves to support it. That is why the Apostle Paul preached using reasons, arguments, and evidence (Acts 17:2-3, 17; 2 Timothy 3:14). He knew that the witness of his words to the ears of his hearers would simultaneously be confirmed by God's natural revelation to men as well as by the special witness of the Holy Spirit. He explicitly relied on God's natural revelation to man as a starting point from which to present the revealed truths of salvation (Acts 14:15-17; 17:22-31). Those who tested his teachings with a correct logical method were praised in Scripture as being "noble-minded" (Acts 17:11).

Paul understood that the gospel is in a sense naturally revealed through preaching and hearing. God uses men's sense perception as a channel through which His divine message about Christ is presented to their minds (Romans 10:14; Colossians 1:5-6). Behind the human words, however, is the divine witness of God's Spirit convicting men in their inmost being (1 Thessalonians 1:5; 1 Corinthians 2:4). All of this assumes a certain rational character and logical element in man. For Paul, the special revelation of the gospel builds on a foundation of God's general revelation in nature.

One should not think it ironic, then, that Paul would assail the human mind as incurably hostile to truth and then demand that we use it as one of the primary tools for establishing and defending the truth. Once the mind is set or focused on the truth (Romans 8:6), it can safely undertake to reason about all things, even spiritual things and matters of salvation.

Paul assumed his readers would use this kind of reason to test the authenticity of claimed revelations. Nowhere did he ever teach that so-called revelations should be accepted without being subject to such a test. He told followers to be "on guard" against those who would "speak perverse things" (Acts 20:28-30). They were to judge prophetic utterances (1 Corinthians 14:29). Since Satan, the great deceiver, can disguise himself as an angel of light (2 Corinthians 11:14), giving men false visions (Colossians 2:18), men must "prove" or carefully test and examine "all things, and hold fast to that which is good" (1 Thessalonians 5:21). They are to beware of the "activity of Satan" (2 Thessalonians 2:9). They need to "rightly divide the word of truth" (2 Timothy 2:15), recognize and avoid "false brethren" (Galatians 2:4), and know even when true Christian leaders make spiritual mistakes (Galatians 2:14).

Thus in the epistemology of the Apostle Paul, the intuitive knowledge that God instills into men is the correct foundation for all discursive human reason. The natural light of intuitive reason becomes then the moral compass by which man's intellect stays on course. If man's thinking agrees with the intuitive reason shined into man by God, man's reason is right reason. If it disagrees with the intuitive knowledge from God, man's reason is wrong reason.

Through Jesus Christ, men receive the Holy Spirit and God's grace that end the bondage of sin. God begins restoring the image of God to man so that with the help of the Holy Spirit, man can again reason discursively in harmony with the intuitive reason placed in man by God. The link between intuitive reason from God and discursive reason in the human intellect begins to be reestablished.

Because God ordained this arrangement to be the normal mode of man's being when He created man in God's image, man inescapably functions in terms of it. God does not seek for man to function in any other way. Therefore, God even presents the gospel to men in such a way as to affirm that they are created in the image of God and are primarily rational creatures. So it is true that at the personal moral level, sin has ruptured the link in man's rationality between God's truth and man's reasoning. But Romans 2:15 makes clear that the link is not totally severed. That is why all men are accountable to God.

I take this to be consistent with the apostle's overall approach. Intuitive reason, since it is from God, is not a product of man's mind and, therefore, is not fallen. Intuitive knowledge registers on man's intellect because God makes it evident to man (Romans 1:19). But immediately man's intellect, through its conspiracy with man's rebellious will, resists, denies, or opposes God's truth in various ways. Thus when man reasons discursively, he inevitably thinks in a fallen way. The rebellion is especially intense where reasoning about God and man's duty to Him are concerned. Man's discursive reason, since it is a product of man, is fallen and corrupted by sin. When man turns to the truth by the grace of God, he is better able to reason discursively in the moral and philosophical sense.

According to Paul, the sin in man's intellect does not completely destroy man's ability to reason about moral matters. Where simple justice and common morality are concerned, God's grace makes it possible for unbelievers to acknowledge and act upon God's eternal moral law, though in a limited and defective way. It can never lead them to salvation. However, Paul's gospel of the Christian faith, while severely indicting the sin in man's intellect, assumed the use of the intellect and reason in its delivery. Paul's gospel required the faithful use of reason as part of man's service to God to test the authenticity of revelation and to keep one clearly within the bounds of the true gospel of Christ (Galatians 1:6-9).

John Locke's Epistemology

I noted earlier that John Locke used the term "self-evident" in his *Essay Concerning Human Understanding*. For Locke, a self-evident truth is one so basic and fundamental that it may be accepted as true without rational proof.[48] His *Essay*, you will recall, was vastly influential in England and America. It contained Locke's epistemology, or theory of knowledge. It is widely held that in the *Essay*, Locke rejected a Biblical view of knowledge and exalted fallen human reasoning over God's divine revelation. Supposedly, his ideas about reason and self-evidence fueled the Enlightenment and hastened the rise of deism in America. His thinking finally affected the Declaration of Independence, which embodied his deistic theory of knowledge. For the reasons that follow, I have serious doubts whether these things are true about Locke.

Locke wrote to refute the concept of innate ideas, a belief made popular by Descartes that had come to mean that men are born with certain innate ideas inscribed in their minds from birth.[49] It had its roots in Plato's doctrine of ideas.

Locke surmised that man's mind was a blank slate at birth, an idea he took from Richard Hooker.[50] Others have discussed very well the political issues at stake in the concept of innate ideas, so I will not address them.[51] What is important here is that Locke distinguished between an idea as an intelligible, rational thought in the mind, and from self-evident knowledge instilled into man by God.[52] For Locke, *idea* was not synonymous with *knowledge*,[53] and *self-evident* and *innate* were not the same thing.[54]

Two points should be noted. Although earlier Christian teaching had used the word *innate* in describing that which is self-evident to man, and although some Christians had always viewed innate knowledge as stamped on the minds of men, for the most part earlier Christians like Aquinas had not used the word to mean what it came to mean just prior to Locke's writing. By Locke's time, the word was being used in almost a deistic way, namely, that God stamps certain true ideas on man's mind at birth and after that does not need to deal further with the mind.

Locke saw that believing this way allowed men to elevate their own opinions to the level of divine revelation if they could claim the idea was from God. It also led men to become arrogantly dogmatic since their pet ideas supposedly were divinely infused. If some ideas were innate in all men, certain folkways or regional attitudes might gain acceptance as God's will since many people in a particular period thought alike. By rejecting innate ideas, Locke was rejecting a foolish and deistic form of thinking. Ironically, he is said to have made himself a deist for doing so.

John Locke, the Bible, and the *Essay*

Locke begins his *Essay* by quoting the Apostle Peter saying that God has given us all things pertaining to life and godliness.[55] Locke immediately explains that God causes all men to have a knowledge of their Maker and their duties to Him. Of course, this corresponds to Paul's writings in Romans 1 and 2 above. At the start of the *Essay*, therefore, Locke appears to base his epistemology on how he read and understood the Bible. For example, he says: "The Candle that is set up in us shines bright enough for all our purposes."[56] Locke is alluding here to Proverbs 20:27: "The spirit of man is the candle of the Lord . . ." His thinking, of course, parallels at this point the epistemology of the Apostle Paul and is clearly within the medieval and Protestant tradition about the natural light of God in men's souls.

Alexander Fraser comments in a footnote that the metaphor was well-known in Anglican theology. Whichcote, Culverwell, and others had spoken this way. Culverwell, in particular, had linked the idea with his overall teaching concerning man being created in God's image.[57] Fraser notes that these men, along with Hooker, had greatly influenced Locke.[58] Locke also uses other terms such as "bright sunshine" here and throughout the *Essay* referring to the light of God's natural revelation that God shines upon men. Fraser directly links these ideas to Locke's view of "self-evident."[59]

For Locke, the "bright sunshine" was the intuitive knowledge God shines on all men: "This part of knowledge is irresistible, and like bright sunshine, forces itself immediately to be perceived, as soon as ever the mind turns its view that way; and leaves no room for hesitation, doubt, or examination, but the mind is presently filled with the clear light of it. It is on this intuition that depends all the certainty and evidence of all our knowledge."[60]

In the chapter on degrees of knowledge, Locke divided human knowledge into intuitive, demonstrative, and sensitive knowledge.[61] The intuitive is from God. The demonstrative is from evidence and logical demonstration, and the sensitive is through man's five senses. All certainty in all forms of knowledge depends on clear intuitive knowledge, that which is divinely placed in man by the action of God: "Certainty depends so wholly on this intuition, that, in the next degree of knowledge which I call demonstrative, this intuition is necessary." [62]

Where moral ideas are concerned, men face a special difficulty in coming to moral truth through demonstration. They would rather hold to lies.[63] Men would be in total darkness "were not the candle of the Lord set up by himself in men's minds."[64] But even with God's gracious gift of intuitive moral knowledge that requires no demonstration or "reasoning," man's ignorance is "infinitely larger" than his knowledge, according to Locke.[65] Whether men seek to understand the laws of motion in the universe or the resurrection of the dead, they can know so little by demonstration and are involved in such darkness that they must ultimately resign all those matters to the will of God.[66]

In Book 4, chapter 10 of the *Essay*, Locke begins a discussion of the knowledge of the existence of God. He starts by quoting Acts 14:17 and continues in words showing the obvious influence of Romans 1. Here he explains what he meant when he said earlier that we know God through demonstration.[67]

Some have thought that he sought to "prove" the existence of God through philosophical argument. But instead he is talking about the way God manifests the knowledge of Himself to men through creation. God does the demonstrating. If we compare Locke's words here with John Murray's, a renowned Protestant theologian, we find that Locke is squarely within orthodox Christian teaching.[68] In paragraph seven, Locke directly quotes Romans 1:20 as the foundation of his argument: "For I judge it as certain and clear a truth as can anywhere be delivered, that 'the invisible things of God are clearly seen from the creation of the world, being understood by the things that are made, even his eternal power and Godhead.' "[69]

Intuitive and Discursive Reason

Locke distinguishes between intuitive and discursive reason in the same way that he distinguishes between intuitive and demonstrative knowledge. In his chapter on reason, Locke first shows how the term *reason* is used in many different ways in common society as well as in philosophy.[70] Then he presents his own view. Like Hooker before him, and in harmony with the Apostle Paul, Locke distinguishes between intuitive and discursive reason. Morton White says: "But there are, he held, two different kinds of reason, one intuitive and the other discursive. The first was used to see the truth of self-evident principles and the second to deduce theorems from them."[71] For Locke, intuitive reason, part of the image of God in man, is the ability God gives man to become mentally aware of the intuitive knowledge shined upon man by God.[72] Discursive reason, on the other hand, is the particularly human mental process of thinking, or inferential reasoning, corresponding to demonstrative knowledge.[73]

Intuitive reason, according to Locke, is "a revelation from God to us by the voice of reason," which causes us to know a natural truth which we had not known before.[74] That sort of natural revelation is quite different from the revealed truth of the Christian religion, Locke says. God declared the truths of the Christian religion "by the voice of his Spirit."[75] No amount of comparing natural maxims self-evident to reason would have brought forth the Christian religion.

Locke has been misunderstood, I think, because he used the terms "intuitive knowledge" and "intuitive reason" almost as synonyms without alerting his readers to what he was doing. Intuitive knowledge, says Locke, is that knowledge that "is certain, beyond all doubt . . . this being the highest of all human certainty."[76] Where through intuitive knowledge one "knows" something to be true, "there is no use of the discursive faculty, no need of reasoning."[77]

He confuses his readers, however, by saying a few pages later: "Intuitive knowledge is the perception of the certain agreement or disagreement of two ideas immediately compared together."[78] The only difference between intuitive knowledge and intuitive reason for Locke is the intervention of a third idea. And when Locke describes the difference between reason and faith, he emphasizes discursive reason while assuming or presupposing intuitive reason as the "conscious or unconscious . . . condition of its operation."[79] Locke risks leaving his reader in a muddle at a crucial point in the argument.

At this very point, Locke begins discussing how to separate truth from error and ward off false teaching that tries to present itself as a divine revelation. He assumes that his reader remembers that God is the source for the veracity of intuitive knowledge. Thus when someone claims to have a revelation from God, the hearer's intuition should agree if the revelation be truly from God, since God is the author of both revelations.[80] If revelation is coming to one man from another man by the natural process of speaking and hearing, the natural light of intuitive knowledge is immediately called into play. When a man is expected to receive a teaching as divine truth, he cannot exercise belief if the witness from God in his mind disagrees. "Therefore," Locke says, "no proposition can be received for divine revelation" or cause a man to truly believe "if it be contradictory to our clear intuitive knowledge."[81]

Locke intended to show how a man in faithfulness to God would protect himself from error by the correct use of intuitive reason. But he goes on in the following pages to use the word *reason* in both senses, intuitive and discursive, expecting his reader to distinguish the difference. Thus, when he reaches the climax of his argument, he assumes the word *reason* to mean "intuitive reason," saying: "Nothing that is contrary to, and inconsistent with, the clear and self-evident dictates of reason, has a right to be urged or assented to as a matter of faith, wherein reason hath nothing to do."[82]

The problem here, of course, is if a reader fails to see that Locke is talking about intuitive reason, the reader will think that Locke is subjecting divine revelation to the control of fallen discursive intellect. Indeed, that is what has happened. In the twentieth century, most historians quote this passage from Locke as evidence that he exalted the mind over the Bible.[83] Because Locke did not take special care in guarding against linguistic confusion while using a word that had two distinct meanings, he has allowed himself to be misunderstood as an enemy of the Bible.

Hooker, Locke, and Reason

One reason that Locke did not foresee that he would be misread was that he was following the argument of Richard Hooker, who was widely read and respected. Hooker had divided God's Eternal law into "nature's law" binding the natural universe; "celestial law" binding the angels; "reason" binding "reasonable creatures in this world, and with which by reason they may most plainly perceive themselves bound"; "Divine law" given by special revelation in Scripture; and "human law," which men legislate in civil government.[84] Hooker believed that the laws of right reason were dictated to man by God.[85] He based his discourse concerning reason on the writings of Paul, particularly Romans 2:14.[86]

Hooker anticipated Locke's views of self-evident or intuitive reason, saying: "The main principles of Reason are in themselves apparent."[87] Hooker boldly asserted:

> Law rational therefore, which men commonly use to call the Law of Nature, meaning thereby the Law which human Nature knoweth itself in reason universally bound unto, which also for that cause may be termed most fitly the Law of Reason; this Law, I say, comprehendeth all those things which men by the light of their natural understanding evidently know . . .[88]

Here Hooker speaks in the same language of Aquinas' *Summa*. Thus either from Aquinas, Hooker, and possibly even Suarez, Locke learned that *law of nature* and *reason* were interchangeable terms, because in this context *reason* is from God and does not refer to man's inferential reasoning process but only to intuitive reason.[89]

Throughout the rest of Hooker's treatise, he repeatedly uses reason as a synonym for the natural revelation described in Romans 1 and 2 and to represent Christian teaching about the natural life of man.

> Wherefore as touching the Law of Reason, this was (it seemeth) Saint Augustine's judgment: namely, that there are in it some things which stand as principles universally agreed upon; and that out of those principles, which are in themselves evident, the greatest moral duties we owe towards God or man may without any great difficulty be concluded.[90]

Hooker also insisted that reason should be used to test the veracity of claimed revelations.[91] Finally, he concluded that "the greatest part of the Law moral (is) easy for all men to know" though men make themselves ignorant of their moral duties through their love of sin and darkness.[92]

So Locke did not think he was doing something novel by relying on self-evident principles of reason or by insisting that reason played an important role in testing claimed revelations. By seeing reason (intuitive reason) as a divine revelation from God, Locke was simply building upon the example of his mentor, Richard Hooker. So it is fair to say that Locke did not originate the ideas of self-evident truths or intuitive reason as a revelation from God, and he did not change them in an Enlightenment direction either. Rather, his epistemology is close enough to that of the Apostle Paul, and certainly close enough to that of Richard Hooker, to maintain that Locke is within the Christian tradition rather than the Enlightenment.

Deism and Self-Evident Truths

Moving to the period just before the American Revolution, we find that the Christian definition of self-evident truths still exerted its influence. The Christian definition of the term dominated colonial thinking, especially in university courses on logic or philosophy. One of the best examples is from the writings of Matthew Tindal, who is generally regarded as a deist. His book, *Christianity as Old as the Creation* (1730), was widely circulated in the colonies. It is said to have had a large impact on the way colonists thought. Some say it helped them move away from Christianity to deism.

However, when we examine how Tindal used the term *self-evident*, we find that he is squarely within the Christian tradition. To him, *self-evident* knowledge is that which is directly infused into men's minds by the inspiration of God. It is "intuitive knowledge" that God communicates to men supernaturally.[93]

> If there were not some Propositions which need not to be prov'd, it would be in vain for Men to argue with one another; because they then could bring no Proofs but what needed to be prov'd. Those Propositions which need no Proof, we call self-evident; because by comparing the Ideas, signify'd by the Terms of such Propositions, we immediately discern their Agreement, or Disagreement: This is, as I said before, what we call intuitive Knowledge, and is the Knowledge of God himself, who sees all Things by Intuition; and may, I think, be call'd 'divine Inspiration,' as being immediately from God; and not acquir'd by any human Deduction, or drawing of Consequences; This, certainly, is that divine, that uniform Light, which shines in the Minds of all Men.[94]

Tindal's words could just as easily have come from Hooker. Indeed, there is no significant difference between Tindal, Hooker, or even Aquinas where the above definition is concerned. Whatever impact deism may have had in other parts of Tindal's philosophy, it had not altered for him the traditional Christian meaning of self-evident truth.

Conclusion

Writers on this subject have almost universally agreed that the words *self-evident truths* in the Declaration of Independence tell us that the founders rejected a Christian view of knowledge and embraced the philosophy of deism. I have shown that the word *self-evident* had a long history in Christian philosophy and was not coined by the Enlightenment. I have also shown that the reasons usually given for a non-Christian meaning of the term are based on a reading of history that is blatantly unhistorical. By undermining that false reading of history, I have immediately questioned the conclusion that the founders rejected the Christian meaning of self-evident.

Historians are right to say as does Morton White that: "(I)n the Declaration the use of the word *self-evident* was directly or indirectly influenced by John Locke's use of the word."[95] White, however, is only one of a mere handful who understand that Locke built on the thinking of Hooker and Aquinas.

I have gone further to demonstrate that Hooker and Aquinas built on the Bible, particularly the writings of Paul. I assume, for reasons discussed in an earlier chapter, that Paul was not merely parroting Stoic notions borrowed from the Greeks, and that Aquinas was not introducing Greek dualism into Christian philosophy. Paul was consistent with the Old Testament doctrine of creation law and man's knowledge of it. For the most part, Aquinas was consistent with Paul. Thus to say, as do many, that Paul, Aquinas, Hooker, and Locke were all using Stoic notions to explain the interrelationship of divine and human law, or that they were using Stoic notions to explain how man knows and relates to unwritten divine law simply misses the point.

Locke used the word *self-evident* in a manner completely consistent with both Hooker and Aquinas. He did not put some new "Enlightenment" twist on it. When Locke spoke of reason in man's intellect, he likewise was consistent with both Hooker and Aquinas. Locke consciously tried to model his view of knowledge and reason on the teaching of Paul. Whether he succeeded is for others to determine. But unquestionably, he succeeded in modeling Hooker's thought. Therefore, Locke's views of reason are not of the Enlightenment, unless we are willing to make Hooker in 1593 the epistemological father of the Enlightenment rather than Locke.

The most serious charge leveled at Locke is that he subjected divine revelation to human reasoning. He did not. He subjected all human ideas about divine revelation to the confirming voice of intuitive, not inferential, reason. As in the writings of Hooker before him, and in the scholastic tradition generally, Locke believed that intuitive reason was not of man or from man, but was from God. It was one of the witnesses given from God's Spirit whereby man could judge between truth and falsehood.[96]

If this idea of Locke's differs from Paul's in 1 Thessalonians 5:21, I cannot perceive it. And it agrees entirely with Hooker's *Ecclesiastical Polity*, Book 2, chapter 7. If others have been right in saying that Locke subjected revelation to human reasoning, they do not go far enough in calling Hooker a rationalist. They should also conclude that Hooker subjected revelation to human reasoning, which of course would be an absurd claim.

If I am right, the rest of the tale of the American Enlightenment begins to tumble like a house of cards. For example, it is wrong to say the colonial Puritans departed from the true faith by studying the classics. By failing to understand that the Bible and Christianity teach the doctrine of the image of God in man, historians have failed to see that the Christian's use of the science and knowledge common to mankind is part of true Christianity and of a Christian's service to God.

Concerning Locke's influence on deism and natural theology, I find it interesting that Matthew Tindal's so-called "Deist Bible" uses the traditional Christian definition of the word *self-evident*. I also find it interesting that in the kinds of materials the founders relied on most in their public speeches and writings in their quest for independence, the idea of "self-evident truth" carried the traditional Christian meaning.

Since I am convinced that the founders were directly influenced by Locke's use of *self-evident*, and likewise am convinced that he used it in the traditional Christian sense, I believe that the founders used a Christian idea when they wrote "self-evident truths" into the Declaration. I cannot agree with those who insist that they rejected the Christian meaning. Unless stronger proof comes from those who think otherwise, I maintain that it is wrong to charge the founders with rejecting Christian teaching about the human mind by writing "we hold these truths to be self-evident."

F O U R

"UNALIENABLE RIGHTS" ENDOWED BY THE CREATOR

THE DECLARATION OF INDEPENDENCE proclaims its rights theory with the words: "We hold these truths to be self-evident: that all men are created equal; that they are endowed, by their Creator, with certain unalienable rights; that among these are life, liberty, and the pursuit of happiness." By 1776 the colonists finally realized that it was useless to depend on their "rights as Englishmen" before the king and Parliament. So in the Declaration, they appealed to a higher standard of rights — "unalienable rights" endowed by the Creator.

These were rights ordained by God in the constitution of the universe. They were conferred by a higher king than King George, and declared by a higher law than Parliament's. Whether or not the British acknowledged them was irrelevant because these rights were "self-evident" — clear and certain.[1] The founders' theory of rights was highly ideological, being based on a comprehensive system of beliefs about God, man, nature, and justice.

Twentieth-century society has lost any foundation for a defensible understanding of "rights." Few today believe that rights are God-given. Most see "rights" as a matter of politics — the government creates rights, and the government can take them away. While there is a great deal of talk about "human rights" and "civil rights," hardly anyone speaks of "unalienable rights." Even in America the concept is all but lost.

Outside Christianity, few *secular* rights theorists have any substance for the language of rights. Except for a handful of these writers, the concept of "rights" has become obsolete. Within modern Christianity the same problem exists. Theologians and preachers speak only the language of "duty." For both Christians and non-Christians the bottom has dropped out of rights theory. This situation signals a crisis in modern political thought and threatens Western freedoms, since the concept of rights is "theory-dependent."[2]

That we have lost the meaning behind the language of rights is especially distressing from a Christian historical perspective. Church leaders in America and the West too often disparage or attack any notion of rights. They seem to be unaware that the Bible and the church gave birth to the Western notions of rights. Christians should be salt and light in the world, including the area of rights theory. But while the world has been losing its way with respect to the meaning of rights, the church has failed to provide a Biblical witness or model.

America was founded on "unalienable rights"—those that a man may not unconditionally sell, trade, barter, or transfer without denying the image of God in himself.[3] God the Creator endows man with these rights, annexing them to the human person. They are inalienable. For to deny these rights in a man is to deny that he is a human being.

The Bible and Christianity, because of their unique view of the importance and value of each person, gave birth to the concept of inalienable rights centuries before it found its way into the Declaration. But confusion abounds about the nature and history of the concept of inalienable rights. Generally, people believe that the founders' understanding of rights came from deism and the Enlightenment, tracing to the Renaissance, and from there to ancient Rome and Greece.[4] In this way of thinking, the concept of inalienable rights is purely of secular origin and has nothing to do with the Bible, Judaism, or Christianity.[5] Many Christians hold a negative view of the Declaration and of the language of rights, because they too are convinced that rights theory has no Biblical foundation.

If we examine the component parts of the founders' concept of inalienable rights and trace those ideas into ancient history, we find that the Bible and the church had more influence on the formation of rights theories than did Greece, Rome, or the Renaissance. That is not to say that the idea of rights is missing from pagan culture. On the contrary, it appears that some of the language of rights is as old as mankind. However, the kind of thinking that gave rise to belief in inalienable rights is distinctively Biblical, going beyond the rights thinking of Greco-Roman and other ancient cultures.

Much has been written about the contributions of twelfth-century humanists, Aristotelian medievalist clergy, and fourteenth-century nominalists in the development of individual rights. I do not deny that they influenced that development. But even their thinking cannot be correctly evaluated apart from the influence of the Bible on Western culture. And Biblical ideas are indispensable for the transition from individual rights to the notion of inalienable rights. Indeed, the concept of inalienable rights traces almost exclusively to the influence of Biblical ideas. So it is fair to say that the concept of rights found in the Declaration of Independence has a Biblical heritage.[6]

To understand the Biblical heritage of Western rights, we must examine four elements. The first is the creation story in Genesis 1 and 2 and its importance for a Biblical model of rights. Second, we must examine how the Hebrew and Greek Scriptures use the language of rights, including how that language differs from secular Greek thought. Third, we must compare the constructs of Greek and Roman political thought with the Biblical model and the Declaration of Independence to determine whether the Declaration agrees with the Greek model or the Biblical model. Fourth, we must survey the history of the development of rights theory to determine what role Christians played in its development.

Genesis 1 and the Biblical Model of Rights

The starting point for a Biblical model of rights theory is Genesis 1 and 2. There we find that in the beginning God created the universe. As Creator or Author, God has the inherent right to decide or dispose of all that He has created. He is sovereign. He is Lord of all, and He governs all. Of Him and through Him and to Him are all things. The created universe is entirely subject to Him and dependent upon Him in everything. We also find in Genesis 1 that God created man. Man is entirely subordinate to God and dependent upon Him for all things. Man is God's creature and servant.

Genesis 1 teaches that God created man in God's own image. God gave man certain faculties, abilities, and capacities that put man in a unique class of beings. According to theologian J. I. Packer, these faculties represent the image of God in four ways. First, man is rational, "able to form concepts, think thoughts, carry through trains of reasoning, make and execute plans, live for goals, distinguish right from wrong and beautiful from ugly, and relate to other intelligent beings. This rationality is what makes us moral beings, and it is the basis for all other dimensions of Godlikeness."

Second, God made us sub-creators under Him, "able and needing to find fulfillment in the creativity of art, science, technology, construction, scholarship, and the bringing of order out of various sorts of chaos."

Third, we are stewards, vice-regents, lords with a small *l*, to have dominion over God's estate, which is His world.

Fourth, man was at one time naturally and spontaneously righteous, actively responding to God by doing what God loves and commands and by avoiding what God hates and forbids.[7]

Not only did God create man in His own image, thus endowing man with certain faculties and abilities, but Genesis 1:28-29 also records that God gave man a decree, a "creation mandate." God commanded man to be fruitful, multiply, fill the earth, and take dominion over the earth and all its resources—the land, the plants, and the animals. God's command immediately endowed man both with the duty to live for God and the authority to live for God. Endowed with God's image and also with God-given authority, man became a lord (small *l*) over God's earth.

The idea that man is created in God's image and has lordship over the earth is the key to the modern notion of subjective rights. Subjective rights are those that are inherent in the individual; they are inseparably part of the human personality. Being made in God's image makes man a being of enormous value and inherent worth. This notion was foreign to all ancient systems of thought and accounts for the lack of any strong concept of subjective rights outside ancient Israel or in non-Christian cultures.

The English word *dominion* used in Genesis 1:28 translates the Hebrew word *rahdah*, meaning to reign or to rule. The word *dominion* derives from the Vulgate Latin verb *dominamini* (*dominare*), from *dominus* meaning lord, or ruler. It shares the stem of the Latin noun *dominium*, meaning property or lordship over possessions and lands. Translators used the word *dominion* in part because it accurately reflects the Biblical idea that property, an attribute of lordship, was given to man before the Fall into sin and is part of the original law of nature.

In Genesis 1, therefore, we find that God reserves ultimate sovereignty to Himself, but has created man in His own image, and has endowed man with authority and dominion. Every man is under an absolute duty to live his life for God, to cultivate the image of God in himself, and to take dominion over the resources of the earth, which God has subjected to man. Every man has an inalienable duty, as it were, to live his life for God—to live out the image of God and to be a steward of God's authority and creation. The image of God in man, and man's possession of the creation mandate with its twin aspects of duty and authority are the starting point for the Biblical model of rights.

Men share that image and authority in common. Thus, all men are created equal. In human terms, no man is higher or better than any other man. No man is lord over any other man. No man may insert himself between God and another man. No man may interfere with another man's righteous effort to fulfill his duty to live out the image of God and take dominion over the earth.

Biblically speaking, then, every man's duty to God gives rise to rights between men. Men have a duty to respect and honor the image of God in other men and the duty to refrain from interfering with another man's righteous efforts to take dominion over the earth. These parallel duties are not passive but active. Men's duties to God are rights toward other men. Men are under a complete duty to God as stewards, and God forbids idolatry. No man is permitted to passively allow another man to usurp God's control or lordship in his life. Every man has a duty to God to resist other

men's attempts to degrade the image of God in him or to interfere
with his dominion activity, except when he chooses to suffer for the
gospel's sake. When one man degrades the image of God in another by murder or other crimes to the person and interferes with
his dominion activity by theft or other trespasses, he tries to take
the place of God in that man's life and makes himself an idol. Likewise a man commits idolatry when he passively allows another man
to take the place of God in his life.

Men's inalienable duties toward God translate into inalienable
rights between men. God gave and commands life, liberty, property, and a life of blessedness or happiness for man. Each man is a
steward under an absolute duty to God for these things. As a steward, trustee, and protector under God, a man may resist other
men's unlawful interference with the performance of that duty.
This is the historical analysis and starting point of the church's doctrine of the right of self-defense and of rights generally.

Genesis 1 and the creation model, therefore, are the Biblical
basis for rights generally and for inalienable rights particularly.
Every man is created in God's image and possesses the creation
mandate. Every man is under an absolute duty to God to live out
the image of God and to take dominion in the earth. God gave
man life, liberty, and property, telling man that he would be
blessed or happy if he lives his life in service and obedience to his
Creator. Men are derelict in their duty to God when they fail to
live out the image of God or to take dominion according to God's
command. They commit idolatry when they passively allow other
men to degrade the image of God in them or interfere with their
lawful and righteous dominion activity. Their duties to God are
rights toward other men.

The Language of Rights and the
Linguistics of Scripture

The word for rights in the Hebrew Old Testament is *mishpat*. It
is the ordinary Hebrew word for justice and occurs about 410 times
in the Old Testament. *Mishpat* is often used in connection with another Hebrew word, *tzedek*, which means both justice and righteousness. A study of all the places these words occur in Scripture
provides enormous insight into what God has established about jus-

tice and rights. The Biblical model of rights cannot be separated from the Biblical teaching about justice.[8]

First of all, God is the God of *mishpat*, or justice and right (Isaiah 30:18). Justice is the essence of His nature and being. He is all-righteous. The character of God Himself is the standard of justice. And God has explained Himself to man, making clear the principles of justice and righteousness in human terms. Justice is what He requires as the norm of all human interaction.

Justice is that which is "right" (Genesis 18:25; Isaiah 32:7). Hence the term *rights*, because Biblical rights are based on a belief about rectitude and normativity.

Justice is something we "do," because justice is active rather than passive (Genesis 18:19; Psalm 119:121). This leads eventually to the notion that rights are active, not merely passive.[9]

God's justice is a standard or law that binds all men.[10] God's justice is the standard of fairness and equity to which all human statutes, ordinances, and judicial sentences must conform.[11]

Justice can also be reflected in custom (Psalm 119:132). True justice always conforms to the manner in which God has created all things and agrees with His purposes and plans for each part of His creation.[12]

Because justice is a norm imposed by God and required of men, it must not be perverted by men (Exodus 23:6; Proverbs 17:23). It binds all men equally and demands equal treatment of all men before the law.[13] Man must judge by principles rather than by expediency or appearances.[14]

The *mishpat* is the Lord's (Deuteronomy 1:17). God is the source of all original authority, rights, and justice.[15]

The word *mishpat* is translated as "cause" or legal case in Numbers 27:5; 2 Samuel 15:4; 2 Chronicles 6:35, 39; Job 13:18, 23:4, 31:13; and Isaiah 50:8. It is translated as a "right" in Deuteronomy 21:17; 1 Kings 8:45, 49; Job 34:6, 36:6; Psalms 9:4, 140:12; Jeremiah 5:28, 32:7-8; Lamentations 3:35; and Ezekiel 21:27. The justice and rights spoken of in these Scriptures are not simply the distributive justice of Aristotle nor the right of nature of the Stoics.[16] They include rightly ordered relationships and a moral order imposed upon those relationships. But they also include the power to act upon one's inherent God-given authority and to make demands of others based on an objectively revealed moral order. These rights are active claims rather than passive hopes. Thus, they are both objective (regulated by law) and subjective (annexed to human nature), whereas in the classical model, rights were almost entirely objective.[17]

The Biblical uses of the word *mishpat* can be divided therefore into two broad meanings. First, *mishpat* is justice: an objectively ordered relationship between God and man, and between men and men, including a body of legal and moral precepts and the right order itself.[18] Second, *mishpat* is a subjective personal right inherent in one's being, part of what it means to be a person since man is created in God's image.[19] Thus, the Bible provides for an objectively revealed moral law from which flows objectively ordered relationships and for individual rights.

For example, God has ordained justice and given the law. He had the right to do this because of who and what He is. He has the authority, or right, to act in certain ways toward men and creation. The nature of His rights is defined by what kind of being He is. His "sovereignty" or "divine right" is part of what it means for Him to be God. Conceptually His "rights" are separate from His justice, but they cannot be separated from His nature.

Men, created in God's image, have been given similar rights, appropriate to their created nature and inhering in that nature by the decree of the Creator. To deny these rights is tantamount to denying what it means to be a human being.

According to the Old Testament, God relates to men in a judicial way and in legal terms. Numerous Scriptures speak of God's lawsuit against men, in which God pleads His case and vindicates His just claims upon men.[20] According to Biblical teaching and usage of the word *mishpat*, God has rights which are active as well as passive, and which are claim-rights—God has the right to demand men's service and obedience.[21]

The Hebrew Scriptures use the same terminology and legal framework of justice, authority, and rights when speaking about men. The only difference is that whatever authority and rights man has are given by God. And man is bound by God's standards of justice. But men do have rights—claim-rights—and men receive justice when those rights are protected.

The verb *shahphat* makes this clear in the numerous instances where it is translated *plead*, meaning to argue, advocate, or pursue. Rights can be pleaded or prosecuted according to the Biblical model. Other Old Testament words that support this analysis are *deen*, meaning judge, plea, and cause; and *yahchach*, meaning to reason, rebuke, reprove, plead, or argue your case.

The New Testament continues this paradigm of rights that we find in the Old Testament, using the Greek words *exousia* and *dikaion*, ordinarily translated authority and right.[22]

"Rights" and the Ancient Greeks and Romans

When we examine the ancients' beliefs about rights we find that their views of rights are quite different and distinct from the kind of thinking that gave rise to the idea of inalienable rights. The Greeks had no concept of inalienable rights. And the ideas of claim rights, subjective rights, and active rights were either weak or nonexistent, depending on what period of history one studies. Yet, all these concepts can be found in the Scriptures.

The Declaration's words "all men are created equal and are endowed by their Creator with certain unalienable rights" cannot be traced to the Greeks for the following reasons. First, the Greeks had no clear concept of a Creator. The Greeks were polytheists who believed in an eternally existing universe in which matter and divinity shared the same essence. The Greeks did not believe in a personal Creator god. The Bible and Biblical religion teach about God the Creator, who is separate and distinct from His creatures. The Declaration rests upon such a concept of the Creator and cannot be Greek.

Second, the overall Greek view of the universe did not allow for the notion that the universe or men were "created." For the most part, the Greeks believed the universe emanated or sprang from an impersonal divine force that permeates the universe. At best, Zeus pervades all things and nature is an extension of his being.[23] All men and things participate in this essence and possess divinity in differing degrees. All men are thus inherently unequal. Some men are more divine than others.

Third, there was no room in Greek philosophy or religion for the notion of "endowment" because creatures and divinity were never separated. Creatures were believed to be visible manifestations of divine energy. Matter was viewed as an infusion and generation of divine force, not as endowed by a transcendent and separate Creator. The Greek worldview provided for a belief in magic and divination whereby men could manipulate cosmic forces and the powers of inferior deities. But it made no place for the belief in a divine endowment of authority or power from a Creator. Greek religion rested on the notion of the "chain of being" in which all things share in the same divine essence. God was the universe, and the universe was divine.

Fourth, the nature of Greek philosophy and religion rendered rights unfixed or "uncertain." Greek mystery religion made truth unknowable and inscrutable. Man's existence was subject to the whim and caprice of the gods and fate. The heart of Greek belief was not certainty but tragedy. Man's status in the universe was always tenuous, never fixed. His "rights," where such were even mentioned, were never "certain."

Fifth, the Greeks could not conceive of "unalienable rights." The same Greek beliefs about mystery, fate, and tragedy made all human characteristics and attributes mutable and alienable. The Greek world operated on the principle of might rather than right. The gods of the Greeks were "heroes" or giants of force, power, and might. The Greeks gloried in might and power. Weak men deserved to be slaves of strong men, because the strong were more like the gods.

Sixth, the Greeks could not conceive of "rights" that were God-given. The Greeks believed that "rights" were a product of society and state. Only free men had rights, because free men were able to participate in the government of the *polis*, the "city." Slaves, women, and children did not share those rights because they had no political voice. What rights men had were created by the state and could be ended by the state. Rights were politically given, and subject to the political process, rather than God-given.

Seventh, only in Biblical religion do we find all the component parts that make up the Declaration's phrase that "all men are created equal and are endowed by their Creator with certain unalienable rights." The message of the Bible is about a Creator who created all men equal because all men are made in the image and likeness of God. He is separate from His creatures and over them in all things. This view of God stands in complete distinction to the Greek belief in an eternally existing universe where god and matter share the same essence.[24] And the Bible's view of man stands in stark contrast to that of the Greeks, in which men belong at different levels in a great mystical hierarchy where they participate in the divine essence of the universe.

Neither Aristotle nor Plato believed that all men were created, or that they were created equal, or that they were endowed by a Creator with rights, or that such rights were inalienable. Both still held to Greek polytheism, which declared all men inherently unequal. Even the gods were unequal for the Greeks.

Aristotle thought that some men ought to be slaves. Plato believed that women and children had no rights because they had nothing to contribute to the political life of the state. Both agreed with the natural character of slavery and with the Greek practice of dividing the human race into distinct and unequal political and ethnic groups. Only males who could make the state a more perfect state had rights. In Greece people were deemed to be inherently unequal.

The Greeks did not believe in rights by nature any more than they believed in law by nature. According to Antiphon, the Sophists held nature to be in opposition to law, custom, and convention.[25] For the Greeks, law was antithetical to nature. Men create law by convention, and whatever rights men have (in the distributive sense) are at the grace of the state. They are state-created. Socrates, for example, believed that rights were a product of convention.[26] The same can be said of Plato. It is impossible to link law and rights in the Greek view the way they are linked in the Declaration.

In the Greek view all rights are alienable because all rights are politically given rather than God-given.[27] Man's right is to receive the justice due him as determined by the state. The state is higher and more important than the man even though the purpose of the state is to "perfect" man. A man is only fully human when he is being directed by another superior man who is a statesman, legislator, or other civil ruler.[28] Of the Greek view, Leo Strauss writes, "Political activity is then properly directed if it is directed toward human perfection or virtue."[29]

It is well-known that the Greeks had no doctrine of equality.[30] Strauss correctly observes: "Equal rights for all appeared to the classics as most unjust."[31] The Greeks, and later the Romans, believed that some men by nature were superior to others and had an inherent right to rule others. The Roman Stoic, Cicero, did not change this view. Thus, equal rights cannot be traced to Cicero either.

The French scholar, Michel Villey, for four decades sought to prove that the Romans did not have any concept of subjective rights, a concept which he claims was birthed by William of Ockham and the Franciscans in the fourteenth century.[32] Medieval specialists Richard Tuck and Brian Tierney, while in general agreement with Villey, have shown that the shift from Roman thought to the modern concept of rights took place several centuries before Ockham, even as early at the twelfth century.[33] Harold Berman has shown that these shifts occurred in response to the papal revolution and Catholic Reformation started by Pope Gregory VII in 1075.[34]

Tuck maintains that the Romans not only had a very weak theory of subjective rights, but they lacked the modern elements of an active-right/claim-right theory.[35] At least the concept of subjective right was very weak in Rome. According to Tuck, all Roman rights were passive rights and as such made "liberty a relatively unimportant concept."[36]

The Romans did not see property as a right at all, much less as an inalienable right.[37] They followed the Greeks for whom "justice (was) incompatible with what is generally understood by private ownership."[38] Tuck says that the notion of *iura ad rem*, or rights in a thing, "would have been utterly incomprehensible to the Roman jurist, but it obviously followed from the idea of a right as a claim."[39] Tuck also says that the "classical Romans did not have a theory about legal relationships in which the modern notion of a subjective right played any part."[40]

The idea of active and subjective claim rights, not merely passive but prosecutable rights, had to come from something other than a Greek or Roman source. Some change in Western thinking had to mark the shift from passive rights to claim rights, where all rights are juridically identifiable and legally redressable. Rights had to become a demand that one man could make on another man who owed him a duty. Without this shift, there could be no concept of inalienable rights.

That shift was initiated in the entrenched Hellenism of Greece and Rome by the coming of the gospel. Prior to the gospel, the state was the religion. The regime was coextensive with creation, and its purpose was to become the "best regime" by making men virtuous.[41] Redemption was to be brought to men through political action and state activism. All this was in the name and service of the local deity, whose chief priest was also the chief magistrate of the city or *polis*. Greek religion knew nothing of the separation of church and state.

Christianity meant that the state was no longer the religion. The purpose of the state became completely transformed in Biblical religion. No longer was the *polis* or government to bring about redemption, but redemption and virtue in man was to be produced by God's supernatural activity.[42] The state became an administrator of justice under God's divine law, and men were to render to Caesar only those things that were Caesar's and to God what was God's. Christ did not equate the kingdom of God with a particular government or political party. Christianity made possible the jurisdictional separation of church and state.

Christianity and the Development of Rights Theory

Christianity did not conquer Hellenism and statism overnight.[43] Christianity was born during the age of empire and flourished only despite it. For centuries the church was under the control of political rulers and emperors. Converted emperors could not bring themselves to renounce the imperio-papal principle, even though Pope Gelasius had advocated the separation of church and state as early as the fifth century.

Not until the Gregorian Reform and the Investiture Struggle (1075-1122) did the Biblical model begin to dominate Western political theory and become the central focus of debate about rights. This was the time in which "the Bishop of Rome sought to emancipate the clergy from the control of emperor, kings, and feudal lords, and sharply to differentiate the church as a political and legal entity from secular politics."[44] The modern Christian theory of rights was born in this period, due to the work of Christian jurists and legal scholars, even though the principles had been present in the linguistics of Scripture for more than a thousand years.[45]

After the Gregorian Reform, we enter an entirely different atmosphere. Whereas the classicists could never easily equate property and right, or *dominium* and *ius*, the "medieval lawyer always regarded property (*dominium*) as a right (*ius*)."[46] Irnerius, who founded the law school at Bologna at the end of the eleventh century, specifically equated *dominium* with *ius*, following the Biblical model.[47] Later, Irnerius's successor Azo insisted that property is not only a right (*dominium* is a *ius*), but a *ius* or right is also a *meritum* (claim). So, Tuck says, by the time of Azo, the concept of claim rights was clearly extant in medieval thinking.[48] Tierney is convinced that claim rights came much earlier than Azo. But Tierney agrees with Tuck's more important point that for the Catholic canonists all rights became claim rights. According to Tuck, "they required other men to act in some way toward" the one asserting the claim.[49]

The "Unalienable Right" to Life

Most important for our purposes is the fact that the Catholic law scholars were the first to articulate the ground for what we now call inalienable rights. The word *unalienable* is a term from property law, and seems to be an odd word to use when speaking of rights. However, the Catholic law scholars of the early thirteenth century used the word *dominium* or property to signify "any right which could be defended against all other men, and which could be transferred or alienated by its possessor."[50] Rights to things were clearly property rights and could be transferred or alienated unconditionally. But rights to one's own person were different.

The development of thinking about rights of the person led to the concept of inalienable rights. Tuck says, "To a large extent, this must be bound up with the increasing elaboration and sophistication of the canon law. It was the canon lawyers who developed and applied such important maxims as the principle that personal *iura* [rights of the person] cannot be transferred to others nor be the subject of contracts."[51]

Tuck notes that the church is designed for charitable purposes, and says it is "not surprising that a theory about rights as claims should have evolved from within an institution which was so concerned with the claims made on other men by the needy or deserving."[52] So it was the church, under the influence of Scripture, that translated its high regard for the person into the belief that every man's life and person was sacred.

Men have rights, such as the right to life. But because a man has a duty to live his life for God, the right is inalienable. He can defend his life against all others, but not destroy it himself. No man has the right to do harm to himself, to commit suicide, or to waste his life. He has a property interest—dominion—in his own life, but not total control.

The "Unalienable Right" of Property

Although the church was united in its belief about the inalienable right to life, various groups within the church disagreed over the inalienable right of property. Gratian in the *Decretum* (circa. A.D. 1140) had said that men only hold all things in common possession. The Franciscans took this to mean that property ownership was a result of man's fall into sin. Property was not part of God's original plan with Adam, or part of the law of nature. Instead, property was the product of civil society and human law and convention.

The Dominicans, following Thomas Aquinas (d. 1274), disagreed. Aquinas pointed out that *before* man fell into sin, God had given man dominion and all that it implied. To own property was not a mark of sin but was a gift of God. For Aquinas, property was part of the law of nature and was not merely the product of civil society and human convention. To own property did not end one's innocence before God.

The Dominican pro-property position undercut the Franciscan teaching about apostolic poverty. Conversely, if the Franciscans were right that some men could live in an innocent way, then all men could. A long and intense struggle ensued between the Franciscans and the Dominicans. Duns Scotus applied his energies to defending the Franciscan position, saying that the law of nature positively ruled out property (*dominium*). Pope John XXII responded by issuing the bull *Quia Vir Reprobus* (1329) defending the Dominican position.

Richard Tuck summarizes the pope's position by saying, "God's *dominium* over the earth was conceptually the same as man's *dominium* over his possessions, and that Adam 'in the state of innocence, before Eve was created, had by himself *dominium* over temporal things.' " "(P)roperty was thus natural to man, sustained by divine law, and could not be avoided. (A)ll relationships between men and their material world were examples of *dominium*: for some lonely individual to consume the products of his countryside was for him to exercise property rights in them. Property had begun an expansion towards all the corners of man's moral world."[53]

William of Ockham tried and failed to refute the pope's position. Thus, the Franciscan side was silenced for the most part while the Dominicans enjoyed the church's official endorsement. For centuries after this debate, the matter was considered settled. *Dominium* or property "was not a phenomenon of social intercourse, still less of civil law: it was a basic fact about human beings, on which their social and political relationships had to be posited."[54] *Dominium* or property dealt with the very character of men and God's plan for men in the world. The Dominican view was received by the Calvinists in the Protestant reformation and by the English common law so that in America and England the right to property was called inalienable. To deny men the right of property is to deny an aspect of their personhood.

The "Unalienable Right" of Liberty

The church for a time was uncertain whether liberty was an inalienable right. Although Scripture clearly taught principles of spiritual liberty, no ancient society promoted personal liberty in the Western sense as an inalienable right. The Romans, for example, had made liberty the contrary of a right, meaning that *libertas* could not be equated with *ius*. The early medievalists failed to link them as well.

Libertas came to be viewed as a *ius* (liberty became a right) between the time of Richard Fitzralph (1350s) and Jean Gerson (1402). Fitzralph insisted that man's natural *dominium* at creation in Genesis 1 was an *auctoritas* or authority. Gerson insisted that at Creation, men's *ius* (right) was not only an *auctoritas* (authority) but a *facultas* (ability). Gerson was then able to "treat liberty as a kind of *dominium*" (liberty as a property).[55] By this time it had been settled already in Christian thinking that *dominium* (property) was a *ius* (right). Gerson helped make it clear that liberty is a right as well and thus, a property right of man.[56]

Since a man's liberty relates directly to his personhood, the question immediately arose whether liberty was an alienable right. As noted earlier, the Dominicans insisted that men had some rights or *dominia* that were transferable and some that were not. Some rights were alienable, some were not. Personal rights were inalienable because these were rights over which man did not have total control or sovereignty. Liberty was thus a right and a property of man, but inalienable, for, as the Dominicans insisted, "men were not . . . in general free to enslave themselves, and they could not rightfully be traded as slaves if the grounds for their servitude were unclear."[57] Once liberty came to be viewed as a right, it quickly passed into the category of inalienable rights for those following Dominican theology. Renaissance humanists, on the other hand, building on Greek and Roman ideas, rejected the notion that liberty is an inalienable right.[58]

In a sense, Gerson and Fitzralph simply emphasized two different parts of the Genesis 1 model. God created man in His own image, endowing man with certain faculties. And He gave man the creation mandate or dominion decree investing man with authority. Both faculties and authority are part of the Biblical model in Genesis 1. Through the Bible's influence on the thinking of men like Gerson, liberty came to be viewed as a property right, part of man's person, and thus inalienable.

The "Pursuit of Happiness"

The Declaration lists the "pursuit of happiness" as one of the "unalienable rights" given to man by his Creator. This, too, is called an Enlightenment idea.[59] Supposedly it replaced the Christianity of colonial America with a secular religion.[60] It appears to many to be a hedonistic rather than Christian assertion.[61] But it, too, has its roots in the Christian common law, the teaching of the Church, and the Bible.

Jefferson took the phrase "pursuit of happiness" from the Virginia Constitution of 1776, which said: "(A)ll men . . . have certain inherent rights, of which, (are) the enjoyment of life and liberty, with the means of acquiring and possessing property, and pursuing and obtaining happiness and safety."[62]

The term *happiness* was a technical term in the English common law. The Framers used it in the same sense as Sir William Blackstone in his *Commentaries on the Laws of England* (1765). There Blackstone explained that God made man and placed man on earth to live according to God's laws and plan. God has "so inseparably interwoven the laws of eternal justice with the happiness of each individual, that the latter cannot be attained but by observing the former; and if the former be punctually obeyed, it cannot but induce the latter."[63]

Happiness, according to Blackstone, referred to man's "felicity," or his sense of well-being and blessedness in his earthly existence that comes from obeying the laws of his Creator.[64] Right living, then, leads to man's "substantial 'happiness,'" which relates not to man's redemption or heavenly rewards, but to whether man pleases God and is blessed in this life.[65] If before God man's actions are right, they "tend to man's real happiness," but if they are displeasing to God, they are obviously "destructive of man's real happiness."[66]

This common-law concept of happiness was not part of some rationalistic faith-in-progress. Rather, it was part of the formal study of ethics in Christian philosophy which for centuries had been based on the teachings of the Bible. The English word *happy* was the equivalent of the Latin word *beatus* used in medieval theology describing the future state of the redeemed in heaven and the earthly life of the faithful. Its importance in the teaching and liturgy of the English Christian tradition is hard to overestimate. It traced its heritage to the beatitudes of Matthew 5 in Christ's Sermon on the Mount and the multitude of Old Testament verses translated by the KJV word *blessed*. Rather than being an Enlightenment term, happiness is the translation of the Hebrew Bible word *esher* in the Old Testament, the Greek Bible word *makarios* in both the Septuagint and the New Testament, and the Vulgate *beatus*.[67]

The history of the word is not hard to uncover. In the Greek Old Testament and in pre-Christian Judaism, the concept of being "blessed" or "happy" played a prominent role.[68] Georg Bertram notes that in both the Old and New Testaments, "Blessedness is fulness of life; it relates first to earthly blessings."[69] In the New Testament, due to the special emphasis on the proclamation of the kingdom of God, most instances of "happy" refer to "the distinctive religious joy which accrues to man from his share in the salvation of the kingdom of God."[70] Nevertheless, the New Testament contin-ues the earlier theme that earthly joy and happiness are gifts from God to man (1 Timothy 4:4; 6:17).

Like other Christian concepts that became part of formal philoso-phy and the common law, the Biblical notion of happiness runs deep within the channels of the common law. Its use is so obvious and extensive in the growth of English legal thought, one wonders whether those today who call it an Enlightenment term have read anything at all from the source materials of the common law, materi-als that were well-known and widely read by the American founders.

The Renaissance

Many scholars today trace the rights theory of the Declaration not to the Catholic canonists, but to the Renaissance humanists. To do so is a mistake. As Richard Tuck clearly shows, the humanists of the Renaissance did not believe in the creation account, natural law, or rights from nature or creation.[71] They rejected the Catholic ideas, based on the Biblical account of creation and society, of the naturalness of rights and the principle of unalienability. They also rejected the link between the law of nature and inalienable rights, the fundamental ground of the Declaration's preamble.

"The humanists instead simply accepted the classical Roman view," says Tuck, "(that) all real moral relationships belonged to the stage of civilisation."[72] They "found it virtually impossible to talk about natural rights."[73] Humanist intellectuals of the Renaissance stood in the quattrocento stream and were positivists: "What was important to them was not natural law but humanly constructed law; not natural rights but civil remedies."[74] Indeed, they viewed the Christian way of thinking about law and rights with "con-tempt."[75] Tuck rightly concludes, "Given the general attitude of the humanist lawyers, there was obviously no place in their thinking for natural rights of any kind. Man's natural life was simply not an appropriate setting for such things as *dominium*."[76]

Tuck reinforces his explanation by showing how Aquinas' view of the naturalness of property rested on "post-classical" (later than Greek or Roman) developments in legal thinking, based on "un-classical" (not Greek or Roman) notions of property and rights.[77] The Catholic developments were of a wholly different kind of thought than that passed down from Greece and Rome. In effect, the Renaissance humanists rejected Christian thought in favor of earlier pagan ideas.

The Christian stream continued through writings of the Protestant Calvinists and the Spanish Dominicans, who linked natural rights to "the laws of nature and God."[78] Over the centuries the Dominicans particularly advocated the principle of inalienable liberty by insisting that "men were not . . . in general free to enslave themselves, and they could not rightfully be traded as slaves if the grounds for their servitude were unclear" because liberty "was given by the law of God."[79]

The humanists, on the other hand, insisted that all rights were state-created, not God-given.[80] The humanists' preoccupation with civil convention and state power limited their ability to think in terms of rights. They were unsympathetic to the view of rights held by America's founders. To them one only has rights in society and only the rights the society recognizes, grants, or permits. It is, therefore, historically erroneous to trace early American law of nature and inalienable rights theory to the Renaissance humanists, since the humanists rejected that entire perspective.

The humanists were true naturalists in the secular sense. They saw nature as impersonal and amoral. Thus, whatever occurred in nature was natural. For the humanist, no law of nature could constrain man. Law was whatever a particular society determined law to be. They did not believe in a transcendent moral order that binds human laws.

The humanist approach and the Christian approach, then, stand in complete distinction from each other. Francois Connan (1540s) limited natural right only to man in a state of nature. Man has meaningful rights only under civil law. Salamonio explained social compact as simply the outgrowth of arrangements among men for the fostering of convenience and civilization. Thus, the theistic and moral base was entirely removed.

These quattrocento ideas led easily to absolutism in Bude, Piccolomini, More, and others. There was no natural dominium and no place for natural rights of any kind. Tuck says, "all rights were thus civil rights: but by saying this, the humanist lawyers immediately diverted attention from the right to the remedy, the civil action which actually secured his objective for the possessor of a right."[81] "The Renaissance concept (of property) belonged to a theory in which the natural life of man was right-less and therefore propertyless, while the Thomist believed that by nature man did possess certain limited rights."[82]

A quick survey of other leading writers of the period between the Renaissance and the Declaration reveals that to the extent one was committed to an Aristotelian – Renaissance – model rather than to the Bible, he leaned toward absolutism, positivism, and the alienability of all rights. Tuck mentions such names as Louis Le Roy (1579) of England, and Johannes Felden of Germany, noting that "Aristotelians . . . were themselves absolutists."[83] He points to Robert Filmer as a defender of absolutism owing to his Renaissance beliefs (and it should be noted that John Locke wrote to refute Filmer).[84]

Turning to England and the development of natural law and natural-rights theories there, we find that John Selden's partial commitment to Renaissance thinking caused him to tend toward absolutism, although he "accepted a non-humanist account of *dominium*."[85] This precisely explains Selden's Erastianism, the belief that the government should control the church.

In chapter 5, Tuck deals specifically with the Tew Circle writers, a group of British humanist intellectuals in the Renaissance stream who followed along the lines of Selden's thought. They wrote specifically to refute the widespread belief that the law of nature provides for the rights of self-defense in a people and for military resistance against a tyrannical king.[86] This inalienable right of revolution traced clearly back to earlier Protestant and Catholic thought. It linked the laws of nature and inalienable rights precisely in the same way as found in the Declaration of Independence, but this way of thinking was rejected by Renaissance-oriented intellectuals.

Other comparisons are pertinent as well. Grotius, for example, departed from the Scholastic stream by making liberty an alienable right and by insisting that a people give up their right of resistance when they enter into a compact of government with a king.[87] The Declaration, on the other hand, makes liberty an "unalienable" right under the laws of nature and God, and argues primarily for the right of a people to resist a tyrannical king. Jefferson's colleagues back home in Williamsburg explicitly rejected the Grotian, humanist model when they wrote Article 1 of the Virginia Constitution of June 12, 1776.[88] There they insisted that men cannot by compact or constitution give away certain rights, including liberty.[89] That Jefferson shared these views with George Mason and other Virginians is questioned by no one.

Other absolutists, such as Hobbes, also believed that the power of the state was more important than the rights of people. Although he finally rejected the idea that people surrender their right of self-defense against bad rulers when they enter into a compact of government, Hobbes still stands in the Renaissance stream. Jefferson and the Declaration, on the other hand, stand in the scholastic, Christian stream. The Thomist/Dominican view as refined by the English common law and the Protestant Reformation is what we find in the Declaration of Independence. And, as Tuck notes, this theory of natural dominium rests on an "unclassical notion."[90] It cannot be traced either to the Renaissance or to the Greeks or Romans.

The Medieval Christian-Rights Heritage

In the previous pages, I have outlined a way to understand the development of Western rights theories. The research in this area is only beginning. Which person introduced which idea in which century will go through many refinements in the coming years as more research takes place. The existing research, even with all its differences, shows compellingly that the kind of rights theory that went into the Declaration of Independence has roots deep in the Western Christian tradition.

Brian Tierney says it best with his conclusions about the link between natural-law and natural-rights theories.

> The doctrine of individual rights was not a late medieval aberration from an earlier tradition of objective right or of natural moral law. Still less was it a seventeenth-century invention of Suarez or Hobbes or Locke. Rather, it was a characteristic product of the great age of creative jurisprudence that, in the twelfth and thirteenth centuries, established the foundations of the Western legal tradition.[91]

If Tierney is right, as I am convinced that he is on this point, then much of what passes for the history of political theory and rights development being taught in colleges and universities in America needs to be tossed in the wastebasket. For example, it is widely taught that natural law and natural rights are contradictory concepts. But this view is simply unhistorical and untenable. And the prevailing notion that all Western rights theory begins in the seventeenth century with Hobbes and Locke is simply laughable, as it always should have been.

Conclusion

Today, the rights theory of the founding fathers and the Declaration of Independence is routinely traced to deism, the Enlightenment, the Renaissance, and from there to ancient Rome and Greece. The great Western achievements made possible by the exercise of these rights are credited to the philosophers of the Enlightenment and the occidental secular tradition. Although the West received the bulk of its political freedoms and scientific vision from the impact of Christianity and the church, the church rarely gets credit for its role in the development of Western political freedoms or science.

Unlike men of the Enlightenment who acted on the ideals of Christianity while denying their source, modern society is trying to act on occidental secular concepts, as well as attribute Western achievements to them. That is why Western society is in the same early stages of dysfunction that preceded the fall of Greece and Rome. Having denied both the source and the rationale for the best in Western culture, we are quickly moving into the twilight era of Western freedom and the ultimate demise of free Christian society.

We are living in a time of a renewed struggle between Jerusalem and Athens. The secular occidental worldview based on power, communalism, and elite classes has come to dominate education, government, and church. It offers a religion of statism, salvation by government as opposed to the Biblical concept of salvation by a God who is no respecter of persons. The secular worldview smothers individual freedoms in its quest to force people to be free.

Why should Americans care that the Biblical roots of our culture have been exchanged for a wholesale commitment to the prevailing secular occidental philosophy? Secular occidental philosophy and politics are based on pagan notions of power, whereas Biblical politics is based on concepts of authority. In the secular view, nothing is ever impermissible because no lines are drawn that cannot be crossed.

Whoever wields power can determine the content of laws, the extent, and even the existence of other people's freedoms. Biblical philosophy, on the other hand, admits to predetermined lines of authority which the civil government is not permitted to cross. Personal rights and freedoms are God-given and inalienable; they do not exist merely for civil convenience or at the discretion of those who hold civil power. This is why only Biblical ethics maintain a proper balance between order in public life and individual freedom.

Occidental secularism knows nothing of God-given inalienable rights limiting a government's civil authority. Instead, it recognizes only conditional "civil liberties," liberties granted by the civil government at its own convenience—and terminated at its own convenience. It can exalt individualism until society is on the brink of anarchy and then crush the individual for the sake of establishing state control. In the hands of a shrewd elite, it can do both at the same time.

GOVERNMENT BY THE "CONSENT OF THE GOVERNED"

THE DECLARATION OF INDEPENDENCE does not use the word *revolu-tion*. The founding fathers did not see themselves as revolutionaries. But today, we call what they did in 1776 a revolution. Such language instantly offends many Christians since the Scriptures condemn rebellion and command obedience to authority. This fact, more than any other, causes many Christians to think that the Declaration of Independence could not possibly rest on Biblical principles or Christian teaching. To these Christians, then, the American Revolution had to have been an anti-Christian event, meaning that the American nation was born illegitimately.

Were they rebels: first to God and then to the king? The bulk of recent writings would lead us to think so. The Bible and Christianity had little to do with the birth of America, according to most. Except for Francis Schaeffer and a handful of others, even Christian scholars link the American Révolution with the currents of pagan irreligion that fueled the French Revolution. This causes some Christians to be ashamed of America's founding and defensive about its foundations.[1]

The theory of revolution in the Declaration of Independence has a Christian heritage. Indeed, the word *revolution* is misleading, because the theory of the Declaration is not about revolution but about lawfully changing the form of government when the present government has become tyrannical. The theory is more akin to the earlier idea of one complete turn of a wheel in a backwards direction, to restore a previous order or balance. The ideas in the Declaration were not new with Jefferson. They grew out of Western Christian political theory and had been developing for seven hundred years.

When we examine the terminology, argument, and logical structure of the Declaration, we find them to be consistent with the Bible and Christian teaching. These ideas were rejected by thinkers from the humanist/rationalist tradition who often get credit for creating them.[2] The ideas were embraced by Christian political writers long before Jefferson was even born.

What the Declaration Says

The argument of the Declaration is really quite simple. First, the laws of nature and of nature's God regulate the lives and relations of all men and nations. Second, these laws make clear that all men are created equal and are endowed with "unalienable rights". Third, the purpose of government is to secure those rights. Fourth, men institute government through consent, or compact. And they consent only to the exercise of just powers. Fifth, tyranny and despotism on the part of the government break the compact, so that the people are free to alter or abolish the form of government and institute a new one.[3]

So the Declaration organizes its argument around the "compact theory of government." Starting from the laws of nature and God, the theory builds to the key ideas of compact, condition, and material breach. According to this theory, the relationship between the king and the colonists was based on a covenant or compact. The essence of the compact was an exchange of promises between the king and the colonists, recorded in the colonial charters. The compact represented the voluntary agreement of the people to vest the king with the just powers of government.

He would rule and they would obey so long as he fulfilled the conditions of the compact. He must rule for the safety and welfare of the people, protecting their inalienable rights, which included life, liberty, and the pursuit of happiness. If the king committed a material breach of his promise, he would lose his right to rule. Tyranny and despotism were a material breach of the promise, stripping the king of governing authority and triggering the people's right of self-defense.

The Declaration then tries to show that the King of England had become a tyrant. Using nearly two-thirds of the entire text, the Declaration lists the king's wrongs as proof he had committed a material breach of his promise by a "history of repeated injuries and usurpations." The Declaration ends with the "representatives" of the people formally declaring the end of the king's government and the intent of the people to defend themselves by force.

The Bible and Compact

The idea of compact traces to the Bible. *Compact* is the English equivalent of *pactum*, one of the Latin words used to translate the Old Testament Hebrew word *berith* (covenant). The word *covenant* occurs 286 times in the Old Testament alone. Almost all God's dealings with man in the Bible were through covenants. God made covenants with Adam, Noah, Abraham, Moses, David, and Solomon. Covenant is so important to God that He provided redemption to man through covenant. Jesus Christ said, "This is the New Covenant in my blood."

A covenant or compact is a formal agreement between two or more persons, sworn by an oath and ratified by a public ceremony. Each party to a covenant promises to perform certain tasks or fulfill certain conditions. A covenant includes mercy so that if a party fails to keep the covenant perfectly, it is still valid. However, a particular kind of failure — a material breach of the terms or conditions — frees the injured party from any further obligations under the agreement.

What constitutes a material breach depends on the nature and terms of the agreement. For example, Adam's eating the forbidden fruit was a material breach of God's covenant of works (Genesis 2:17). Idolatry was a material breach of God's covenant of law on Mount Sinai (Exodus 32). Adultery is a material breach of the covenant of marriage (Matthew 19:9). Tyranny is a material breach of the covenant of government (2 Chronicles 23).

The Bible and "the People"

Part of God's covenant dealings with man was to recognize the human race as "the people." Early in the book of Genesis, God made a covenant with Noah and his sons (Genesis 9:9). God put in their hands the police power, the central feature of civil governing authority (Genesis 9:6). They were not yet a nation, but were the parents of all humanity, meaning that civil authority is vested in the human race generally. That authority passes to each of Noah's descendants individually and to all people equally. "The people" were given governing authority long before there were kings. Later God divided them into political units, or nations (Genesis 10), making them distinct peoples (Acts 17:26).

Once nations are formed, the police power is exercised through rulers rather than private individuals (Leviticus 19:18; Romans 12–13). Still, civil rule is government "by the people." No one is exempt from the duty to see that civil rulers obey God's decrees about civil justice (Deuteronomy 16:18-20). God holds "the people" directly responsible for the well-being of the nation: "If you continue in sin, you and your king will be destroyed" (1 Samuel 12:24).

The Bible and the "Consent of the Governed"

"Government" is ordained by God (Romans 13:1-4). But "a government" is a "human creation" (1 Peter 2:13). Particular governments, or particular forms of government, are instituted by men through their common consent, not by direct divine decree. The Bible shows that a man lawfully becomes a ruler only by being selected by his fellow countrymen (Deuteronomy 17:15; 2 Samuel 3:21), the office becoming effective when he enters into covenant with the people (2 Samuel 5:1-3; 1 Chronicles 11:3). God does not make kings directly. Even David was anointed king by God years before he was made king by the people (2 Samuel 3:21; 5:1-3; 1 Chronicles 11:3).

Civil rulers do not have an absolute right to rule (1 Samuel 13:13–14). God has commanded civil rulers to honor those who do right and punish those who do wrong (1 Peter 2:14; Romans 13:4). They are sent by God to help those who are doing right (Romans

13:4). Their purpose is to uphold justice in the nation for everyone (Deuteronomy 17:18–19; Proverbs 31:5, 8–9; Psalm 72:12–14; Jeremiah 22:3-4). They govern "for the people," not for their own benefit or to increase their own power and wealth. If they put themselves above the people, doing evil rather than justice, they lose their right to rule (Proverbs 16:12).

The Bible and Lawful Revolution

The story of the tyrant queen, Athaliah, shows how these ideas come together in the Bible. God had given Israel a covenant or compact of government in the book of Deuteronomy (Deuteronomy 29:1-21). The covenant provided for male leadership only (Deuteronomy 17:15). Athaliah, mother of King Ahaziah, made herself Queen of Israel by trying to kill all the royal line of Judah when her son died (2 Chronicles 22:10). Only the infant Joash survived, hidden by Jehoiada the priest (2 Chronicles 22:11).

When Joash reached the age of seven, Jehoiada made covenants with the leaders of Israel to remove Athaliah from the throne (2 Chronicles 23:1-5). In a public ceremony, they crowned Joash king (2 Chronicles 23:11). Athaliah screamed "treason" but was arrested and executed (2 Chronicles 23:15). The whole people then ratified the revolution by entering into covenant with King Joash (2 Kings 11:17).

In this example, the form of government had been established by a covenant or compact. The person in the office violated the conditions of the covenant through acts of despotism and tyranny. She had no right to rule. The lower rulers and representatives of the people covenanted together to institute new government. Their revolution was forceful, but lawful. Joash was made king by the people when he entered into covenant with them.

The Christian Theory of Revolution

The Christian theory of revolution rests on Scripture passages like those noted above.[4] What is the Christian theory of revolution? Stated simply, if through acts of tyranny the highest ruler in a country forfeits his right to rule, lower officers who still have a right to rule can declare a change of government. Those who have a right to rule must be representing the law and "the people," because the people can resist tyrants only through lawful representatives. Lower rulers must act to defend the covenant or compact of government. Once the lower rulers declare a change of government, "the people" in self-defense of their rights may use force to remove the tyrant from office. Such force can be used only under the direction or authority of lawful rulers. "The people" cannot become a destroying mob, acting apart from the direction of lawful representatives. If they do, they lose their right to resist.

This theory of revolution is known by the term "interposition." Some have called it "resistance to tyranny through lower magistrates." It occurs when lower rulers—the lower magistrates who have remained faithful to the law—"interpose" themselves between a despotic higher ruler and the people he is oppressing.

The Catholic Roots of Interposition

The Christian theory of interposition, based on Scripture, has its practical beginnings in the Gregorian Reform, or the papal revolution from A.D. 1075-1122 begun by Pope Gregory VII.[5] Before the time of Pope Gregory, the church and state in the West were usually merged, the churches being controlled by "the state" or emperors, kings, and feudal lords. The Gregorian Reform and the Investiture Struggle made up a movement to free the church from the control of secular political powers and make the church a self-governing independent entity.

Michael Lessnoff, senior lecturer in politics at the University of Glasgow, has traced the social contract element of the theory to Manegold of Lautenbach in Alsace about the year 1080. Manegold wrote:

> No man can make himself king or emperor, the people raise a man above them in this way in order that he may govern them in accordance with right reason, give to each one his own, protect the good, destroy the wicked, and administer justice to every man. But if he violates the contract (*pactum*) under which he was elected, disturbing and confounding that which he was established to set in order, then the people is justly and reasonably released from its obligation to obey him. For he was the first to break the faith that bound them together.[6]

Manegold was a Catholic scholar picked by Pope Gregory VII to explain why Emperor Henry IV could lawfully be deposed. Manegold, drawing on the Bible and medieval feudalism, explained that Henry IV had broken his contract with the people and was in material breach of the conditions of the contract through tyrannically destroying peace and justice. The people, represented by all the princes collectively, were absolved from allegiance to him and free to depose him.[7]

Harold Berman, in *Law and Revolution* (1983), has shown how the Gregorian Reform initiated the intellectual life of the modern West as we know it. In the two centuries after Pope Gregory, his impact and ideas influenced the direction of all of Christian thought. During this period, numerous writers copied Manegold's theme of social contract and widely discussed his ideas of tyranny as a breach of contract. Michael Lessnoff remarks that "a contractual relationship between peoples and their secular rulers became the stock-in-trade of medieval thinkers."[8]

From Manegold to the Magna Carta (1215)

William the Conqueror invaded England in 1066, only seven years before Gregory VII became pope. The Norman kings consolidated their power not only over the whole of England but over the churches in England as well. The selfish and tyrannical rule of the Norman kings and their royal domination of the church stood starkly opposed to the ideals of the Gregorian Reform. The contest came to a head under King John in 1215.

King John was a hard but inept ruler. He lost a war with France (1199–1206), sought to dominate the church (1206–13), and lost favor with the barons and lords by ruining the economy and denying their traditional civil rights.[9] To finance his mistakes he confiscated church property, destroying the only source of aid for the poor. He surrounded himself with an expensive and inefficient bureaucracy. When the barons refused to support a renewed war with France, he decided to make war against the barons.

Stephen Langton, Catholic Archbishop of Canterbury, took the side of the barons, instructing them on Manegold's theory of social contract and resistance to tyranny.[10] The barons, acting on Langton's advice, renounced allegiance to John and elected Robert

Fitz-Walter as their leader on May 5, 1215. The barons and bishops, the "lower magistrates," presented the king with the choice of affirming known rights by means of a written compact and ending oppression of the church by the state, or face armed resistance which they themselves would lead.

Helplessly outnumbered, John agreed to meet the demands of the lower rulers and the people, and signed the Magna Carta at Runnymede on June 15, 1215. When it appeared later that Pope Innocent III would not bind John to the Charter, the barons invited Louis of France to replace John on the English throne, an act of religious dissent as well as civil disobedience. However, both John and Innocent died suddenly. The new pope confirmed the Magna Carta, and Henry III was made king.[11]

The Magna Carta and the American Revolution

The influence of the Magna Carta on the development of English common law is well known. Its "profound influence" upon the American founding fathers is "an accepted fact."[12] Of the many valuable books on the Magna Carta, two are particularly helpful on this point. Richard Perry's *Sources of Our Liberties* (1978) traces the impact of the Magna Carta on the development of the English common law and its subsequent influence on the charters, declarations, and constitutions of early America. Louis Wright's excellent little book, *Magna Carta and the Tradition of Liberty* (1976), tells how the Magna Carta directly influenced the legal tradition of the American colonies and became a cornerstone of the American Revolution. Wright's book is a condensed treatment of the more detailed work of A. E. Dick Howard in *The Road From Runnymede: Magna Carta and Constitutionalism in America.*

Perry shows how Sir Edward Coke's detailed treatment of the Magna Carta in his *Second Institute* (1628) "influenced not only the legal thinking of his own day but also helped shape the constitutional theories which developed in America during the seventeenth and eighteenth centuries."[13] Perry says:

> Magna Carta played an essential part in the history of American constitutional development. It came to be regarded by the colonists as a generic term for all documents of constitutional significance. Among the documents framed by the colonists as counter-

parts of Magna Carta were the Massachusetts Body of Liberties, the New York Charter of Liberties and Privileges, the Pennsylvania Charter of Privileges, the instructions to Sir George Yeardley, popularly known as "The Great Charter," and the Carolina "Great Deed of Grant." In addition, the colonists frequently embodied the provisions of Magna Carta, particularly chapter 39, into their own legislation. Although the enactments were often vetoed by King George III, who feared that his prerogative would be threatened by any concession, the colonists always claimed the rights which they considered were to be found in Magna Carta. Thus the Stamp Act was denounced by John Adams as a violation of Magna Carta, and its provisions were cited in support of the principle "no taxation without representation."[14]

Wright shows how some of the earliest settlers in America cited the Magna Carta in their letters and writings.[15] He notes: "All of the English colonies looked back to Magna Carta as the source of fundamental liberties, which they had inherited. Before the Declaration of Independence, when colonials were arguing that they had all the rights of Englishmen, they constantly invoked Magna Carta."[16]

Massachusetts' first state seal showed a patriot holding a copy of Magna Carta and fighting for liberty.[17] William Penn, founder of Pennsylvania, invoked the Magna Carta in his trial of 1670 in England for preaching Quaker doctrine.[18] Later he incorporated Magna Carta's provisions into documents relating to the laws of the colony of Pennsylvania, and had copies of the Magna Carta published and distributed in the colony. Of the American Revolution, Wright says: "The writings of the founding fathers and their speeches frequently cite Magna Carta and Coke's *Commentary*. . . . John Adams . . . was often to refer to Magna Carta and its guarantees in legal arguments and constitutional debates."[19]

Since the Magna Carta was such an all-pervading influence in the political and legal thought of colonial America, it is fair to assume that it influenced more than how the colonists viewed constitutionalism and procedural justice. In light of the Declaration of Independence and the fact of the American Revolution, it is safe to say that Magna Carta's revolutionary theory was not lost on the founding fathers either.

The Protestant Reformation and Interposition

Harold Berman is probably correct to say that the Gregorian Reform was more than a reformation, it was a revolution: "the papal party and the imperial party fought it out in bloody wars for almost fifty years."[20] But if it was the papalists who produced the theory of interposition, it was the Protestants who perfected it. Developments in the Christian theory of revolution after the Protestant Reformation bore directly on the kind of thinking that went into the Declaration of Independence.

Martin Luther started the Protestant Reformation when he nailed his 95 theses on the door of the Castle Church of Wittenberg on Oct. 31, 1517. But Luther's influence was not strongly felt outside Germany. His support for the theory of interposition was overshadowed by his denunciations of mob violence in the Peasant's War (1524-26). Even today many writers erroneously conclude that Luther had no theory of civil disobedience.[21]

John Calvin's influence, however, was felt over all of Europe and later in the American colonies as well. In his *Institutes of the Christian Religion* (1536), Calvin says that while private individuals cannot resist tyranny with a mob uprising, lower magistrates who represent the people have a duty to resist.[22] The people may appoint "popular magistrates . . . to curb the tyranny of kings."[23] The people may then act at the direction of the magistrates. These representatives have a duty to "restrain the willfulness of kings," even if it means they must "overturn . . . their intolerable governments."[24] Will Durant called Calvin's *Institutes* "One of the ten books that shook the western world."[25] John T. McNeill, editor of the standard work on Calvin's *Institutes*, shows how Calvin's views of resistance to tyranny were "to prove powerfully influential" in the development of Western democratic thought.[26]

That influence was felt almost immediately through the French Calvinist manifesto, *Vindiciae Contra Tyrannos* (*Defense of Liberty Against Tyrants*). The *Vindiciae* was written in response to the St. Bartholomew's Day Massacre (Aug. 24, 1572), when the Catholic rulers of France killed thirty thousand French Calvinists known as Huguenots.[27]

The Defense of Liberty Against Tyrants

The *Defense of Liberty Against Tyrants*, written in 1579, is a landmark of Protestant political thought.[28] Written under the name Stephen Junius Brutus, the 164-page book became the most famous and most quoted of the many Protestant tracts on interposition, or resistance to tyranny through lower magistrates, from the late sixteenth through early seventeenth centuries. Along with Calvin's *Institutes*, it was the authority upon which most of later Puritan revolutionary thought was based.

It is important to note that the *Vindiciae* is full of Scripture, the author clearly intending to show that his political ideals have the support and sanction of the teachings of the Bible. Each proposition rests on page after page of Biblical examples and citations, showing that the law is above the king, that the people are above the king, that governing authority is based on compact, and that the people can depose the king if he becomes a tyrant, breaking the compact. Many of the key terms and ideas of the *Vindiciae*, as well as its central argument, show up later in the Declaration of Independence.

First, says Brutus, rulers are bound by the law of God: the Ten Commandments and the law of nature.[29] If a king commits a felony against God's divine law, he must be punished, and God has placed the power of punishment in the people.[30] By "the people," he means those who hold their authority from the whole people, namely, the lower magistrates.[31] This includes the "assembly of the estates" or the "states."[32] "(A)s it is lawful for a whole people to resist and oppose tyranny, so likewise the principal persons of the kingdom may as heads, and for the good of the whole body, confederate and associate themselves together; and . . . (when) the better part of the most principal have acted . . . (it is deemed) that all the people had their hand in it."[33]

Second, the people have the authority to punish tyrannous kings because kings are made by the people and the people are above the king.[34] Although God has ordained the general authority of government, he gives to the people the duty to elect and empower the king of their own choice.[35] Government by the consent of the governed is a Biblical idea for Brutus.[36]

Third, kings are created to serve, to be under a duty rather than to serve themselves.[37] Their duty is to "maintain by justice, and to defend by force of arms, both the public state, and particular persons from all damages and outrages, . . ."[38] Their duty is "to provide for the people's good."[39] The king is subject to the law and depends upon the law; his will is not law.[40] The welfare and happiness of his kingdom and people rest on his obedience to law.[41]

Fourth, the king's authority rests on covenant, or compact, specifically the second of the two kinds of compacts recorded in 2 Kings 11:17.[42] The king is bound by the Biblical pattern where Israelite kings promised in a compact with the people of Israel to govern justly and uprightly for the benefit of the people.[43] His right to rule is conditioned on his performance of his sworn duties. But if he fails to keep his promise to the people "the whole people (is) the lawful punisher of (his) delinquency . . . or the estates, the representative body thereof who have assumed to themselves the protection of the people."[44] The people can only agree to those kingly powers allowed by the law of nature, they cannot consent to tyranny.[45]

The covenant or compact between the people and the king obliges the king to rule justly and the people to obey:

> There is ever, and in all places, a mutual and reciprocal obligation between the people and the prince; the one promises to be a good and wise prince, the other to obey faithfully, provided he govern justly. The people therefore are obliged to the prince under the condition, the people simply and purely. Therefore, if the prince fail in his promise, the people are exempt from obedience, the contract is made void, the right of obligation of no force.[46]

But Brutus makes it clear that if the king violates the condition upon which the people allowed him to rule, he loses his right to rule.

Incompetent rule must be endured, and merely bad or somewhat unjust rulers must be honored.[47] But if the king goes beyond being a merely bad king to becoming a tyrant, he may be deposed, if the people have tried all lawful means short of revolution to solve the problem.[48] At that point, it becomes the duty of lower officers and representatives of the government to interpose against the king and suppress his tyranny.[49]

The lower rulers must be sure that the king has indeed become a tyrant. Brutus explains tyranny, saying:

> But if a prince purposely ruin the commonwealth, if he presumptuously pervert and resist legal proceedings or lawful rights, if he make no reckoning of faith, covenants, justice nor piety, if he prosecute his subjects as enemies; briefly, if he express all or the chiefest of those wicked practices we have formerly spoken of; then we may certainly declare him a tyrant, . . . We . . . speak of a prince . . . absolutely bad . . . of one malicious and treacherous . . . of one perversely bent to pervert justice and equity . . . of one furiously disposed to ruin the people, and ransack the state.[50]

If the lower rulers find that the king has become a tyrant within the terms described by Brutus, they must publicly declare that they hold the king to be a tyrant and intend to resist him.[51] Private persons cannot act as a mob or use force in their private capacity to overthrow the king.[52] They must act under the direction of lawfully elected lower rulers who also have been vested with governing authority to uphold the law, individual rights, and public safety.[53]

So in the *Vindiciae*, the cornerstone of Protestant revolutionary theory in the century of the Reformation, we find the components upon which the Declaration of Independence builds. The laws of God and nature bind governments. Governments are put in place by men to protect justice, rights, and civil happiness. Mediocre government must be obeyed but not tyrants who are bent on destroying their own subjects. The people are above the king and have a right to replace him if he becomes a tyrant. But the people must act through representatives, "lower magistrates" of the "states," who interpose themselves between the tyrant and the oppressed people. Those magistrates must formally declare that the king has become a tyrant, and only then may they take up arms in self-defense against him, replacing his government with another of their choice.

The Reformation and English Revolutionary Theory

Samuel Rutherford's *Lex Rex* (1644)

While France in the late 1500s suffered civil war leading to absolutism and the rejection of the Reformation, England experienced the comparatively enlightened rule of Elizabeth I, who embraced many Reformation ideas.[54] But England soon entered a period of absolutism under King James I (1603-25) and his son Charles I (1625-49). Both James and Charles believed that they ruled by "divine right," that is, by the direct authority of God, rather than by the choice of the people.[55] James and Charles were ruthless, controlling all matters of religion and public life. James did not call Parliament from 1611-21, and refused to work with it when in session.[56] Charles did not call Parliament from 1629-40.

The domineering rule of James I and Charles I, particularly their suppression of Protestantism, bred severe discontent in England among Presbyterians and Puritans.[57] After his misrule had wrecked the economy, Charles finally convened Parliament in 1640 only to find that the members were ready for revolution. At first, the revolution aimed only to repudiate the "divine-right" theory of government and reform the English church. Eventually, full-scale civil war erupted, and Charles was beheaded (1649) by Puritan radicals.

Samuel Rutherford's *Lex Rex*, or *The Law and the Prince* (1644), appeared in the early stage of the civil war. *Lex Rex* was a major force in the development of the revolution. Written to refute Robert Maxwell's defense of the "divine right" of kings, *Lex Rex* adapted and expanded the argument of the *Vindiciae*, applying it to the English situation.[58] Although *Lex Rex* was only one of dozens of such tracts asserting the right of resistance to tyranny, it is important for being exhaustive; it was widely known, and it contained the principles of revolution upon which all major Protestant parties in England agreed.[59] *Lex Rex* is typical of Reformed thought about revolution from the Puritan era. Its major legal principles are essentially identical to the principles proclaimed in the Declaration of Independence 130 years later. It is simply wrong to say that the ideas in the Declaration are opposed to America's Calvinistic heritage.[60]

Like the Declaration, Rutherford's *Lex Rex* insists that civil government is based on the "law of nature," a divine law binding the conscience, and on the law of God, or the moral law in Scripture.[61]

The laws of nature and of Scripture, says Rutherford, declare that all men are equal, that they have rights that they do not surrender when they enter into a compact of government, and that government is formed by their consent, organized to exercise its powers as the people see fit.[62] Similarly, the Declaration of Independence maintains that because of the laws of nature and of nature's God, men are created equal and endowed with certain rights which government cannot take away but is sworn to protect. Men do not surrender these rights to government when men by their common consent enter into a compact of government.

According to Rutherford, men institute particular governments, while God ordains the proper scope and authority of civil government by divine law.[63] God places "the power of the people above the king."[64] "The people," not the king, are sovereign in the political/legal sense.[65] These ideas too have their parallel in the Declaration, which says that governments are instituted among men, deriving their just powers from the consent of the governed under the laws of nature and of nature's God. Many assume that Jefferson's words in the Declaration are anti-Biblical. Rutherford traced them to 1 Peter 2:13 in the New Testament, which calls government a "human creation."[66] For Rutherford as for Jefferson, "there floweth something from the power of the people."[67]

Lex Rex and the Compact Theory of Government

Like the Declaration, Rutherford's *Lex Rex* builds its argument on the compact theory of government which prevailed among Calvinists from the time of the *Vindiciae* to the Puritan Revolution. Again, the key ideas are compact, condition, and material breach. Rutherford explained that a ruler obtains his office by entering into an agreement, a compact, with the people.[68] The compact is an exchange of promises whereby the people promise to obey and the ruler promises to rule for their well-being according to the laws of nature and of God.[69]

The compact is not open-ended but conditional.[70] If the king fails to live up to his promise he can lose his right to rule by breaking the compact.[71] But he cannot break the compact by simply being a bad, unjust, or incompetent ruler. More is required before he can be put out of office. He must break his promise in a material way.[72] Arbitrary rule, despotism, and tyranny amount to a material breach of the promise.[73]

One act of tyranny is not enough.[74] There must be a series of tyrannous acts before the people have a right to put the king out of office. Also, the people cannot act as a mob, they must act through representatives.[75] The representatives must formally declare that the king is a tyrant, publicly naming the wrongs that the king has committed.[76] Only after such a public declaration has been made can the people take up arms against the ruler to dethrone him.[77]

Of course, Rutherford makes many more points than these in the 234 pages of *Lex Rex*. Many of them speak to that particular crisis facing his land in his day. But all of them build on the ideas shown above. These ideas were the common coin of Calvinist political thinking in the decade of the Puritan revolution. And it is fair to say that every idea found in the Declaration of Independence relating to the right of revolution and the reasons that justify revolution are found 132 years earlier in Rutherford's *Lex Rex*. The Declaration did in few words and in practice what *Lex Rex* had explained in great detail as a matter of theory. The only difference being that Rutherford called for a state-established church, an idea which even many Presbyterians had rejected by 1776. Small wonder, then, that a number of British observers termed the American revolution "the Presbyterian revolt."[78]

John Locke's *Second Treatise of Government*

That John Locke's *Second Treatise of Government* (1688) influenced the political thought of the colonies and the writing of the Declaration of Independence is widely known. It is important then to determine whether Locke's ideas build upon or reject the medieval "social compact" theory as developed through the *Vindiciae Contra Tyrannos* (1579) and *Lex Rex* (1644). Certainly Locke was familiar with both.[79] His writing is consistent with them, whether or not he drew directly from them.[80]

Some doubt whether Locke's "social compact" ideas are consistent with them, however. For example, Carl Becker, in his famous book on the Declaration of Independence, insisted that Locke rejected the position of the *Vindiciae*:

The idea that secular political authority rested upon compact was not new—far from it; and it had often been used to limit the authority of princes. It could scarcely have been otherwise indeed in that feudal age in which the mutual obligations of vassal and overlord were contractually conceived and defined. Vassals were often kings and kings often vassals; but all were manifestly vassals of God who was the Lord of lords and King of kings. Thus medieval philosophers had conceived of the authority of princes as resting upon a compact with their subjects, a compact on their part to rule righteously, failing which their subjects were absolved from allegiance. . . .

Popular resistance to kings was commonly taught both by the Jesuits and the Protestant dissenters: . . . Calvin was one of the writers. . . .

In 1579, another Frenchman . . . that wrote the "*Vindiciae contra tyrannos*" gave greater precision to this idea. Subjects are not bound to obey a king who commands what is contrary to the will of God. But are they bound to resist such a king? According to the "*Vindiciae*" they are. When kings were set up, two compacts were entered into: in the first, God on the one side, and the people and king on the other, engaged to maintain the ancient covenant which God has formerly made with his chosen people of Israel; in the second, the king contracted with his subjects to rule justly, and they with him to be obedient.

Here was a "version of the original compact" which Locke might have used to justify the Revolution of 1688. He might have said, with any amount of elaboration, that the people had a compact with God which reserved to them the right to rebel when kings ruled unrighteously. Why was Locke not satisfied with this version? . . .

The truth is that Locke . . . had lost that sense of intimate intercourse and familiar conversation with God which religious men of the sixteenth and seventeenth centuries enjoyed. . . In the eighteenth century as never before, "Nature" stepped in between man and God so that there was no longer any way to know God's will except by discovering the "laws" of Nature, which would doubtless be the laws of "nature's god" as Jefferson said. . . .[81]

Did Locke reject the *Vindiciae*? No, Becker misread the *Vindiciae*. Becker took the two compacts in the Bible, the first between God and the nation, and the second between the king and the people, to mean that if the king violated the first covenant, the people could dethrone the king. But the *Vindiciae* says:

> In the first covenant or contract there is only an obligation to piety; in the second, to justice. In that, the king promises to serve God religiously: in this, to rule the people justly. By the one he is obliged with the utmost of his endeavors to procure the glory of God: by the other, the profit of the people. In the first, there is a condition expressed, "if thou keep my commandments": in the second, "if thou distribute justice equally to every man." God is the proper revenger of deficiency in the former, and the whole people the lawful punisher of delinquency in the latter, or the estates, the representative body thereof who have assumed to themselves the protection of the people. This has always been practiced in all well-governed estates.[82]

According to the *Vindiciae*, God alone punishes the king for breaking the first covenant. The people can only punish the king for breaking the second.

As shown earlier, even the *Vindiciae* grounds the second covenant, the one between the king and the people, on the law of nature and the moral law of Scripture.[83] For Locke to focus on the compact with the people, and how the compact is grounded on the law of nature and the moral law of God, is not inconsistent with the *Vindiciae*.[84]

Likewise Becker overlooked what Calvinist writers like Rutherford had said about the place of the law of nature in revolutionary theory. A main theme in *Lex Rex* was that "the covenant betwixt the king and the people is clearly differenced from the king's covenant with the Lord."[85] Rutherford dedicated chapter 14 of *Lex Rex* to showing that the king's covenant with the people to do justice was grounded on the law of nature and the law of God. If the king breaks the second covenant through tyranny, the people have a right and duty to disobey.[86] When Locke wrote the *Second Treatise*, the law of nature argument had long been a fundamental part of Puritan and Presbyterian political thought. It was not deistic.

It is appropriate also to note that most of Locke's arguments are found, at least in elemental form, in *Lex Rex*. Locke's arguments in chapter one against divine right of kings and natural inheritance from Adam occur earlier in *Lex Rex*. His ideas about the scope of political power and the public good also are in *Lex Rex*. The ingredients of Locke's "state of nature" theory in chapter 2 are all found in *Lex Rex*; including what he says about equality, liberty versus license, the place of reason in the law, and that men surrender the duty of punishing criminals to the magistrate.

Locke's ideas about the condition of slavery in chapter 4 and his description of the right of property in chapter 5 are found in *Lex Rex*. His ideas about paternal power in chapter 6, and analysis of political and civil society in chapter 8 are also in *Lex Rex*. His use of Scripture explaining the beginning of political societies in chapter 8 has countless parallels in *Lex Rex*.

But it is also clear that Locke's *Second Treatise* covers ground untouched by *Lex Rex*. This is true in part because Rutherford wrote to refute John Maxwell, and Locke wrote to refute Robert Filmer. Naturally there were some different emphases. Also, Rutherford was a rock-ribbed Calvinist. Locke was a latitudinarian, more comfortable with the moderate tones of Richard Hooker than with the harsh excoriations spewed by his father's Puritan friends. And Locke spoke of the separation of powers, a point to which Rutherford gave little attention. Nevertheless, Locke's final chapters on prerogative, conquest, usurpation, and tyranny build on the same foundation as *Lex Rex*. This is not to say that Locke was consciously following *Lex Rex*, but that the argument was well established before Locke wrote.

John Locke: Compact, Condition, and Material Breach

Like the *Vindiciae* and *Lex Rex*, Locke's *Second Treatise* insists that all lawful government is by the consent of the governed. Locke says:

> (T)hat which begins and actually constitutes any political society is nothing but the consent of any number of freemen capable of a majority to unite and incorporate into such a society. And this is that, and that only, which did or could give beginning to any lawful government in the world.[87]

That consent is given by compact: "And this power has its original only from compact and agreement, and the mutual consent of those who make up the community."[88]

The compact is conditional. Tyranny, despotism, and arbitrary rule break the condition making the compact null and void:

> (D)espotical power is an absolute, arbitrary power one man has over another to take away his life whenever he pleases. This is a power which neither nature gives—for it has made no such distinction between one man and another—nor compact can convey, for man, not having such an arbitrary power over his own life, cannot give another man such a power over it; but it is the effect only of forfeiture which the aggressor makes of his own life when he puts himself into the state of war with another. . . . (A) despotical power . . . arises not from compact, . . . (F)or what compact can be made with a man that is not master of his own life? What condition can he perform? . . . (A)s soon as the compact enters, slavery ceases. . . . Voluntary agreement gives . . . political power, to governors for the benefit of their subjects, to secure them in the possession and use of their properties. . . .

> Now this power . . . is to use such means for the preserving of his own property as he thinks good and nature allows him, and to punish the breach of the law of nature in others so as . . . may conduce to the preservation of himself and the rest of mankind. So that the end and the measure of this power . . . can have no other end when in the hands of the magistrate but to preserve the members of that society in their lives, liberties, and possessions; and so cannot be an absolute arbitrary power over their lives and fortunes, . . . (S)o tyranny is the exercise of power beyond right, which nobody can have a right to.[89]

Locke goes on to explain that certain acts of tyranny end the king's right to rule. If the king dissolves the legislature, sets up his own arbitrary will in the place of law, stops the legislature from meeting, alters electoral rules without public consent, subjects the people to foreign domination, abandons the office, or combines with the legislature to act contrary to the public trust, he has committed those acts which make lawful revolution to his rule an appropriate response.[90]

Like Rutherford, Locke insists that a king's incompetence is not a sufficient ground for revolution: "(S)uch revolutions happen not upon every little mismanagement in public affairs."[91] He must commit repeated acts of tyranny, "a long train of abuses, prevarications, and artifices, all tending the same way" which "make the design visible to the people" that the king intends to destroy them and their land.[92] When it becomes evident to the people that the king will not turn from his plan, they, through their representatives, may set up a new government.[93]

Unlike Rutherford, Locke neglects to explain the process of revolution.[94] He fails to mention how the representatives of the states must gather to find by process of law that the king is a tyrant. He does not explain that those representatives must make a formal public declaration that the king is out of office.

Locke appears to be more concerned with the moral rightness of the people's act. Once more, he cites the Bible—Judges 11—for his working principle. If the people in good faith and in the integrity of their hearts are convinced that the king is a tyrant and about to destroy them, they may call upon God, the "Supreme Judge," to support their armed resistance against the king.[95] Again, this is not deistic language. Rutherford also had insisted that in these matters the king is not the "supreme judge," but God is the "Supreme Judge."[96]

The similarities in theory of Locke's *Second Treatise* and Rutherford's *Lex Rex* dramatically outweigh the differences between them. The core of the compact theory of government is identical in the two. They contain the same view of the laws of nature, of human rights, property, and the political authority of government. There are differences, but the revolutionary theory is the same. Locke openly relies on Richard Hooker's writings, but it is obvious that Locke is consistent with the basic revolutionary theory coming from the medieval era: first through the Catholics, then through the French Huguenots, then through English Calvinists. If Locke were rejecting his Calvinist heritage, there should be glaring contradictions between the *Second Treatise* and *Lex Rex* or the *Vindiciae*. There are none because they are branches of the same tree.

Rutherford, Locke, and the
Declaration of Independence

The theory of revolution and the principles of Christian revolution are the same in *Lex Rex* and the *Second Treatise*. Those principles are the skeleton that organizes the arguments of the Declaration of Independence. The Declaration says that governments are formed by compact. Those compacts are conditional. The condition is that the government rule for the safety, well-being, and protection of the people. When the government destroys people's lives and rights, it becomes tyrannical. Tyranny is a material breach of the compact.

The king of England is a tyrant, the Declaration pleads. He has committed a series of tyrannical abuses: obstructed justice; acted contrary to the public good; suspended or impeded legislatures; interfered with elections; corrupted the judiciary; wasted public and private wealth; enforced martial law in time of peace; spied on the people; broken the charters; left government to others who had no right to rule; waged war against unarmed towns and cities; and perpetrated continued acts of theft, murder, and barbarity. In short, he has denied the laws of nature, denied divine law, denied the laws of England, and repudiated his charters.[97] He is thus a tyrant who can lawfully be deposed. He has materially broken his promise.

The Declaration was formal and public as required by *Lex Rex*. It was written by "representatives" of the "states," lower magistrates who had assembled to interpose themselves between the king and. the people whom he sought to destroy.[98] It thus followed the theory of the Magna Carta, as well as the *Vindiciae*, *Lex Rex*, and the *Second Treatise*. These representatives appealed to the "Supreme Judge of the world" — on the principle of Judges 11, in words used both by Locke and Rutherford. The framers closed the Declaration with a new oath creating a new compact: "we mutually pledge . . ."[99] By this deed, they birthed a new government based on a new compact, formed by the representatives of the people.

Conclusion

Today many believe that the American Revolution was "extralegal" and not based on Christian principles.[100] Most feel it was certainly un-Biblical if not anti-Biblical. Yet, the procedure the colonists used to set up the Continental Congress, the acts Congress carried out, and the principles they proclaimed through the Declaration of Independence all rested on a Christian common-law base that was centuries old. That common law grew out of the strong influence of medieval Christian theology, particularly where the compact theory of government was concerned.

The American Revolution, as enshrined in the terms of the Declaration of Independence, was both legal and Christian. It was legal in that it was carried out on principles which had been part and parcel of the British law tradition for centuries. It was "Christian" in that all the principles included in the Declaration of Independence agreed with, and probably grew directly from, the Biblical teaching about revolution as formulated by major Catholic and Protestant theorists over a span of seven hundred years.

Every idea in the Declaration's compact theory of government finds precedent in the Bible. Through the Catholic Church, especially during the Gregorian Reforms of the eleventh through thirteenth centuries, those Biblical precedents were infused into western culture and political thought. They underlie the Magna Carta in 1215, which has clear and direct historical links to the American Revolution and the Declaration of Independence.

Protestant writers also contributed. Beginning with Calvin's *Institutes*, through the *Vindiciae* of the French Huguenots, to Rutherford's *Lex Rex*, the impact of Calvinist thinking on the English political experience is clear. John Locke's *Second Treatise* continued to employ the major outlines of that thinking without substantial changes. Despite some claims to the contrary, Locke continued to rely on Scripture and law of nature arguments as did the Calvinists before him. He based his most critical points about the timing and manner of revolution directly and consciously on Scripture. Thus, there is also a direct link from the Bible by way of Calvinism and English Protestantism to the Declaration.

To say the ideals of the American Revolution as embodied in the Declaration were "Christian" does not mean that all who took part were Christians. Nor does it mean that they always acted according to Christian principles. But the theory of the revolution was "Christian" in the sense that the principles of the American

Revolution, whether rightly or wrongly applied, were an inheritance left to colonial Americans by earlier generations of Christian writers.

Of course it would be clearly wrong and extreme to suggest that the influences on the American Revolution and the Declaration were exclusively Christian. It is equally wrong and extreme to suggest that Christianity had nothing to do with the Revolution and the Declaration. Curiously, though, there is a nearly universal silence about the Christian roots of American Revolutionary theory in prevailing scholarship. Those Christian roots are historically evident, logically compelling, and easily researchable. This makes the overwhelming volume of denial in prevailing scholarship of the Christian influence even more inexplicable.

Because so much scholarship goes the other way, there is no real danger that the Christian links will be overstated without being roundly challenged. At present, they are radically understated if recognized at all. To redress the imbalance, this chapter is an attempt to demonstrate those links, and has concluded: (1) At the very least, if all the Biblical and Christian sources in history for compact theory were removed, the Declaration could not have been written the way it was. (2) It is probably more accurate to say that without the Bible and Christianity, the Declaration could not have been written at all, since it depends so heavily on the Judeo-Christian stream of political thought.

S I X

GOD AS SUPREME JUDGE AND DIVINE PROVIDENCE

THE FINAL CHALLENGE raised against Christian ideas being found in the Declaration is based on the founders' use of *Supreme Judge* and *Divine Providence* as names for God. In the last paragraph of the Declaration, the signers call upon "the Supreme Judge of the world" for the "rectitude" of their intentions and on "Divine Providence" for their protection. They did not use the word *God* nor the name *Jesus Christ*. That failure supposedly reveals that they had a deistic rather than a Christian conception of God.

Some popular writers today believe that deists changed God's name to Providence in the late 1700s. They imply that *providence* was always a deistic term. Many scholarly writers, on the other hand, admit that providence was at one time a Christian term, but insist that the founders used it in a deistic rather than a Christian way.[1] So it is widely held that the use of "Supreme Judge" and "Divine Providence" in the Declaration are clear proofs that the founders had a deistic rather than Christian view of God and that the Declaration itself is deistic.

A separate problem has arisen with the word *providence* in the twentieth century. Providence was a technical term in Stoic philosophy in the several centuries before the birth of Christ. It became a technical term in Christian theology through the writings of the early church fathers. Although providence was deemed a Christian term by both Catholics and Protestants until the nineteenth century, some today feel that it should no longer be used. They think that it borrows from Stoicism in an illegitimate way. The founders, then, by using the word *providence* showed that they were being influenced by Stoic ideas. They were, therefore, not truly Christian in their thinking, even if they seriously intended to be Christian.

This chapter will show that the founders' use of "Supreme Judge" and "Divine Providence" as names for God was not deistic. To speak of God this way was perfectly legitimate in terms of Christian theology. It expressed a fully Christian view of God and His relationship to men and nations.[2] The chapter will also show that it is wrong to associate Stoic notions of providence with the later Christian use of the term.

Supreme Judge

Chapters 2 and 5 already have addressed the issue of God as "Supreme Judge" in some detail. But a brief review here is in order. First, the idea of calling upon the "Supreme Judge" was a major part of John Locke's overall theory of revolution in the *Second Treatise*.[3] The founders surely had Locke's argument in mind when writing the last paragraph of the Declaration. Locke drew his principle from the account of Jephthah in Judges 11:27. By following Locke, who was following the Bible, the founders themselves were applying a political idea drawn from Scripture.

Furthermore, the idea was not original with Locke. Numerous Puritan political writers had talked about God as Supreme Judge. One notable example was Samuel Rutherford, whose *Lex Rex* referred to God as Supreme Judge in ways almost identical to those of John Locke.[4] Calling upon God as Supreme Judge was part and parcel of Calvinist and Puritan political theory. For the Declaration to employ the term *Supreme Judge* in a like manner is clear evidence of Calvinist influence, not of deism.

But one crucial point was not addressed in earlier chapters, namely, the theological significance of seeing God as Supreme Judge. The importance relates to the fact that John Locke studied Hebrew and sought to master the Old Testament. That the idea of

God as Judge was important to him and to others of that time shows how strongly they were influenced by the Old Testament.

Gottfried Quell has shown that the concept of God as Supreme Judge is central to all Old Testament theology.[5] The Old Testament views God as "Judge of the whole earth" (Genesis 18:25). He posits the law, and to challenge His law is to violate nature itself.[6] Quell remarks: "In such declarations Yahweh is undoubtedly thought of in terms of His office as Ruler and Judge."[7] To view God as the Judge who intervenes in human affairs to protect the weak from wrongdoers is particularly a mark of Biblical religion.[8]

For Rutherford, Locke, and the Declaration to speak of God as Supreme Judge is not deistic. Kittel's *Dictionary* notes that "Deism did not regard judgment . . . as one of the truths of natural religion."[9] To believe that God intervenes as judge in the affairs of men is incompatible with the deistic view of God that holds Him to be aloof to human events.

To speak of God as Supreme Judge is not Greek either. The Greeks, for the most part, believed in fate rather than in divine judgment.[10] Judaism, on the other hand, held that: "It is one of the cardinal articles of faith . . . that God judges, that He does not just let evil occur without resisting it, that He upholds with punishments and rewards His holy Law . . . that He enforces it irresistibly in face of those who despise it."[11] Therefore, the view of God as Supreme Judge in the Declaration cannot be traced to deism or to Greek thinking. It can only be traced to the influence of Biblical religion.

Divine Providence

It is difficult to overstate the importance of the words *Divine Providence* in colonial religion. The earliest settlers were Calvinists and Anglicans. For both groups, divine providence represented the heart of their belief in God, namely, that God was the ever-active, moment-by-moment governor of the universe.

The colonists often named towns, cities, roads, and settlements by words that held special religious significance in their lives. *Providence* was such a word. For example, one cannot study the history of New England without learning of Providence, Rhode Island, or of Providence Plantations.[12] Sermons, letters, speeches, and records of all sorts from the earliest days of the colonies are filled with repeated references to "providence."

William Ames, whose *Marrow of Theology* (1623) became a measure of correct Puritan doctrine, found the Biblical root of providence in Ephesians 1:11, saying: "The providence of God is that efficiency whereby he provides for existing creatures in all things in accordance with the counsel of his will."[13] He went on in his famous book to outline twenty-six points of correct doctrine concerning God's providence.

Providence was a major tenet of the various reformed creeds. For example, the Westminster Confession (1646) defined Providence in chapter 5:

> God, the great Creator of all things, doth uphold, direct, dispose, and govern all creatures, actions, and things from the greatest even to the least, by his most wise and holy providence.[14]

Similar statements occur in the other Reformed creeds going as far back as the Second Helvetic Confession in 1566.[15]

The Reformed Church's preoccupation with the doctrine of providence came about due to their commitment to a Calvinistic theology. John Calvin, in his *Institutes of the Christian Religion* (1559), used the last three chapters of Book 1 to explain and apply his doctrine of God's providence. According to Calvin, "providence means not that . . . God idly observes from heaven what takes place on earth, but that . . . as keeper of the keys, he governs all events."[16]

Calvin was involved in a complicated debate wherein he was refuting early deists of the Renaissance as well as opponents who accused him of embracing pagan ideas of chance and fate. For Calvin, to confess belief in God's providence is immediately to deny deism:

> It were cold and lifeless to represent God as a momentary Creator, who completed his work once for all, and then left it. . . . (W)ithout proceeding to his Providence, we cannot understand the full force of what is meant by God being the Creator, . . . (who) is also a Governor and Preserver . . . by . . . Providence sustaining, cherishing, superintending, all the things which he has made.[17]

To speak of God's providence, says Calvin, rules out a deistic view of God and His relationship to the world because "providence consists in action."[18] Therefore, the truly pious man will, as Augustine said, "refer everything to Divine Providence."[19]

Providence then, insists Calvin, is completely foreign to the Greek views of chance and fate because "God's providence, as it is taught in Scripture, is opposed to fortune and fortuitous happenings."[20] He continues saying:

> Those who wish to cast odium upon this doctrine defame it as the Stoics' dogma of fate. This charge was once hurled at Augustine. . . . We do not, with the Stoics, contrive a necessity out of the perpetual connection and intimately related series of causes, which is contained in nature; but we make God the ruler and governor of all things, who in accordance with his wisdom has . . . decreed what he was going to do, and now by his might carries out what he has decreed. . . . (N)ot only heaven and earth and the inanimate creatures, but also the plans and intentions of men, are so governed by his providence that they are borne by it to their appointed end.[21]

In Book 1, chapter 17, section 9, of the *Institutes,* Calvin ends by saying that the man with a "godly mind" when facing future dangers and difficulties "will entrust himself to God's wisdom, . . . For he will always hold his mind fixed upon God's providence alone," committing to the Lord the determination of the outcome.[22]

It is worth noting at this point, that the final paragraph of the Declaration of Independence does exactly what Calvin counseled in chapter 17 of the *Institutes.* The founders, looking at the difficulties ahead of them, but believing that their course was just, relied on the protection of divine providence. To do so is clearly Calvinistic, reflecting the influence of Calvin's theology, which pervaded the colonies. It certainly is not deistic. One does not rely on a static deistic providence that sits idly in the heavens. A deistic providence does not actively intervene in men's affairs to protect the innocent.

Providence and Christian Teaching

That providence is one of the oldest cornerstones of Christian teaching is beyond dispute. The doctrine of providence is so universally held among all Christian groups that G. C. Berkouwer has observed:

> God's providence seems to be one of the most self-evident articles of the Church's confession. The confession of the churches contain a common witness to the Providence of God over "all things," those of the Roman Catholic as well as those of the Lutheran and Reformed, churches. In Protestant confessions there is a remarkably uniform definition. In the handbooks of theology, too, the definitions and distinctions appear in striking consensus. We read in all of them of sustenance, and rule, and of God's embracing in his prescient government all that occurs in the universe.[23]

Indeed, the unanimity of the church, both Catholic and Protestant, on the doctrine of providence since the days of the church fathers is striking. From Augustine (354-430) through Aquinas (1225-74), Luther (1483-1546), Calvin (1509-64), and until the twentieth century, the doctrine of providence has been one teaching upon which Catholics and Protestants have agreed more than disagreed.[24] Since the Bible and Christianity were interwoven within the fabric of American culture in 1776, one should presume that the words *divine providence* in the Declaration carry the ordinary Christian meaning of the term unless there is clear evidence to the contrary. Such evidence is lacking.

It is well-known that founders such as Washington, Madison, and Franklin used the term "divine providence" as a name for God quite often in their public addresses.[25] Most have concluded such language to be deistic, or at least little more than literary flourish.[26] Certainly the word *providence* was used from time to time by some colonists as little more than a pious-sounding label. But it is the logical fallacy of taking the part for the whole to assume, as Catherine Albanese has done, that because some people used the word as mere religious metaphor, therefore all uses by the founders were devoid of sincerity and meaning.[27]

Deists of the eighteenth century sometimes used the word *providence*, but only to deny it. Louis Berkhof, in his *Systematic Theology*, described the deistic conception of providence this way:

According to Deism God's concern for the world is not universal, special and perpetual, but only of a general nature. . . . At the time of creation He imparted to all His creatures certain . . . properties, . . . and left them to work out their destiny by their own inherent powers. Meanwhile He merely exercises a general oversight, not of the specific agents that appear on the scene, but of the general laws which He established. The world is simply a machine which God has put in motion, and not at all a vessel which He pilots from day to day.[28]

John Orr, professor of Bible at Westminster College, in his *English Deism: Its Roots and Its Fruits*, also concluded that deists deny "providence" along with all other Christian doctrines.[29] But, says Orr, George Washington did not deny that providence:

Although "The Battle of the Biographers" goes merrily on, the Washington that emerges from the smoke appears to have been just a normal member of the Church of England in his religious views. He certainly left no writing that supports any position championed by the Deists.[30]

Of Ben Franklin's use of religious language, Orr writes:

Indeed Franklin's views on providence and prayer were quite inconsistent with the Deistic conception of an absentee God who does not and who could not, in consistency with the perfection of his work of creation and his impartial nature, interfere in the affairs of men.[31]

For deists, providence was "simply the way the world turned."[32] The deistic conception of providence was one where God had created the world with inherent qualities and potencies. The world was autonomous, though under immutable law, and left to function on its own. God was viewed as a mere spectator. Providence, then, consisted in general motion and superintendence of the universe by forces implanted in nature itself.[33] Providence, in the deistic sense, meant that men were left to their own devices.

This deistic notion of providence, which is in reality a denial of providence, is not what we find in the Declaration of Independence. The Declaration views God as the superior who by His own will has given rules binding inferior creatures. He has posited a law of nature that stands for the totality of His acts which He has ordained for the cosmos. He is the Supreme Judge who, through His divine providence, governs all things by the laws of nature. This view of God, law, nature, and providence is unquestionably the Christian view of providence.[34]

Supreme Judge and Divine Providence: Substitute for Names of God?

Did the founders show themselves to be deists by writing "Supreme Judge" and "Divine Providence" in the Declaration rather than "Jesus Christ" or "God"? There are those who think so.

Some charge that, since the Declaration does not contain the words, "Our Lord and Savior Jesus Christ," it must, therefore, be deistic and not Christian. The response to such a charge is simple. No Puritan document in American history is more famous than the Mayflower Compact of 1620. No one questions that it was based on Christian ideas and principles. Yet nowhere in the document does it mention the name Jesus Christ.[35] The Pilgrims on the Mayflower could hardly be called deists. Furthermore, in the history of Christian legal documents, the naive view that one must always use the name *Jesus Christ*, lest a document be impiously written, was never prominently held.

The more serious charge is that, by using *Supreme Judge* and *Divine Providence* instead of the word *God,* the founders demonstrated some sort of contempt for God. The opposite is true. Using substitute names for God was a way of showing respect and reverence for God's name in colonial religion. The practice arose for several reasons. One was the impact of the Hebraic Biblical tradition on colonial religion.

The most important name for God in the Old Testament was Yahweh. In Hebrew, it was written with the four letters *YHWH.* The name was held in such respect and reverence that pious Jews were never supposed to say "The Name" aloud nor even try to think the sound of the word while reading the Bible. Scribes who made copies of the Bible wrote the vowels of another word *Adonai,* meaning "lord," above the 5,321 entries of *YHWH* in the Old Testa-

ment.[36] Readers thought and pronounced *Adonai* rather than
YHWH lest they somehow take God's name in vain, thus violating
the Third Commandment.

The respect for "The Name" continued in the New Testament
among Christian Jews where the Greek word *theos* was used to
translate the Hebrew *YHWH* or *God*. This becomes most obvious by
comparing the Gospel of Luke, who was a Gentile, and the Gospel
of Matthew, who was a Jew. When Luke wrote of the kingdom proclaimed by Jesus Christ, Luke used the words "the kingdom of
God."[37] But Matthew, consciously respecting "The Name," wrote
"kingdom of heaven" instead of "kingdom of God."[38] Using the
word *heaven* as a metaphor for *God* did not make Matthew a deist,
but showed his reverence for God's name.[39]

In the first five centuries of the early church and particularly in
the Byzantine Empire, Christians treated the Greek name for God
with the same respect as *YHWH*. Numerous ancient manuscripts of
the New Testament have the divine names *Theos* (God) and *Kurios*
(Lord) abbreviated with a single slash mark across the tops of the
first and last letters of the name.[40]

Eventually, fifteen different Greek words associated in various
ways with the name of God received this special treatment in the
Greek texts.[41] These words have come to be called *nomina sacra* or
"sacred names" by Greek experts. A. H. R. E. Paap traces their
origins to Jewish Christians since "for them the Greek word for
'God' had exactly the same value as the Tetragrammaton and for
that reason was entitled to a distinction in its written forms."[42]

This kind of high regard for the name of God occurs in various
ways in Christian culture throughout the centuries. In colonial
America, it became a common practice in Puritan Christianity and
especially in Anglican Christianity, to speak of God by some majes-
tic metaphor as a way to show reverence and respect toward Him.
Besides the Hebraic influence and traditional Christian reverence
for "The Name," polite culture in England with its increasing aris-
tocratic emphasis on manners and protocol encouraged referring
to God indirectly.[43]

Also, at that time French was the language of culture. The
French aversion for expressing familiarity with a superior and the
conscious practice of self-effacement also made its influence felt in

the colonies. In such a setting, where Old Testamentalized religion mixed with British manners and French etiquette, for an ordinary man to speak of God directly rather than indirectly in certain contexts was viewed as disrespectful.

However peculiar such language and custom might strike us today, in colonial culture to speak of God by metaphor rather than by name was a mark of piety. Pastors and priests could always speak directly of God because they were spokesmen for God. In some contexts, it was proper for laymen to speak directly of God without appearing disrespectful. But in everyday affairs, while acknowledging God was considered every man's moral duty, it was also deemed inappropriate to use the divine name casually or with the appearance of too much familiarity.

Particularly among Anglicans, but among other Christian groups in the colonies as well, customary piety required men to show respect for God by avoiding a direct and familiar reference to His name. This differs little from Jewish practice or Christian practice in earlier centuries. So the Declaration does not have a less than Christian view of God merely by using "Supreme Judge" and "Divine Providence" to refer to the Deity.

An Essay on the Nature of Language.
"Providence" Borrowed From The Stoics?

Like so many other Christian concepts, providence is being questioned as authentically Christian. Some today trace it to the Greeks and Stoics, charging that Christians borrowed the idea from the Greeks. We are told that even though Christians for centuries used *providence* as a Christian term, today we know better and should no longer speak of providence. The modern confusion about whether it is proper for Christians to use the word *providence* is evident, for example, in the writings of the Dutch Christian philosopher, Bob Goudzwaard:

> The term "divine providence" does not appear in the Bible. Rather, it has been derived from the literature of the Stoics. . . . The Stoic idea of providence is borrowed by Augustine (354-430); however, he grafts it on a Christian root.[44]

Not everyone accepts that "grafting" a Stoic idea onto a Christian root makes any difference. Scholars like Cornelius Van Til and Rousas Rushdoony have dedicated their lives to purging Christianity of Greek and Stoic influences since any merger of Greek and Christian thought corrupts Christianity. Lesser reformers have sometimes thrown out the Christian baby with the pagan bath water by tracing Christian ideas to the Greeks.

Here is the dilemma Christians face. When God gave the New Testament, He chose to have it written in Greek, the common language of trade and culture in the first-century Roman empire. Except for the word *maranatha* and a handful of other Hebrew and Aramaic loanwords, most of the 5,436 different Greek words in the New Testament had a pagan past in Greek philosophy and mythical religion. The same thing is true for the Septuagint, or LXX, the Greek translation of the Old Testament, which was the Bible of the early Christians.[45]

When Jesus said "Blessed are the pure in heart," for *blessed* the Bible used the word *makarios* which in pagan Greek referred to the happy state of the gods living on Mt. Olympus.[46] It was from the noun *makar*, which in the plural meant "the gods." When Matthew wrote "the kingdom of heaven," the Greek word for *heaven* was *ouranos*, the name for Uranus, the Greek god of the sky.[47] Did Matthew think that Jesus had come to declare the "kingdom of Uranus"? Of course not.

Earlier chapters mentioned that the New Testament word for *justice* was *dike*, which signified a Greek goddess of the same name. John called Jesus the divine *logos*, a word with particular significance in the philosophy of Heraclitus. The list of New Testament words with pagan historical significance goes on and on. Few words in the Greek New Testament were not commonly used in unchristianized Hellenistic culture with pagan meanings. Christ and the apostles took those words, filled them with Christian meaning, and used them to proclaim the revealed truth of God.

When evangelists and translators put the message of the Bible into Latin and other languages, they faced the same situation. The languages of the nations were filled with words having meanings based on pagan worldviews. Unless those words could be transformed and given new meaning, it would be impossible to give men the gospel in their own tongues. This is a historical fact of the nature of language and linguistics.

Yet, many writers today fail to understand the nature of language and the ordinary principles of linguistics. Therefore, they assume that if Christians use a word that was used prior to Christianity by Greek or Stoic philosophers, the Christians must be borrowing from the Greeks.[48] To be logically consistent, those who make this mistake should also assume that since the entire New Testament is in Greek, the New Testament writers must have used Greek ideas by the simple fact that they used Greek words.

To be truly Christian, then, Christ and the apostles should have invented a wholly new language, but then no one would have understood it. To be consistent with this false linguistic principle—the misuse of etymology—the New Testament could never have been written in Greek and the gospel could never have been preached in any language other than a pure one created by the Holy Spirit.

However, this wrong view of the nature of language is widespread among modern writers. That is why the apostles, the church fathers, the medieval scholastics, the reformers, and even the colonial Puritans in America have been misunderstood. For example, B. F. Brown has said: "St. Paul, St. John Chrysostom, St. Augustine, and St. Isidore of Seville . . . all . . . borrowed Stoic ideas in describing the interrelationship between natural and supernatural laws."[49] Because Brown has not recognized that Paul and the church fathers were trying to put the gospel into the language of their hearers, thus fundamentally altering the concepts carried by the words, he has made Paul into a humanist who merges Jerusalem and Athens.

The same mistake is made in interpreting Augustine and Aquinas. Most historians believe that Augustine merged Christ with Plato, thus platonizing Christianity, and that Aquinas merged Christ with Aristotle. William Ebenstein has said, for instance:

> Of the two giants of the Christian tradition, St. Augustine and St.
> Thomas Aquinas, the first, St. Augustine, was thoroughly imbued
> with Platonic ideas; he was a Platonist. . . . Although St. Thomas
> Aquinas died before he was fifty . . . his lasting accomplishment
> (was) the incorporation of Aristotelianism into Christian

thought. . . . Augustinianism is the fusion of Plato and Christianity. Thomism is the synthesis of Aristotle and Christianity.[50]

Ebenstein could just as easily have said that John was imbued with Heraclitean ideas by referring to Christ as the logos in John 1:1. Or he could have said that Paul incorporated Aristotelian thought into Romans 1 with the word *phaneros*, Aristotle's term for "self-evident."[51] The same could be said of Paul's use of the Greek word *phusis*, or nature.

This is not to say that Augustine and Aquinas made no mistakes. Aquinas, in particular, used Aristotle in some wrong ways. Usually, though, Aquinas used a word only after giving it a Christian meaning. But his readers often ignore Aquinas's change in definition and read the earlier Greek philosophical meaning into the *Summa*. Thus, it appears that Aquinas sought to merge Aristotle and Christ, when instead he was trying to bring Aristotelian philosophy captive to the gospel.

The point is, the New Testament presents an entirely different picture of God, the world, man, and nature than we find in Greek philosophy and pagan religion. But it does so while using the very words and thought forms of the pagan culture itself. It claims words and meanings for Christ, transforming them with Christian worldview concepts, thus changing a culture by Christianizing its dictionary. Augustine and Aquinas tried to do the same thing in their writings. So did Luther, Calvin, and the Reformers.

The miracle of the New Testament is that God in His providence chose to use Greek, one of the most religiously and philosophically corrupt languages in history, as the vehicle by which to communicate the gospel of Jesus Christ. The purest and most important message God ever gave to man was recorded and transmitted to posterity in a language which was blighted and distorted by sin and superstition. The gospel stands for the proposition that God redeems and restores even man's fallen vocabulary.

The Stoics and Divine Providence

The Stoics were polytheists who rejected monotheism as a diminution of God.[52] For the Stoics as for earlier Greeks, the *cosmos* itself was divine.[53] Gods were gods, and men were gods, and matter was part of god. Stoics in particular emphasized that "impersonal

metaphysical powers and forces" innate in the *cosmos* were "god" in
the neutral sense of merely being "divine."[54] The Stoic god was not
a personal Creator God who was separate from His creation and
who was Lord over it. God for the Stoics was little more than an
impersonal, rational force of destiny.

In Stoicism, god was the divine spirit that was synonymous with
life and order in the cosmos, for "God and the *cosmos* are identical. . . ."[55] The "gods" were reduced to "metaphysical and cosmic
concepts."[56] Zeus, for example, was simply the "comprehensive law
of the world."[57] Thus, the Stoic view of God was highly rationalistic
and abstract, completely unlike the Biblical view of God.

The most important title for god in Stoicism was the Greek
word *pronoia*, or providence.[58] *Pronoia* is from the verb *pronoeo*
meaning to know in advance or know beforehand.[59] Translated
into Latin, it becomes *praevidere*, to see in advance, or "to make
provision for."[60] Providence for the Stoics was "The original divine
power immanent in the world (that) interrelates all things."[61] Thus
in early Stoicism, god was little more than a rational idea that
somehow was active in ordering and giving life to all cosmic phenomena. It was "providence" in that it provided for the harmony
and balance of all events.

In later Stoicism, the idea extended even to making meaningful
the meaningless events of chance, destiny, and fate.[62] But in Stoicism generally, providence was a cosmic divine force inherent in
the world itself which rationally orders the organism which is the
universe. Providence was world-centered and man-centered. It was
a rational idea, which, as a divine force, gave form to matter.

The Biblical notion of providence is completely different because the Biblical idea of God is different. The Bible presents God
as a person, not an impersonal force. He is more than a divine
principle; he is the transcendent almighty God who created all
things. The *cosmos* exists because He made it, but God is completely
separate from His creation. He orders all things by His will and
word, not simply by some rational deistic form or principle. His
will is law for all that he has created, which He actively governs,
sustains, upholds, and protects. All creatures are entirely dependent upon Him for all things.

This summary, which only covers part of the overall Biblical teaching about God, is enough to show the vast difference between the Christian view of God and that of the Greeks. When the LXX and the New Testament use Greek language, Greek religious terms, and Greek philosophical terms to proclaim the word and ways of the God who creates, sustains, and governs all things, the meanings of the words inevitably are radically transformed. To use the only words available in a language, particularly those which, at least formally, have some conceptual similarities to the ideas one seeks to express, is not to borrow from paganism but to redeem it.

The Bible and Divine Providence

In the beginning of this section, Bob Goudzwaard was quoted as saying that the Bible does not speak of *providence*.. He was mistaken. The Greek word *pronoia* occurs both in the Greek Old Testament and in the New Testament. The first instance is in the Old Testament Book of Wisdom, in the Apocrypha:

> But it is thy providence, O Father, that steers its course, because thou hast given it a path in the sea, and a safe way through the waves.[63]

Some commentators allege that the writer here has imported Stoic concepts by using the Greek word *pronoia*, or providence.[64]

In the New Testament the Apostle Paul uses *pronoia* in the ordinary sense of "to provide for" when he exhorts his disciples to "make no provision for the flesh to fulfill its lusts" (Romans 13:14). Although not using the word in a strict philosophical sense, Paul is still using a word that very clearly had pagan implications in Stoic philosophy. He did not regard the pagan use as an obstacle to his using the word in a legitimate way.

No one questions that the book of Genesis, the first book in the Bible, predates the Stoics. Genesis 22 tells how God tested the faith of the patriarch Abraham, the father of the Jews. At a crucial moment, God provided a ram for Abraham to use as a sacrifice. Abraham named the mountain *YHWH-jireh* — "The Lord Will Provide" (Genesis 22:14). The word translated "to provide" is the Hebrew word "to see," a parallel of the later Latin *providere*, to foresee, or to provide. When Augustine spoke of providence he did not need to borrow from the Stoics. God had shown himself to be the Provident One, the provider, roughly 1,600 years before Zeno the Stoic began teaching. We may safely assume that Augustine read the Bible.

Many writers have shown that the Bible clearly teaches the doctrine of providence regardless of Greek and Latin language considerations. In his excellent treatise on providence, Wilbur Fisk Tillett observes: "(T)he doctrine indicated by the term *providence* is one of the most significant in the Christian system, and is either distinctly stated or plainly assumed by every Biblical writer."[65] Protestant and Catholic scholars alike universally agree that the doctrine of providence is in the Pentateuch, the historical books of the Old Testament, the Psalms, the wisdom literature, the book of Job, the major and minor prophets, the apocalyptic literature, the Gospels, Acts, the Epistles, and the rest of the New Testament writings.[66]

Augustine did not borrow the Stoic doctrine of providence. He gave the pagan world the true doctrine of providence as taught in Scriptures and the early church creeds.[67] He was fulfilling the mission of the church to give the clear message of God that the nations of the world grope blindly for. Using the language of fallen men to convey to them God's truth is not contrary to the Christian faith but is part of the *modus operandi* of the Great Commission. Because God has made men verbal and has given them speech and language, to require Christians not to use the language of fallen men is absurd as well as un-Biblical.

Conclusion

When the founders used "Supreme Judge" and "Divine Providence" as names for God in the Declaration of Independence, they were squarely within the Christian mainstream. Both titles were fully acceptable as designations for God in Biblical Christianity, whether Catholic or Protestant. Furthermore, the idea of providence as found in colonial Christianity does not trace to the Stoics nor display any trace of Stoic philosophical influence. To think that it does rests on a flawed understanding of the nature of language and the principles of linguistics.

The Stoic use of the word *providence* and the meaning conveyed in Stoic thinking about providence is fundamentally different from the Christian concept. The Christian concept of providence is what one finds in the Declaration of Independence. For all these reasons, the use of "Supreme Judge" and "Divine Providence" in the Declaration should be accepted as marks of Christian influence on the founders rather than as evidence of deism, irreverence, or of Stoic influence.

EPILOGUE

ONE LAST POINT MUST BE MADE. The American Revolution is not over. The ideals enshrined in the Declaration for which the founders fought and died — ideals of law, justice, equality, liberty, inalienable rights, self-government — are barely understood in America today, much less in the rest of the world. We have all but forgotten what the words mean and what America is all about.

We think the American Revolution ended with the peace treaty of 1783. But it had not ended for American blacks whose equal creation and inalienable rights under God were systematically denied for two-hundred years. It had not ended when Abraham Lincoln heard Jefferson Davis and southern secessionists deny the ideals of the Declaration and deny that it had any relevance for American law. And it had not ended when Martin Luther King stood in Washington D.C., among monuments to the founding fathers, to declare with them that "all men are created equal."

The American Revolution was more than a contest with England. It was and is a war of ideas, a contest for the hearts and minds of men. It was and is a war to defend a vision about law, rights, justice, and the God-given dignity of man. The vision was inspired over time by the words of the Bible and the teachings of Christianity but applies to all men everywhere regardless of their faith.

At different times in different lands, men saw different parts of the vision. Parts of it were even put into practice in some of their countries, but never before 1776 had all of its ideas been implemented at one time. The American Revolution is unique because it began by declaring all these ideas as part of the foundation of a nation. A new political order was born on the earth.

Now, however, the Declaration's ideas are scoffed at by philosophers, misrepresented by historians, attacked by clergymen, ridiculed by law professors, held in contempt by power hungry politicians, and ignored by the people. As long as this continues, the American Revolution is not over.

We understand that the communist revolution did not end in the 1920's. It is a world revolution driven by a vision for world domination. Many such ideologies are abroad today. But we fail to see that the American Revolution is also a world revolution, guided by a view of the world and man which exchanges the iron heel of statism for the rod and staff of justice.

So, it is important, particularly for Christians, to know that the Declaration stands in the Judeo-Christian stream of political theory. Its legacy must be defended, since it is different both in degree and in kind from its secular counterpart, the French Revolution. Its legacy must be proclaimed, since political liberty is a corollary of spiritual liberty in Christ.

The American Revolution, then, will not be finished until in Tiennanmen Square, Red Square, and in all the town squares of the nations freedom rings as it did in July, 1776.

DECLARATION OF INDEPENDENCE
July 4, 1776

The Unanimous Declaration
of the Thirteen United States of America

WHEN, IN THE COURSE OF HUMAN EVENTS, it becomes necessary for one people to dissolve the political bands which have connected them with another, and to assume, among the powers of the earth, the separate and equal station to which the laws of nature and of nature's God entitle them, a decent respect to the opinions of mankind requires that they should declare the causes which impel them to the separation.

We hold these truths to be self-evident: that all men are created equal; that they are endowed, by their Creator, with certain unalienable rights; that among these are life, liberty, and the pursuit of happiness. That to secure these rights, governments are instituted among men, deriving their just powers from the consent of the governed; that whenever any form of government becomes destructive of these ends, it is the right of the people to alter or to abolish it, and to institute a new government, laying its foundation on such principles, and organizing its powers in such form, as to them shall seem most likely to effect their safety and happiness. Prudence, indeed, will dictate, that governments long established, should not be changed for light and transient causes; and accordingly all experience hath shown, that mankind are more disposed to suffer, while evils are sufferable, than to right themselves by abolishing the forms to which they are accustomed. But when a long train of abuses and usurpations, pursuing invariably the same object, evinces a design to reduce them under absolute despotism, it is their right, it is their duty, to throw off such government, and to provide new guards for their future security. Such has been the patient sufferance of these colonies; and such is now the necessity which constrains them to alter their former systems of government. The history of the present King of Great Britain is a history of repeated injuries and usurpations, all having in direct object the establishment of an absolute tyranny over these states. To prove this, let facts be submitted to a candid world.

He has refused his assent to laws the most wholesome and necessary for the public good.

He has forbidden his governors to pass laws of immediate and pressing importance, unless suspended in their operation till his assent should be obtained; and when so suspended, he has utterly neglected to attend to them.

He has refused to pass other laws for the accommodation of large districts of people, unless those people would relinquish the right of representation in the legislature; a right inestimable to them, and formidable to tyrants only. He has called together legislative bodies at places unusual, uncomfortable, and distant from the depository of their public records, for the sole purpose of fatiguing them into compliance with his measures.

He has dissolved representative houses repeatedly, for opposing, with manly firmness, his invasions on the rights of the people.

He has refused for a long time, after such dissolutions, to cause others to be elected; whereby the legislative powers, incapable of annihilation, have returned to the people at large for their exercise; the state remaining, in the mean time, exposed to all the dangers of invasions from without, and convulsions within.

He has endeavored to prevent the population of these States; for that purpose obstructing the laws for naturalization of foreigners; refusing to pass others to encourage their migrations hither, and raising the conditions of new appropriations of lands.

He has obstructed the administration of justice, by refusing his assent to laws for establishing judiciary powers.

He has made judges dependent on his will alone, for the tenure of their offices, and the amount and payment of their salaries.

He has erected a multitude of new offices, and sent hither swarms of officers, to harass our people, and eat out their substance.

He has kept among us, in times of peace, standing armies, without the consent of our legislatures.

He has affected to render the military independent of, and superior to the civil power.

He has combined with others to subject us to a jurisdiction foreign to our constitution, and unacknowledged by our laws; giving his assent to their acts of pretended legislation:

For quartering large bodies of armed troops among us;

For protecting them, by a mock trial, from punishment for any murders which they should commit on the inhabitants of these States;

For cutting off our trade with all parts of the world;

For imposing taxes on us without our consent;

For depriving us, in many cases, of the benefits of trial by jury;

For transporting us beyond seas to be tried for pretended offences;

For abolishing the free system of English laws in a neighbouring province, establishing therein an arbitrary government, and enlarging its boundaries, so as to render it at once an example and fit instrument for introducing the same absolute rule into these colonies;

For taking away our charters, abolishing our most valuable laws, and altering fundamentally the forms of our governments;

For suspending our own legislatures, and declaring themselves invested with power to legislate for us in all cases whatsoever.

He has abdicated government here, by declaring us out of his protection, and waging war against us.

He has plundered our seas, ravaged our coasts, burnt our towns, and destroyed the lives of our people.

He is at this time transporting large armies of foreign mercenaries to complete the works of death, desolation, and tyranny, already begun with circumstances of cruelty and perfidy, scarcely paralleled in the most barbarous ages, and totally unworthy the head of a civilized nation.

He has constrained our fellow-citizens, taken captive on the high seas, to bear arms against their country, to become the executioners of their friends and brethren, or to fall themselves by their hands.

He has excited domestic insurrections amongst us, and has endeavoured to bring on the inhabitants of our frontiers the merciless Indian savages, whose known rule of warfare is an undistinguished destruction of all ages, sexes, and conditions.

In every stage of these oppressions we have petitioned for redress in the most humble terms. Our repeated petitions have been answered only by repeated injury. A prince, whose character is thus marked by every act which may define a tyrant, is unfit to be the ruler of a free people.

Nor have we been wanting in attentions to our British brethren. We have warned them, from time to time, of attempts by their legislature to extend an unwarrantable jurisdiction over us. We have reminded them of the circumstances of our emigration and settlement here. We have appealed to their native justice and magnanimity, and we have conjured them by the ties of our common kindred to disavow these usurpations, which would inevitably interrupt our connexions and correspondence. They too have been deaf to the voice of justice and of consanguinity. We must, therefore, acquiesce in the necessity which denounces our separation, and hold them, as we hold the rest of mankind, enemies in war, in peace friends.

We, therefore, the representatives of the UNITED STATES OF AMERICA, in General Congress assembled, appealing to the Supreme Judge of the world for the rectitude of our intentions, do, in the name, and by authority of the good people of these colonies, solemnly publish and declare, That these United Colonies are, and of right ought to be, FREE and INDEPENDENT STATES; that they are absolved from all allegiance, to the British crown, and that all political connexion between them and the state of Great Britain is, and ought to be, totally dissolved; and that, as FREE and INDEPENDENT STATES, they have full power to levy war, conclude peace, contract alliances, establish commerce, and to do all other acts and things which INDEPENDENT STATES may of right do. And for the support of this Declaration, with a firm reliance on the protection of DIVINE PROVIDENCE, we mutually pledge to each other our lives, our fortunes, and our sacred honour.

JOHN HANCOCK, et al.

A   P   P   E   N   D   I   X   B

THE BIBLE AND "SELF-EVIDENT" TRUTHS

THE APOSTLE PAUL TAUGHT THAT GOD has two messages for men. One is that men are not righteous (Romans 1:18), the other that there is a way for men to become righteous before God (Romans 1:16). The revelation that men are not righteous is a general revelation given to all men everywhere (Romans 1:18). The way to be righteous comes by special revelation and is known only through hearing and believing the preaching of the gospel (Romans 1:16-17). The truth known through general revelation is sufficient only to make men know that they are under God's wrath for wrongdoing (Romans 1:18). The gospel tells men how to be released from God's wrath (Romans 1:16-17).

The Apostle then explains what general revelation contains, so that the knowledge of this general revelation makes men eternally accountable for their thoughts and actions. First, God has revealed the "truth" to men, but since men are corrupted by sin, they suppress the truth with unrighteousness.[1] That truth includes "what can be known about God."[2] This knowledge about God is "evident" to men, because God himself supernaturally steps past man's fallenness and sin and causes man to know it.[3]

This truth about God—what can be known about God—involves things that are "invisible," since no one has seen God.[4] Yet, because God himself causes men to know this truth, there is a sense in which the invisible is made "visible," indeed "clearly seen."[5] God's invisible attributes are not only clearly seen, they are also "clearly understood."[6] And they are clearly understood *tois poiemasin*, signifying both "by means of the things that are made," (that is, understood by observing the order of nature), and "by the things that are made," (understood by men themselves, who are created beings).[7]

According to the Apostle Paul, all men know and understand God's eternal power and deity.[8] In fact, they know "the God"—the living and true God.[9] Since they know the real God, not merely *a* god, they are "without excuse."[10] They know that the "incorruptible God" should be worshipped.[11] For His sake they should live godly, moral lives, honoring their bodies.[12] They should not give themselves up to passion nor do things contrary to nature, such as homosexual acts.[13]

This knowledge that God gives to all men is *epignosis*—a full knowledge, or complete knowledge.[14] It includes an understanding of what is *kathekonta*—that which is according to the order or plan of things, that which is "fitting" or "proper."[15] It includes a specific awareness of the evil nature of specific wrong deeds.[16]

Finally, according to the Apostle Paul, men who have sunk to the lowest possible level of depravity still "fully understand" the "righteous ordinance" of God and—as lawbreakers—deserve to die.[17] This is a remarkable claim by Paul in Romans 1:32, for he declares that even the vilest men not only know, but fully know, the *dikaioma* or the "righteous ordinance" of God. This is a law of God which is everywhere known by all men. They have this law "by nature," and the "requirement of the law" is "written in their hearts."[18]

Thus according to the teachings of the Apostle Paul in the written Scripture, there are many things that all men know in their natural state apart from special revelation. First, they know *the* God. Second, they know "what can be known" about God. He is the "eternal," "incorruptible," "all powerful" God who only is "God." Third, although God is invisible, these truths about God are clearly seen and fully known and understood. Fourth, they know that they should worship and serve Him. Fifth, they know that they should live clean and pious lives. Sixth, they fully know and understand the basic principles of God's eternal moral law. Seventh, they know that nature is a witness of that law and to violate the order of nature is to break God's law. Eighth, they know that they are under God's wrath and that there will be future rewards and punishments.

All these things are "evident" to men "by and through nature." But in his natural state, man only knows God as Creator and Judge. He does not know God as Redeemer, Savior, and loving Father. He knows God and yet does not "know" God. He is not reconciled to God, nor can he become reconciled without divine help. He does not know how to save himself and is incapable of saving himself. Morally and eternally he is lost and spiritually dead. He can come to know how to be righteous with God and actually become righteous before God only by hearing and believing the gospel. In his natural state, man only has a general revelation of things pertaining to creation. He lacks the special revelation of things pertaining to redemption. Until redeemed by Christ, he can understand nothing concerning the kingdom of God or truth concerning redemption.

Historically, the Apostle Paul's teaching of what is "evident" to all men gave rise to the Christian use of the term *self-evident.* When the Apostle Paul preached, he assumed that his hearers already were cognizant of all that is contained in general revelation. Frequently, Paul used that general revelation as a tool of apologetics when presenting the gospel to a pagan audience.[19] Later Christian preachers and apologists followed Paul's example.

END NOTES

INTRODUCTION

1. John Orr, *English Deism: Its Roots and Its Fruits* (Grand Rapids: Eerdmans, 1934), 13: "(T)he deist maintained that God endowed the world at creation with self-sustaining and self-acting powers and then abandoned it to the operation of these powers acting as second causes." For a more elaborate and technical discussion of deism, see Philip P. Weiner, ed., *Dictionary of the History of Ideas* (New York: Charles Scribner's Sons, 1973), s.v. "Deism," by Roger L. Emerson. [Hereafter, *Dictionary of the History of Ideas*.]
2. Carl Becker, *The Declaration of Independence* (New York: Vintage Books, 1970), 37.
3. Ibid.; and Arnold Smithline, *Natural Religion in American Literature* (New Haven: College & University Press, 1966), 9.
4. Charles Francis Adams, ed., *The Works of John Adams*, 10 vols. (Boston: Charles C. Little and James Brown, 1850, text-fiche), 2:6-7, LAC 20284.
5. Ibid., 7-8.
6. Adams to Jefferson, 28 June 1813, in Lester J. Cappon, ed., *The Adams-Jefferson Letters*, 2 vols. (Chapel Hill, N.C.: University of North Carolina Press, 1959, text-fiche), 2:339-340, LAC 22139.
7. Paul Leicester Ford, ed., *The Writings of Thomas Jefferson*, 10 vols. (New York: G. P. Putnam's Sons, 1892, text-fiche), 8:227-228 (divinity of Christ), 8:225, n. (infallibility of Scriptures), LAC 22701.
8. Ibid., 10:68, letter to George Logan, 12 November 1816, LAC 22702.
9. Ibid., 8:294, letter to Joseph Priestly, 29 January 1804, LAC 22701.
10. Andrew M. Allison, Pt. 1, "Thomas Jefferson, Champion of Liberty: A History of His Life," in *The Real Thomas Jefferson*, 2d ed., American Classics

Series, vol. 1 (Washington, D.C.: National Center for Constitutional Studies, 1983), 300.

11. Quoted in Henry Steele Commager, *Jefferson, Nationalism, and the Enlightenment* (New York: George Braziller, 1975), 10.

12. Perry Miller, *The New England Mind: From Colony to Province* (Cambridge: Harvard University Press, 1953), 417-436. [Hereafter, 1 Miller.]

13. Paul Conkin, *Self-evident Truths* (Bloomington: Indiana University Press, 1974), 5.

14. Vernon L. Parrington, *The Colonial Mind 1620-1800* (New York: Harcourt Brace Jovanovich, 1954), 152.

15. Perry Miller, "The Marrow of Puritan Divinity," in *Essays in American Intellectual History*, ed. Wilson Smith (Hinsdale, Ill.: Dryden Press, 1975), 13-17. [Hereafter, Miller, "Puritan Divinity".]

16. Perry Miller, *The New England Mind: The Seventeenth Century* (Cambridge: Harvard University Press, 1954), 192-93. [Hereafter, 2 Miller.]

17. Ibid., 194-96.

18. Ibid., 195.

19. Samuel Eliot Morison, *The Intellectual Life of Colonial New England* (Ithaca, N.Y.: Cornell University Press, 1956), 17.

20. 2 Miller, 73.

21. Miller, "Puritan Divinity," 28.

22. Merrill D. Peterson, *Thomas Jefferson and the New Nation* (London: Oxford University Press, 1970), 51.

23. Parrington, 152.

24. Smithline, 10; Herbert M. Morais, *Deism in Eighteenth Century America* (New York: Columbia University Press, 1934), 17, 36–37.

25. Ibid., 10.

26. Merle Curti, *The Growth of American Thought* (New York: Harper & Brothers, 1943), 108. See also Catherine Albanese, *Sons of the Fathers: The Civil Religion of the American Revolution* (Philadelphia: Temple University Press, 1976), 35-36.

27. Winton U. Solberg, *Cotton Mather, "The Christian Philosopher," and the Classics*, reprinted from the *Proceedings of the American Antiquarian Society*, vol. 96, pt. 2, Oct. 1986 (Worchester, Mass.: American Antiquarian Society, 1987), 332.

28. Smithline, 9, says: "In 1721 Cotton Mather wrote the *Christian Philosopher*, a book anticipating deism. . . . Mather's book represents probably the earliest expression in any consistent form of deistic thought in America."

29. 1 Miller, 417-20; Albanese, 34; Curti, 113; Smithline, 14; Morison, 270.

30. Curti, 75; Roland Bainton's, "Jonathan Edwards: 'The Great Awakening'" in Smith, *Essays*, 61-62, describes Edwards' religion in terms of neoplatonic gnosticism.

31. See Parrington, 152.

32. Morais, 40.

33. Ibid., 85 et seq.

34. See Peter Gay, *The Enlightenment: An Interpretation, The Rise of Modern Paganism* (New York: Alfred A. Knopf, 1967), intro. and chap. 1.

35. Smithline, 10; Albanese, 11, 38, 77-79.

36. Albanese, 18.

37. For a different type of critique of the American Enlightenment thesis see, Daniel J. Boorstin, "The Myth of the American Enlightenment," in *America and the Image of Europe: Reflections on American Thought* (Gloucester, Mass.: Peter Smith, 1976), chap. 3.

38. *Dictionary of the History of Ideas*, 1:647.

39. See Richard R. Lovelace, *The American Pietism of Cotton Mather: Origins of American Evangelicalism* (Grand Rapids: Christian University Press, Eerdmans, 1979), 5, 53-54.

40. E.g., Morais, 113-15.

41. Merwyn S. Johnson, *Locke on Freedom: An Incisive Study of the Thought of John Locke* (Austin, Tex.: Best Printing Company, 1978).

42. Ibid., chap. 7.

43. Ibid., 162, n. 10.

44. Mark Noll, Nathan Hatch, and George Marsden, *Search for "Christian" America* (Westchester, Ill.: Crossway Books, 1983), 20, 23.

45. Ibid.

46. Ibid., 18, 70.

47. Ibid., 81.

48. Ibid., 84.

49. Ibid., 90.

50. John Witherspoon, *Lectures on Moral Philosophy*, ed. Varnum Lansing Collins (Princeton, N.J.: Princeton University Press, 1912, text-fiche), 1, LAC 14281.

51. Noll, et al., 95, 100.

52. John Woodbridge, Mark Noll, and Nathan Hatch, *The Gospel in America* (Grand Rapids: Zondervan, 1979), 31.

53. Mark Noll, "The Image of the United States as a Biblical Nation, 1776-1865," in *The Bible in America: Essays in Cultural History*, ed. Nathan Hatch and Mark Noll (New York: Oxford University Press, 1982), 46. But see Clarence B. Carson, *The Rebirth of Liberty: The Founding of the American Republic, 1760-1800* (New Rochelle, N.Y.: Arlington House, 1973), 44: "To virtually all Americans, their religious background provided the framework through which they winnowed their ideas and in terms of which they builded." Noll's position has changed very little with his most recent book. In *One Nation Under God? Christian Faith and Political Action in America* (San Francisco: Harper and Row, 1988), x, he says that America can be called a "Christian nation" with a distinctive "Christian heritage" only "in a carefully qualified sense" that some "Christians played central roles in the story of the nation and that Christian values have been important in the country's public life." (Intro at). This is short of saying that any of the structural ideas or theoretical principles were Christian and were embraced by both Christians and non-Chrisians.

54. C. Gregg Singer, *A Theological Interpretation of American History*, rev. ed., (Phillipsburg, N.J.: Presbyterian and Reformed Publishing Co., 1981), 36-37, 40.

55. See Richard M. Gummere, *The American Colonial Mind & The Classical Tradition* (Cambridge, Mass.: Harvard University Press, 1963).

56. Gummere observes that Bible and English common law more strongly impacted the colonies than the Greek and Roman tradition, ibid., xii.

CHAPTER 1: FOUNDING AMERICA

1. For a helpful history of this period, see John A. Garraty, *The American Nation: A History of the United States to 1877*, 5th ed. (New York: Harper & Row, 1983), 70-96.
2. Garraty, 70-71.
3. This position was taken by the Massachusetts General Council as early as 1640. That Parliament had no authority to levy taxes directly on the colonies was explicitly reaffirmed in 1692 by Massachusetts. For an account of the dispute over this point see Alden Bradford, ed., *Speeches of the Governors of Massachusetts, From 1765 to 1775; and the Answers of the House of Representatives to the Same; with Their Resolutions and Addresses for that Period* (Boston: Russell and Gardner, 1818, text-fiche), 4, 14, LAC 15249.
4. Ibid., 45 et seq.
5. Garraty, 78.

CHAPTER 2: THE LAWS OF NATURE AND OF NATURE'S GOD

1. For the text of the Declaration see Appendix A. See also Richard L. Perry, ed., *Sources of Our Liberties: Documentary Origins of Individual Liberties in the United States Constitution and Bill of Rights*, rev. ed. (Chicago: American Bar Foundation, 1978), 319.
2. For a survey of the major historical schools of thought about Jefferson and the Declaration see Richard K. Matthews, *The Radical Politics of Thomas Jefferson* (Lawrence, Kan.: University Press of Kansas, 1984), chap. 1; and, Bernard Bailyn, *The Ideological Origins of the American Revolution* (Cambridge, Mass.: Belknap Press, 1982), vi-vii.
3. This chapter surveys the historical background of the phrase "laws of nature and of nature's God." In the more than six-hundred-year development of the ideas embodied in the phrase, a good deal of flexibility existed in the terminology. Some writers spoke of the "laws of nature," others of the "laws of nature and God," and the "laws of God and nature." Many other variations occurred as well. These variations are largely stylistic rather than substantive. They reflect idiomatic peculiarities of time, region, and author. Yet, in context, there is a core of agreement or common theme running like a thread through the centuries.
4. See e.g., Catherine L. Albanese, *Sons of the Fathers: The Civil Religion of the American Revolution* (Philadelphia: Temple University Press, 1976), 114-20.
5. See e.g., Morton J. Frisch, Richard G. Stevens, eds., *American Political Thought: The Philosophic Dimension of American Statesmanship*, 2d ed. (Itasca, Ill.: F. E. Peacock Publishers, 1983), 28-29: "(T)he Declaration (at least in Jefferson's understanding) seems hostile to revealed religion" by speaking of the laws of nature and especially of nature's God.
6. Thomas J. Schlereth, *The Cosmopolitan Ideal in Enlightenment Thought* (Notre Dame: University of Notre Dame Press, 1977), 81. Henry Steele Commager, *Jefferson, Nationalism, and the Enlightenment* (New York: George Braziller, 1975). At 81, Commager says, "When Jefferson wrote that the Declaration was 'an expression of the American mind,' what he referred to was almost

certainly the Preamble. That Preamble was an expression of more than the American mind; it was an expression of the mind of the Enlightenment." See also Henry Steele Commager, *The Empire of Reason: How Europe Imagined and America Realized the Enlightenment* (New York: Oxford University Press, 1982). But cf., Lewis Perry, *Intellectual Life in America: A History* (New York: Franklin Watts, 1984), 149-55.

7. On Locke's "deism" see Herbert Morais, *Deism in Eighteenth Century America* (New York: Columbia University Press, 1934), 33–38.

8. Peter Gay, *The Enlightenment: An Interpretation, The Rise of Modern Paganism* (New York: Alfred A. Knopf, 1967), xi-xii, 11, 13. Adrienne Koch, *The American Enlightenment: The Shaping of the American Experiment and a Free Society* (New York: George Braziller, 1965), 23, 26-27. Cf. Merrill D. Peterson, *Thomas Jefferson & The New Nation* (London: Oxford University Press, 1970), 48-49.

9. See e.g., C. Gregg Singer, *A Theological Interpretation of American History*, rev. ed. (Phillipsburg, N.J.: Presbyterian and Reformed Publishing Co., 1981), chaps. 1, 2. Cf. Mark Noll, Nathan Hatch, and George Marsden, *The Search for "Christian" America* (Westchester, Ill.: Crossway Books, 1983), chap. 4.

10. Cf., e.g., Merle Curti, *The Growth of American Thought* (New York: Harper & Brothers, 1943), 5: "The doctrine of the higher law, or the supremacy of the law of God and nature over all human law, though of course not exclusively English in origin, was transmitted to the new American nation through British channels. The common law, modified though it was in some respects by colonial conditions, was of English derivation."

11. Cited in Alden Bradford, ed., *Speeches of the Governors of Massachusetts, From 1765 to 1775; and the Answers of the House of Representatives to the Same; With Their Resolutions and Addresses For That Period* (Boston: Russell and Gardner, 1818, text-fiche), 50, LAC 15249.

12. Ames wrote the immensely influential *Medulla Theologica*, or *Marrow of Theology* in 1623. For the importance of Ames, see William Ames, *The Marrow of Theology*, trans. John D. Eusden (Boston: Pilgrim Press, 1968), 1-66.

13. Quoted in Perry Miller, *The New England Mind: The Seventeenth Century* (Cambridge: Harvard University Press, 1954), 193. [Hereafter, 2 Miller.] On the "law of nature" see ibid., 193-98; and, Perry Miller, "The Marrow of Puritan Divinity," in *Essays in American Intellectual History*, ed. Wilson Smith (Hinsdale, Ill.: Dryden Press, 1975), 14-18, 21, 26, 31. [Hereafter, Miller, "Puritan Divinity".] On covenantalism see Perry Miller, *The New England Mind: From Colony to Province* (Cambridge: Harvard University Press, 1953). [Hereafter, 1 Miller.]

14. Miller, "Puritan Divinity," 21.

15. Richard L. Perry, ed., *Sources of Our Liberties, Documentary Origins of Individual Liberties in the United States Constitution and Bill of Rights*, rev. ed. (Chicago: American Bar Foundation, 1978), 44. [Hereafter, Perry, *Sources Of Our Liberties*.]

16. Ibid., 35.

17. See generally Carl Stephenson and Frederick George Marcham, *Sources of English Constitutional History: A Selection of Documents From A.D. 600 to the Interregnum*, vol. 1 (New York: Harper & Row, 1972); Samuel Rawson Gardi-

ner, ed., *The Constitutional Documents of the Puritan Revolution 1625-1660* (Oxford: Clarendon Press, 1979); and Perry, *Sources of Our Liberties.*

18. See John A. Garraty, *The American Nation: A History of the United States to 1877,* 5th ed. (New York: Harper & Row, 1983), 82.

19. See Merle Curti, *The Growth of American Thought* (New York: Harper & Brothers, 1943), 118-19.

20. Daniel J. Boorstin, in *Hidden History* (New York: Harper & Row, 1987), 35, rightly says, "During the very years when the Revolution was brewing, Jefferson was every day talking the language of the common law. We cannot but be impressed not only at the scarcity in the Jefferson papers of anything that could be called fresh inquiry into the theory of government but also by the legalistic context of Jefferson's thought. We begin to see that the United States was being born in an atmosphere of legal rather than philosophical debate."

21. The Declaration of Independence was written to accomplish the limited political goal of explaining why the colonists were justified in declaring independence from England. It was a culminating document, the last in a series put forth by the Continental Congress. It must be read in light of the resolutions of the Stamp Act Congress (1765), the Declaration and Resolves of the First Continental Congress (1774), the Declaration of the Causes and Necessity of Taking Up Arms (1775), and the various circular letters distributed throughout the colonies by the various colonial legislatures. It is consistent with these, even though shifting to a different primary ground of law and rights as a last resort after all other attempts had failed.

22. Singer, 36. Singer fails to see that the founders appealed to the "laws of nature," not to "natural law." In the 1770s there were important differences between the two concepts. "Law of nature" meant the objectively revealed moral law of God, first in nature (called "general revelation" by Christian theologians), then in the positive moral law of Scripture. "Natural law" denoted the fallen understanding or mental perception in man's mind of the laws of nature. Some deists used the term "natural law" to speak of man's ability to reason his way to a perfect understanding of natural justice. If Jefferson had wished to equivocate, or to promote deism, he could have used the phrase "natural law." He did not. Deists and Enlightenment rationalists, building on the earlier Renaissance quattrocento school of thought, did not believe in any other source of law than "natural law," that is, their own reason. They did not believe in "laws of nature and of nature's God," a fixed moral law posited by God. This meant that the content of natural law was always subject to debate since men's reason produces varying ideas about law. For them, the only true law could only be positive law, the product of convention and man's political activity.

23. Ibid., 40.

24. See John Murray, "The Epistle to the Romans," 2 vols., in F. F. Bruce, gen. ed., *The New International Commentary on the New Testament* (Grand Rapids: Wm. B. Eerdmans, 1959, 1964), vol. 1, chaps. 1-8. See particularly 44 (natural law), 74-75, 189, 190-91 (law of nature). [Hereafter, Murray, *Romans.*]

25. *"Lege naturae vel divina,"* or "by the law of nature or God," quoted in Richard Tuck, *Natural Rights Theories: Their Origin and Development* (Cambridge: Cambridge University Press, 1979), 21, n. 43. [Hereafter, Tuck, *Natural Rights Theories.*]

26. For "law of nature" as "creation law" see John Calvin, *Institutes of the Christian Religion* (1536), 2 vols., trans. Henry Beveridge (Grand Rapids: Wm. B. Erdmans, 1981), 1:41, 45, 47, 49, 65, 174, 180, 237, 241, 317, 319, 358. [Hereafter, Calvin's *Institutes.*] Even for John Calvin the "law of nature" was the "will of God" and was a technical term for God's "creation law." See also Albert M. Wolters, *Creation Regained: Biblical Basics for a Reformational Worldview* (Grand Rapids: Eerdmans, 1985), 14-15 (laws of nature), 17-18, 21, 24-25, 27. In this section I have used Beveridge's edition as a matter of convenience. The standard work on the subject is John T. McNeill, ed., *Calvin: Institutes of the Christian Religion*, 2 vols., trans. Ford Lewis Battles, vol. 20, *The Library of Christian Classics* (Philadelphia: Westminster Press, 1960).

27. Sir William Blackstone, *Commentaries on the Laws of England* (1765), ed. St. George Tucker (Philadelphia: William Young Birch and Abraham Small, 1803; reprint, South Hackensack, N.J.: Rothman Reprints, Inc., 1969), 1:38-39, *passim*, [Hereafter, Blackstone's *Commentaries.*] Cf., Calvin's *Institutes*, vol. 1, bk. 1, chap. 2. Blackstone's line of argument is identical with Calvin's, not so much because Blackstone was following Calvin, but because both started from a Biblical worldview model.

28. Blackstone's definition represents the influence of John Buridan's commentaries on Aristotle's *On the Heavens.* Buridan rejected Aristotle's doctrine of the eternity of motion and insisted that only a Biblical view of creation and nature was acceptable for the laws of physical science. For the significance of Buridan see Stanley L. Jaki, "God and Man's Science: A View of Creation," in *The Christian Vision: Man in Society*, ed. Lynne Morris (Hillsdale, Mich.: Hillsdale College Press, 1984), 43.

29. "This law of nature, being co-eval with [i.e., existing as long as] mankind and dictated by God himself, is of course superior in obligation to any other. It is binding over all the globe, in all countries, and at all times; no human laws are of any validity, if contrary to this; and such of them as are valid derive all their force, and all their authority, mediately or immediately, from this original." Blackstone's *Commentaries*, 1:41. Compare Blackstone's words with those of John Calvin writing about God's eternal moral law: "The moral law . . . is the true and eternal rule of righteousness prescribed to the men of all nations and of all times, who would frame their life agreeably to the will of God. . . . (Human laws that contravene the moral law) I do not think entitled to be considered as laws. . . ." Calvin's *Institutes*, 2:663-665, bk. 4, chap. 20, secs. 15-16. Blackstone's "voluntarist" understanding of law models Calvin's. Calvin also wrote, "The Lord, in delivering a perfect rule of righteousness, has reduced it in all its parts to his mere will, and in this way has shown that there is nothing more acceptable to him than obedience." Calvin's *Institutes*, 1:319, bk. 2, chap. 8, sec. 5.

30. "(The whole office of reason) is to discover . . . what the law of nature directs . . . . (I)f our reason were always, as in our first ancestor before his

transgression, clear and perfect, unruffled by passions, unclouded by prejudice, unimpaired by disease or intemperance, the task would be pleasant and easy; . . . But every man now finds the contrary in his own experience; that his reason is corrupt, and his understanding full of ignorance and error. This has given manifold occasion for the benign interposition of divine providence; which in compassion to the frailty, the imperfection, and the blindness of human reason, hath been pleased, as sundry times and in divers manners, to discover [reveal] and enforce its laws by an immediate and direct revelation. The doctrines thus delivered we call the revealed or divine law, and they are to be found only in the holy scriptures. These precepts, when revealed, are found upon comparison to be really a part of the original law of nature, . . . But we are not from thence to conclude that the knowledge of these truths was attainable by reason, in its present corrupted state; since we find that, until they were revealed, they were hid from the wisdom of ages. As then the moral precepts of this law are indeed the same original with those of the law of nature, so their intrinsic obligation is of equal strength and perpetuity. Yet undoubtedly the revealed law is . . . of infinitely more authority than what we call the natural law. Because one is the law of nature, expressly declared so to be by God himself; the other is only what, by the assistance of human reason, we imagine to be that law. If we could be as certain of the latter as we are of the former, both would have an equal authority; but, till then, they can never be put in any competition together." Blackstone's *Commentaries*, 1:41-42. Compare this line of argument with John Calvin in Calvin's *Institutes*, vol. 1, bk. 1, chaps. 3-6. Again, Blackstone is summarizing the main points of an orthodox Christian approach to understanding God, man, the world, and nature.

31. Quoting Romans 2:14, Romans 13:1, and an unnamed theologian, in Calvin v. Smith and Another. Trin. 6 Jac. 1. 7 Coke's Reports, 1. Coke became Chief Justice of the Court of Common Pleas in 1606, and Chief Justice of King's Bench in 1613. He died at the age of 80 in 1634. To see that Coke's ideas are orthodox compare Murray, *Romans*, 1:73-75.
Compare Coke's explanation with the words of the Reformer, John Calvin, two generations earlier: "Now, as it is evident that the law of God which we call moral, is nothing else than the testimony of natural law, and of that conscience which God has engraven on the minds of men, the whole of this equity of which we now speak is prescribed in it. Hence it alone ought to be the aim, the rule, and end of all laws." Calvin's *Institutes*, 2:664, bk. 4, chap. 20, sec. 16.

32. Blackstone's *Commentaries*, 1:41-42. Note that Blackstone equates the "law of nature" with the written "law of God" in Scripture but insists that "law of nature" and "natural law" are not the same. "Natural law" in man's fallen mind "can never be put in any competition" with the "law of nature." Thus, when Blackstone says that the law of nature and the law of God are the two foundations upon which the validity of all human laws rest, he explicitly excludes "natural law" as part of the foundation. Man's fallen mind is not a proper source of law or ethics, according to Blackstone.

33. *"Lege naturae vel divina, non sunt rerum distincta domina pro statu inncoentiae [sic], imo tunc omnia sunt communia . . ."* Reply of Duns Scotus to Thomas Aquinas in *"Quaestiones in librum Sentatiarum,"* quoted in Tuck, *Natural Rights Theories,* 21.

34. For example, B. F. Brown writes: "St. Paul . . . borrowed Stoic ideas in describing the interrelationship between natural and supernatural laws." In *New Catholic Encyclopedia,* 1967 ed., s.v. "Natural Law," by B. F. Brown.

35. Psalm 119:89-91.

36. Job 8:8-10, 12:3, 13:1 (cf. Psalm 78:2-3), and 15:7-10. See R. K. Harrison, *Introduction to the Old Testament* (Grand Rapids: Wm. B. Eerdmans, 1969), 1022, 1032, 1040-42.

37. See Job 12:7-9, 20:27; Psalm 19:1-9, 94:10, 97:6, 102:25, 104:5-9, 105:7, 111:7-8, 148:5-6; and Isaiah 24:5.

38. See e.g., Genesis 20:3; Job 4:12-13; 33:13-18; Daniel 2, 4, 5. See also Matthew 2:1-12.

39. See Romans 3:2.

40. Rousas John Rushdoony, *Foundations of Social Order* (Fairfax, Va.: Thoburn Press, 1978), 6.

41. The trinitarian principle means that the church condemns all forms of subordinationism as heresy. In Christology, for example, the Son is subject to the Father, but not subordinate to the Father.

42. Blackstone thought that both phrases, "law of nature" and "of God," were necessary because they represented two different forms of God's revelation of His law. The "law of nature" was God's eternal law revealed in the design and operation of the world and nature. The law "of God" is that same law but specially revealed in the Holy Scriptures. The two phrases used together expressed the link between general and special revelation. Students of Blackstone reading the Declaration would have no reason to think that Jefferson was saying anything different than the law of nature and the law of revelation as explained by Blackstone.

43. Perry, *Sources of Our Liberties,* 318.

44. Louis Wright, *Magna Carta and the Tradition of Liberty* (U.S. Capitol Historical Society and the Supreme Court Historical Society, 1976), 45.

45. See Daniel J. Boorstin, *Hidden History* (New York: Harper & Row, 1987), 103.

46. From Selden, OPERA, III, col. 2041, quoted in Tuck, *Natural Rights Theories,* 92.

47. Gabriel Sivan of Hebrew University in Jerusalem says this about the Bible and Selden's approach: "An analysis of the Hebrew Bible does, in fact, substantiate the claim that laws governing the conduct of states and relations between nations can be deduced from Scripture. . . . [Numerous examples given] . . . Texts such as these, when combined with the Roman doctrine of *jus gentium* ('law of nations'), transformed the original concept of a universal and unchanging 'Natural Law' into the foundation of international law and justice. Furthermore, Grotius and Selden were both equipped to dig deep into post-Biblical Jewish lore as well, the former, citing the Talmud, Targum, Rashi, and Mainomides; the latter, displaying all the wealth of his remarkable Rabbinic learning—the cause of the 'law of nature and of na-

tions.'" Gabriel Sivan, *The Bible and Civilization* (New York: New York Times Book Co., 1973), 140-41.

48. Again, this is assuming a particular brand of deism and the movement related to it in the late 1600s and early 1700s. I am not referring to the deism castigated by Calvin in the *Institutes*. Nor am I referring to the deism coming from Italian Renaissance naturalism attacked by Pierre Viret's *Instruction Christienne* (1564). See Roger L. Emerson, *Dictionary of the History of Ideas*, 1:648.

49. Many of those writers who are ordinarily associated with the rise of natural theology and deism maintained the same symmetry of expression. For example, Matthew Tindal favorably quoted Archbishop Sharp as saying: "(T)hat religion which is from God . . . is not a thing to be altered at Pleasure; both the Law of Nature, and the Law of God; both the natural Dispensation under which all Men are born, and the reveal'd Dispensation as we have either in the Old or New Testament; . . ." Matthew Tindal, *Christianity as Old as the Creation* (London: n.p., 1730; reprint, New York: Garland Publishing, 1978), 84.

50. Compare this thrust of the common law with the Westminster Confession of Faith, chap. 19, and the Westminster Larger Catechism, qs. 91-151. The Confession and the Catechism both maintain that the eternal moral principles of the decalogue, rather than the explicit regulations of the political and ceremonial law of the Bible, comprise the "law of nature," and are binding on all men and nations.

51. Francis Schaeffer, *How Shall We Then Live?* (Old Tappan, N.J.: Fleming H. Revell, 1976), 52.

52. St. Thomas Aquinas, *Summa Theologica*, 5 vols., trans. Fathers of the English Dominican Province, 1920 rev. ed. (Westminster, Md.: Christian Classics, 1981 reprint). Pt 1, Q 86, Art 2, rep obj 1; Pt 1, Q 86, Art 2, answer; Pt 1, Q 1, Art 1, answer; Pt 1 of 2, Q 83, Art 4, answer; Pt 1 of 2, Q 109, Art 8, answer; Pt 1 of 2, Q 74, Art 5, rep obj 2; Pt 1 of 2, Q 75, Art 3, answer; Pt 1 of 2, Q 19, Art 5, rep obj 2; Pt 1 of 2, Q 79, Art 3, answer and rep obj 1; Pt 1 of 2, Q 19, Art 6, rep obj 2.

53. *Summa Theologica*, Pt 1 of 2, Q 94, Art 5, rep obj 1. I have supplied the word different for the word some.

54. *Summa Theologica*, Pt 1 of 2, Q 91, Art 4, answer.

55. *Summa Theologica*, Pt 1 of 2, Q 83, Art 4, answer.

56. *Summa Theologica*, Pt 1 of 2, Q 109, Art 8, answer.

57. *Summa Theologica*, Pt 1, Q 1, Art 5, rep obj 1.

58. Compare the teaching of the Spanish Jesuit Francisco Suarez (1548-1617) on the Catholic doctrine of the use of nature in Gwladys L. Williams, Ammi Brown, and John Waldron, trans., Francisco Suarez, *Selections From Three Works: De Legibus, Acts Deo Legislatore*, 1612; *Defensio Fidei Catholicae, et Apostolicae Adversus Anglicanae Sectae Errores*, 1613; *De Triplici Virtute Theologica, Fide, Spe, et Charitate*, 1621; Vol. 2, James Brown Scott, ed., *The Classics of International Law* (Oxford: Clarendon Press, 1944): "Finally, the Catholic faith teaches not only how far we must obey God when He commands in the supernatural order; it teaches also what nature forbids, commands, or permits; furthermore, it clearly reveals to us the extent to which we must sub-

mit to the higher powers (in the words of Paul) and, indeed, the extent to which we must observe both ecclesiastical and secular laws. From these foundations of the faith, then, it is for the theologian to deduce what should be held, with respect to this or that system of laws." Pref., at 14.

"But theology embraces all these functions on a loftier plane. For it takes into consideration the natural law itself in so far as the latter is subordinated to the supernatural order, and derives greater firmness therefrom; whereas it considers the civil laws only by way of determining, according to a higher order of rules, their goodness and rectitude, or by way of declaring, in accordance with the principles of faith, . . ." Pref., at 16.

We can see from writers such as Suarez that before the rise of Deism, the Catholic faith was examining both Scripture and nature as revelations from God, and was subordinating the natural law to the reveal⌐d standard.

59. See generally Merwyn S. Johnson, *Locke on Freedom: An Incisive Study of the Thought of John Locke* (Austin, Tex.: Best Printing Company, 1978); and John Orr, in *English Deism: Its Roots and Its Fruits* (Grand Rapids: Eerdmans, 1934), 30, n, 12; 99.

60. For a careful analysis of Locke's religious beliefs and view of Scripture see Orr, 83-109. Orr concludes at 99: "Locke made a strong statement concerning his own acceptance of the Bible. He read the Scriptures with full assurance that all therein is true and yielded a submission to its inspired authors that he would give to no other writers. . . . This attitude of Locke toward revelation was certainly very different from that of all the Deists and makes it very evident that Locke . . . was not himself a Deist." See also, Johnson, *Locke on Freedom,* 12: "The standard treatments of Locke's religious views have stereotyped him in a rationalist mold which itself needs to be challenged across the board."

61. See e.g., Vernon L. Parrington, *The Colonial Mind 1620-1800* (New York: Harcourt Brace Jovanovich, 1954), 241-45.

62. See Henry Steele Commager, *The American Mind: An Interpretation of American Thought and Character Since the 1880's* (New Haven: Yale University Press, 1950), 26. But see Adrienne Koch, *The American Enlightenment* (New York: George Braziller, 1965), 41.

63. Carl Becker, *The Declaration of Independence: A Study in the History of Political Ideas* (New York: Vintage Books, 1958).

64. Ibid., 51.

65. Ibid., 35.

66. Ibid., 36-37.

67. Ibid., 37.

68. Ibid.

69. John Locke, *The Second Treatise of Government,* ed. Thomas Peardon (New York: Liberal Arts Press, 1956), 14, chap. 3, sec. 21. [Hereafter, *Second Treatise.*]

70. Ibid.

71. Becker, 35-36.

72. In a later chapter I will deal with Locke's use of the term "reason" and its relation to the Bible, involving a more complex definition of deism. For purposes of this chapter, deism is limited to the definitions given above.

73. *American Heritage Dictionary*, 1970 ed., s.v. "Deism."

74. See e.g., *Second Treatise*, secs. 21, 24, 25, 31, 32, 39, 52, 109, 176, 196, 241.

75. Ibid., 62-63, sec. 109; 100, sec. 176; 138, sec. 241.

76. Ibid., 63, sec. 109.

77. See, John Locke, *"The Reasonableness of Christianity," with "A Discourse on Miracles" and part of "A Third Letter Concerning Toleration,"* ed. I. T. Ramsey (Stanford, Calif.: Stanford University Press, 1958). [Hereafter, Locke, *Reasonableness*.]

78. John Locke, *An Essay Concerning Human Understanding*, 2 vols., ed. Alexander Campbell Fraser (New York: Dover Publications, 1959), 2:120. [Hereafter, Locke, *Essay*.]

79. Ibid., 2:279.

80. Ibid. This is in contrast to natural truth which God can reveal to man by the light of reason: "When we find out an idea by whose intervention we discover the connexion of two others, this is a revelation from God to us by the voice of reason." Whether God leads man to divine truths about the Christian faith through special revelation, or to natural truths through the ordinary revelation of reason, each is "a revelation from God to us by the voice of his Spirit, . . ." Ibid.

81. Ibid., 2:311.

82. Ibid., 2:383.

83. Ibid.

84. Ibid., 2:425.

85. Ibid., 2:438.

86. Ibid., 2:439.

87. Ibid., 2:440. Cf. Richard Hooker, *Of the Laws of Ecclesiastical Polity*, ed. A.S. McGrade and Brian Vickers, abridged ed. (London: Sidgwick & Jackson, 1975), 130, bk. 1, ch. 8, sec. 8. [Hereafter, *Ecclesiastical Polity*.]

88. Quoted in, Locke, *Essay*, vol. 1, prolegomena at 1. Also cited in Orr, *English Deism*, 99. For the modern reader I have modernized the original word *assent* to *belief* and *want* to *lack*. For a discussion of what Locke meant by "assent" see, Locke, *Essay*, vol. 1, Prolegomena, cxxi. Cf., Locke, *Reasonableness*, 33, secs. 27, 29.

89. Locke, *Reasonableness*, 52, sec. 227.

90. Ibid., 35, sec. 40 (justification by faith); 32, secs. 26, 27, 28 (Messiah); 33, secs. 30, 35, 38 (Son of God).

91. *Second Treatise*, 52, sec. 92.

92. Locke, *Reasonableness*, 44, sec. 167.

93. Ibid., 33, secs. 28-29; secs. 73 and 143; 31, sec. 33-34.

94. See Johnson, *Locke on Freedom*, chaps. 2, 7.

95. See Becker, *Declaration*, 64. Compare von Leyden in, John Locke, *Essays on the Law of Nature*, ed. W. von Leyden (Oxford: Clarendon Press, 1954), 40. [Hereafter, Locke, *Law of Nature*]: "Culverwel was as emphatic as Locke in asserting that the formal obligation of laws does not lie in their inherent rationality but must be sought in a supreme will. . . . They accordingly believed that the reason why the law of nature as a divine law is actually binding does not lie so much in the equity of its commands as in God's sovereignty."

96. Locke, *Law of Nature*, 42-43, 50-51; 111, sec. 4; 183, sec. 1; 185-189(2). See also, *Second Treatise*, chap. 2, sec. 11.
97. See, Locke, *Law of Nature*, 28, 133, 187; and Johnson, 27.
98. *Second Treatise*, 3, sec. 1(3).
99. Locke, *Reasonableness*, 29, sec. 19. See also, *Second Treatise*, 8, chap. 2, sec. 11. Cf., *The Westminster Larger Catechism* (1647), Q 2, and notes 1-2, in *The Confession of Faith; The Larger and Shorter Catechisms 1647* (London: Wycliffe Press, 1962), 129. [Hereafter, *Westminster Confession and Catechisms*.]
100. See infra 57, n. 123.
101. For a scholarly treatment of the general revelation, special revelation question see G. C. Berkouwer, *General Revelation, Studies in Dogmatics* (Grand Rapids: Wm. B. Eerdmans, 1955, 1983 reprint).
102. See W. von Leyden in Locke, *Law of Nature*, 17, 67.
103. Hooker, *Ecclesiastical Polity*, bk. 3, sec. 9, quoted in Locke, *Second Treatise*, 77, n. 3. For Hooker's definition of law of nature see Richard Hooker, *Ecclesiastical Polity*, 113, 115, 131.
104. Locke, *Essay*, 1:475.
105. Ibid., 1:475.
106. Ibid., 1:475.
107. Locke, *Second Treatise*, vii.
108. Johnson, *Locke on Freedom*, chap. 2.
109. Locke, *Law of Nature*, 40-43, 50-51, 76-78.
110. Ibid., 30-32.
111. See Fraser's note on Locke's understanding of the eternal and immutable moral law of nature and its relationship as part of the revealed divine law, in Locke, *Essay*, 1:78.
112. Locke, *Reasonableness*, 31, sec. 23.
113. Ibid., 30, sec. 22.
114. "God gave to Adam a law, . . . This law, after his fall, continued to be a perfect rule of righteousness; and, as such, was delivered by God upon mount Sinai in ten commandments, . . . Beside this law, commonly called moral, God was pleased to give to the people of Israel . . . ceremonial laws, . . . To them also, as a body politic, he gave sundry judicial laws, which expired together with the state of that people, not obliging any other, now, further than the general equity thereof may require." In, John Leith ed., *Creeds of the Churches* (Atlanta: John Knox Press, 1982), 213-14. [Hereafter, Leith, *Creeds*.]
115. See Q 91-99, and Scriptural proofs in *Westminster Confession and Catechisms*, 178-82.
116. "We must attend to the well known division which distributes the whole law of God, as promulgated by Moses, into the moral, the ceremonial, and the judicial law, and we must attend to each of these parts, in order to understand how far they do, or do not, pertain to us. Meanwhile, let no one be moved by the thought that the judicial and ceremonial laws relate to morals. For . . . the two latter classes can be changed and abrogated without affecting morals. (The ancients) gave this name (moral law) specially to the first class, without which, true holiness of life and an immutable rule of conduct

cannot exist. The moral law . . . is the true and eternal rule of righteousness prescribed to the men of all nations and of all times, who would frame their life agreeably to the will of God. . . . The ceremonial law of the Jews was a tutelage . . . until the fulness of time . . . of those things which were adumbrated by figures. . . . The judicial law, given to them as a kind of polity, delivered certain forms of equity and justice, by which they might live together innocently and quietly. . . . Now it is evident that the law of God which we call moral, is nothing else than the testimony of natural law, and of that conscience which God has engraven on the minds of men, the whole of this equity of which we now speak is prescribed in it. . . ." In Calvin's *Institutes*, 2:663-664, bk. 4, chap. 20, secs. 15-16. Cf., Hooker, *Ecclesiastical Polity*, 135-141, bk. 1, ch. 10, secs. 1-8. According to Calvin, as well as Locke, Gentile nations are not bound by the express terms of ceremonial or political laws in the Bible, but all nations are bound by the moral precepts and principles embodied even in ceremonial and political ordinances. And according to both Calvin and Locke, the testimony of natural law is the same as the written moral law of Scripture.

117. In the *Summa Theologica*, Pt 1 of 2, Q 98-105, Aquinas also divided the law of the Bible into moral, ceremonial, and judicial (or political). According to Aquinas, the ceremonial law was done away in Christ, and the judicial ordinances bound only the nation of Israel in the land which God had given them. However, every eternal moral principle and precept wherever found in Scripture, properly deduced and formulated, binds Gentile nations for all time. See *Summa Theologica*, 2:1025-1103.

118. Supra 36, n. 13; and infra 57, nn. 120, 123.

119. Locke, *Reasonableness*, 31, sec. 23. Winthrop S. Hudson in *Religion in America*, 3d ed. (New York: Charles Scribner's Sons, 1981), 94, is correct to say that "Locke's political views were little more than a distillation of concepts that had long been current coin in Calvinist political theory—a fact which John Adams had acknowledged—and had become fundamental postulates of a large portion of the English people in earlier conflicts between King and Parliament."

120. Locke, *Reasonableness*, 31, sec. 23.

121. Ibid., 46, sec. 180.

122. Locke explained that God can and does alter the law of nature by amending it in the Holy Scriptures: "The law of nature, that we should obey every positive law of God, whenever he shall be pleased to make any such addition to the law of . . . nature." Ibid., 31, sec. 23.

123. "Thus the law of nature stands as an eternal rule to all men, legislators as well as others. The rules that they make for other men's actions must, as well as their own and other men's actions, be conformable to the law of nature—i.e., to the will of God, of which that [nature] is a declaration. . . ." *Second Treatise*, 77, sec. 135. "(P)rinces . . . owe subjection to the laws of God [i.e., Scripture] and nature. Nobody, no power, can exempt them from the obligations of that eternal law." Ibid., 109, sec. 195. "And upon this is grounded that great law of nature, 'Whoso sheddeth man's blood, by man shall his blood be shed.'" Ibid., 8, sec. 11, quoting Genesis 9:6. See also

chap. 5, p. 16, sec. 25, where Locke contrasts natural reason and "revelation, which gives us an account of those grants God made of the world to Adam, and to Noah and his sons; it is very clear that God, as King David says (Psalm CXV. 16), 'has given the earth to the children of men, . . .' " At 19, sec. 31, he equates the "law of nature" with the Scriptural statement "'God has given us all things richly' (I Tim. VI. 17), . . ." In chap. 6, sec. 52, at 30, Locke defines the "positive law of God" by quoting Exodus 22:12; Leviticus 20:9; Leviticus 19:5; and Ephesians 6:1, carefully noting that this law is contained in both "the Old and New Testament." Indeed the entire fabric of Locke's *Second Treatise* rests on the assumption that the law of God in nature and the law of God in Scripture are in complete harmony.

124. Cf., chap. 21, sec. 7 of the Westminster Confession (1646): "As it is of the law of nature . . . so, in his Word, by a positive, moral, and perpetual commandment, binding all men in all ages. . . ." In Leith, *Creeds*, 218.

125. Ramsey, *Reasonableness*, 31, sec. 23.

126. Ibid., 30, sec. 22.

127. Does this conclusion apply even to Thomas Jefferson? Yes, it does. Jefferson had a high regard for the moral law in Scripture in spite of his unorthodox view of Scripture. In 1803, in his third year as President, Jefferson personally assembled a collection of all the moral sayings of Jesus from the New Testament. In a letter to Joseph Priestly, dated 29 January 1804, Jefferson explains what he did: "I had sent to Philadelphia to get two testaments of Greek of the same edition, & two English, with a design to cut out the morsels of morality, and paste them on the leaves of a book, . . ." As President, he read from those nightly to keep his sense of moral judgment clear. Later, in a letter to his friend Charles Thomson, the Founding Father who translated the first American edition of the Greek Old Testament, Jefferson called the four gospels the "fountain of pure morals." Jefferson then went on to say, "I, too, have made a wee-little book from the same materials, which I call the Philosophy of Jesus; it is a paradigma of his doctrines, made by cutting texts out of the book, and arranging them on the pages of a blank book, in a certain order of time or subject. A more beautiful or precious morsel of ethics I have never seen; . . ."

In 1816, he published them with parallel texts in four languages, calling his book the *Morals of Jesus*. Historians today emphasize that Jefferson cut the miracles out of the Bible. But Jefferson told his friends that the purpose was to have a handy collection, topically arranged, of moral principles taught by "our Savior." He did not cut out the moral law of Scripture. Jefferson doubted the miracles of the Bible but not its moral law, and civil government is not built on miracles but on God's moral law. At least Jefferson respected in a very real sense that part of the Bible which guides the public life of a nation. See Paul Leicester Ford, ed., *The Writings of Thomas Jefferson*, 10 vols. (New York: G. P. Putnam's Sons, 1892, text-fiche), 8:282 LAC 22701 (letter to Priestly); 10:5 LAC 22702 (Letter to Charles Thomson, 9 January 1816); Andrew M. Allison, pt. 1, *Thomas Jefferson: Champion of Liberty, A History of His Life*, in *The Real Thomas Jefferson*, 2d ed., American

Classics Series, vol. 1 (Washington, D.C.: National Center For Constitutional Studies, 1983), 300.

128. Morton White, *The Philosophy of the American Revolution* (New York: Oxford University Press, 1978), 157.

129. See e.g., C. Gregg Singer, *A Theological Interpretation of American History*, rev. ed. (Phillipsburg, N.J.: Presbyterian and Reformed Publishing Co., 1981), 4 and chap. 2.

130. The Westminster Confession, chap. 21, sec. 7, in Leith, *Creeds*, 218.

131. Ibid., 213-15. Compare Locke, supra 56, n. 113.

132. *Westminster Confession and Catechisms*, 130, and n. 2.

133. Ibid., 178-179, Qs 92-95.

134. Ibid., 182, Q 99, and notes.

135. See, Ibid., 430, index: law, and light of nature.

136. Calvin's *Institutes*, 2:663-664, bk. 4, chap. 20, secs. 15-16. By comparison, the Westminster Confession does not use the term "natural law" per se, but it does use parallel terminology associated with the concept. "Although the light of nature, and the works of creation and providence, do so far manifest the goodness, wisdom, and power of God, as to leave men inexcusable; . . . (W)hich are to be ordered by the light of nature. . . . (H)aving the law of God written in their hearts, . . . Beside this law written in their hearts, . . . The light of nature showeth that there is a God, . . . As it is of the law of nature. . . ." From the Westminster Confession, in Leith, *Creeds*, 193, 196, 199, 216, 218. Samuel Rutherford, one of the leading Westminster divines, had this to say about the relation of "light of nature" and "law of nature": "What is warranted by the direction of nature's light is warranted by the law of nature, and consequently by a divine law; for who can deny the law of nature to be a divine law?" Samuel Rutherford, *Lex Rex*, or *The Law and the Prince* (London: John Field, 1644; reprint, Harrisonburg, Va.: Sprinkle Publications, 1982), 1, Q 1. [Hereafter, *Lex Rex*.]

137. See Albert M. Wolters, *Creation Regained: Biblical Basics for a Reformational Worldview* (Grand Rapids: William B. Eerdmans, 1985), chap. 2, particularly 14-15, 17-18, 21, 24-25, 27.

138. See Perry Miller, supra 36, n. 13.

139. *Lex Rex*, 1, Q 1.

140. For an excellent contrast of Renaissance humanism with Christian medievalism see Tuck, *Natural Rights Theories*, chaps. 1, 2, 5, 7.

141. *Lex Rex*, 1-3, Q 2. Cf. Schaeffer, 55 et seq., and 109.

142. *Lex Rex*, 1. In Question 1 Rutherford asks whether government be warranted by a divine law, to which he answers yes, due to Romans 13 and the law of nature which is a divine law. In Question 2 he asks whether government is warranted by the law of nature, again answering yes.

143. Ibid., 128, Q 26, Arg 1.

144. Ibid., 1.

145. Ibid., 2.

146. Ibid., 3. If we are to take Rutherford seriously as a spokesman for Calvinistic political theory, insisting that government must be grounded on the law

of nature, how can we conclude that Jefferson and the American founders were being anti-Calvinistic by relying on the same arguments?

147. Ibid.

148. Herbert M. Morais, *Deism in Eighteenth Century America* (New York: Columbia University Press, 1934), 40. Also see, John Orr, *English Deism: Its Roots and Its Fruits* (Grand Rapids: Wm. B. Eerdmans, 1934), 53.

149. Matthew Tindal, *Christianity as Old as the Creation* (London: n.p., 1730; reprint, New York: Garland Publishing, 1978), 103.

150. See Matthew 22:37-40; Romans 13:8, 10; Galatians 5:14; James 2:8; 1 John 4:20.

151. Calvin's *Institutes*, 2:663, bk. 4, chap. 20, sec. 15.

152. Tindal, 83-84. Tindal is quoting Archbishop Sharp. Winthrop Hudson, in *Religion in America*, 93, appropriately notes: "The alliance of Christians with Deists in carrying forward the Revolution was not as strange as it may seem to be, for Deists did little more than appropriate Puritan political ideas."

153. Quoted in Sydney E. Ahlstrom, *A Religious History of the American People* (New Haven: Yale University Press, 1972), 366.

154. Locke, *Reasonableness*, 31, sec. 13.

155. For example, Christian historians Rockne McCarthy, James Skillen, and William Harper in *Disestablishment a Second Time: Genuine Pluralism for American Schools* (Grand Rapids: Christian University Press, 1982), 30, have written: "The ancient Stoics conceived of the order of the universe as an eternal, rational, moral law-order. Human beings, in other words, could find and understand their place and identity in the world by coming to an understanding of the rational 'natural law.' This philosophy was revived and enjoyed great influence between the Renaissance and the Enlightenment, and it had a tremendous impact on Jefferson by way of John Locke and Scottish Common Sense philosophy. (Carl) Becker provides a valuable background description of this development, pointing to the general influence of Locke as a transmitter of the modernized Stoic outlook: . . ." They agree with Will Herberg that "nothing is more striking than the fact that, whereas the purpose of Puritan education was Christian, its philosophy and psychology were humanistic, harking back to Athens rather than to Jerusalem." Ibid., 139, n. 19.

156. Aristotle, for example, spoke of *dikaion phusikon* but not *nomos phusikos*. So, too, the later Stoics. See, Gerhard Kittel and Gerhard Friedrich, eds., *Theological Dictionary of the New Testament*, trans. Geoffrey W. Bromiley (Grand Rapids: Wm.B. Eerdmans, 1974), s.v. "*Phusis*," by Helmut Koster, 9:260. [Hereafter, *TDNT*.] This article by Koster gives an excellent short treatment of the concept of "nature" in the history and development of Greek language and thought. I am indebted to his article for the framework of my argument. I also acknowledge that my own ten years of Greek study hardly qualifies me to speak authoritatively on this matter. I have found that the task is endless, almost a bottomless pit. Any mistakes here are my own.

157. Koster, *TDNT*, 9:261.

158. Ibid.

159. Ibid., 9:253-263.

160. Hermann Kleinknecht, "*Theos*," in *TDNT*, 3:79.

161. Koster, *TDNT*, 9:259.
162. Ibid., 9:263.
163. See Michael Bertram Crowe, *The Changing Profile of the Natural Law* (The Hague: Martinus Nijhoff, 1977), 39.
164. Koster, *TDNT*, 9:259.
165. "The very rich Stoic conception of rules for conduct according to nature are still put in terms of individual ethics . . . and simply grant that man must be aware of his character as a social being. There is no real move towards social ethics, . . ." Koster, ibid., 9:265.
166. Michel Villey, "Turns and Movements in the Natural Law Tradition: Answer to Questions" (Interview), *Vera Lex: Historical and Philosophical Study of Natural Law and Right*, vol. 6, no. 1 (Pleasantville, N.Y.: Natural Law Society, Pace University, 1986), 10.
167. "(R)eal natural law is firstly not a morality but is jurisprudence. . . ." Ibid., 10.
168. Ibid.
169. Koster, *TDNT*, 9:269, n. 184.
170. Ibid., 9:265. But the English translation here can be misleading, for as Koster says, after a review of several examples, "These findings show that for Greek-speaking Stoics the two spheres of *nomos* and *phusis* could not be combined without further ado to give the concept of natural law." Ibid., 9:266.
171. Gottlob Schrenk shows how Plato's view of law and nature "gives the character of right to even the most arbitrary act. Natural law culminates in the dominion of the strong" in *TDNT*, 2:211, s.v. "*Dike*," by Gottlob Schrenk.
172. Quoted in Crowe, *Changing Profile of the Natural Law*, 37-38.
173. Ibid., 37; and, [Cicero], *Cicero in Twenty-Eight Volumes*, vol. 16, Eng. trans. Clinton Walker Keys, in *The Loeb Classical Library*, ed. G. P. Goold (Cambridge, Mass.: Harvard University Press, 1977; London: William Heinemann, 1977), 210-11, *The Republic*, bk. 3, chap. 22, in Lactantius *Insti. Div.* VI, 8. 6-9.
174. Ibid., 38, n. 28.
175. Koster, *TDNT*, 9:266.
176. Indeed, it may be that the Greeks were influenced by Jewish thought if it is true that both Zeno and Chrysippus were Jews. See Virginia Black, "Did Stoicism Have a Hebrew Origin?" in *Vera Lex: Historical and Philosophical Study of Natural Law and Right*, vol. 2, no. 2 (Pleasantville, N.Y.: Natural Law Society, Pace University, 1986), 24. See also Emanuel Rackman, "The Church Fathers and Hebrew Political Thought," Ibid., 11. Rackman is chancellor of Bar-Ilan University in Israel. See also David Novak, "Reply to Levitas' 'Natural Law' in the Jewish Tradition," ibid., 9.
177. See Hermann Kleinknecht, "The Logos in the Greek and Hellenistic World," *TDNT*, 4:81, 84, 90-91; Otto Procksch, "The Word of God in the Old Testament," *TDNT*, 4:98-99; Gerhard Kittel, "Word and Speech in the New Testament," *TDNT*, 4:128 et seq.
178. See generally, George Eldon Ladd, *The New Testament and Criticism* (Grand Rapids: William B. Eerdmans, 1967), 93, 101-02; and, John Hope Moulton, *A Grammar of New Testament Greek* (Edinburgh: T. & T. Clark, 1963), vol. 3, *Syntax*, by Nigel Turner.

179. Crowe, 4.
180. See Gottfried Quell, "The Concept of Law in the Old Testament," *TDNT*, 2:174-178; and Gottlob Schrenk, "The Idea of Law in the Greek and Classical World," et seq., *TDNT*, 2:178-225.
181. See *"Nomos,"* *TDNT*, 4:1022-1085.
182. Villey ridicules John Locke for extending himself "wrongly in the philosophy of law." To Villey, Locke was doing little more than using natural law as a 'label,' since Locke was approaching law confessionally, and completely outside the stream of Aristotelian natural jurisprudence. Locke believed in a transcendent jural order decreed by God. This is Hebraic and Christian rather than Aristotelian. Villey, an adherent of Aristotelian natural jurisprudence, has to reject Locke. Yet, this very rejection by a scholar of Villey's stature implies that both Locke and the Declaration of Independence lie outside the Greek and Stoic stream of thought. See Michel Villey, *Vera Lex*, supra, vol. 6, no. 1 (1986), 18.

CHAPTER 3: SELF-EVIDENT TRUTHS

1. Rockne McCarthy, James Skillen, and William Harper, *Disestablishment a Second Time: Genuine Pluralism For American Schools* (Grand Rapids: Christian University Press, 1982), 21: "By Jefferson's time . . . the old Stoic natural law philosophy had become a natural rights doctrine. It was a tenet of Enlightenment faith that nature's laws for human beings actually inhere in each individual and in the moral sense as a natural right. . . . Jefferson's appeal here (for a ground of firm truth and authority) is neither to God nor to God's eternal law nor to the Bible. It is simply to what is 'self-evident' within the mind and common conscience of humanity; . . ."
2. See e.g., James Skillen, "The Republican Vision of Thomas Jefferson," in Jerry S. Herbert, ed., *America, Christian or Secular?: Readings in American Christian History and Civil Religion* (Portland, Ore.: Multnomah Press, 1984), 154.
3. "(T)hose principles . . . Jefferson . . . called 'self-evident truths.' That phrase, too, is an expression not only of the American mind, but of the mind of the Enlightenment. . . ." Henry Steele Commager, *Jefferson, Nationalism, and the Enlightenment* (New York: Braziller, 1975), 82.
4. The best book I have seen on this topic is Morton White's *The Philosophy of the American Revolution* (Oxford: Oxford University Press, 1978). He devotes the entire book to tracing, understanding, and interpreting the word *self-evident*. I highly recommend White's book, both for his excellent treatment of John Locke, and for his discussions of "self-evident truths" and the "laws of nature and of nature's God" even though I see more of a direct Biblical and Christian influence on all three than does White.
5. See, for example, St. Thomas Aquinas, *Summa Theologiae*, Thomas Gilby and Blackfriars, trans. (London: Eyre & Spottiswoode, 1964), vol. 2, ia. 2, I, art. 1, at 4 and 5, citing St. John of Damascus. [Hereafter, Blackfriars, *Summa Theologiae*.]
6. For the powerful impact of the book of Romans on history see, F. F. Bruce, *The Letter of Paul to the Romans: An Introduction and Commentary*, vol. 6, 2d ed.,

The Tyndale New Testament Commentaries, ed. Leon Morris (Grand Rapids: William B. Eerdmans, 1985), 56-58.

7. White, 20-21.

8. For the influence of Aquinas on Hooker see Richard Hooker, *Of the Laws of Ecclesiastical Polity*, ed. A. S. McGrade and Brian Vickers (London: Sidgwick & Jackson, 1975), 113, [Hereafter, *Ecclesiastical Polity*]; and, John Locke, *Essays on the Law of Nature*, ed. W. von Leyden (Oxford: Clarendon Press, 1954), 36, [Hereafter, Locke, *Law of Nature*].

9. On Locke and reason see John W. Yolton, *Locke: An Introduction* (Oxford: Basil Blackwell, 1985), chap. 2. In chap. 5 Yolton deals with Locke's religious beliefs and in chap. 6 with Locke's epistemology.

10. For examples of the use of "self-evident" in a Christian context, see Gerhard Kittel and Gerhard Friedrich, eds., *Theological Dictionary of the New Testament*, trans. Geoffrey W. Bromiley (Grand Rapids: Wm. B. Eerdmans, 1964), s.v. "*Dike*," by Gottlob Schrenk, 4:190; "*Ethnos*," by Karl Ludwig Schmidt, 4:369; "*Ergon*," by Georg Bertram, 4:650. [Hereafter, *TDNT*.]

11. For historical examples of the use of "self-evident" see *The Oxford English Dictionary*, 1933 ed., 9:418-19.

12. *Oxford Latin Dictionary*, ed. P. G. W. Glare (Oxford: Clarendon Press, 1982), 1327, sec. 15.

13. *The Oxford English Dictionary*, 1933 ed., s.v. "*per*," 7:666-667, sec. 9.

14. "God, however, did not leave us in absolute ignorance. For the knowledge of God's existence has been implanted by Him in all by nature. This creation, too, and its maintenance, and its government, proclaim the majesty of the divine nature. . . . (T)he knowledge of the existence of God is implanted in us by nature." St. John of Damascus, *An Exact Exposition of the Orthodox Faith*, trans. S. D. F. Salmond, in vol. 9, *The Nicene and Post-Nicene Fathers*, ed. Philip Schaff and Henry Wace (Grand Rapids: Wm. B. Eerdmans, 1979), 1-2, bk. 1, chap. 1, par. 2, and chap. 3, par. 1.

15. See Blackfriars, *Summa Theologiae*, Ia 2, I, n. 2, p. 4.

16. St. Thomas Aquinas, *Summa Theologica*, 5 vols., trans. *Fathers of the English Dominican Province*, 1920 rev. ed. (Westminster, Md.: Christian Classics, 1981 reprint), P 1, Q 2, Art 1, obj, at vol. 1, p. 11. [Hereafter, Dominican Fathers, *Summa Theologica*.]

17. Augustine, *De Trinitate*, XII, 2, 4, cited in Dominican Fathers, *Summa Theologica*, ibid., 451; P 1, Q 88, Art 3, objs 1 and 3.

18. Blackfriars, *Summa Theologiae*, Ia2ae 100, 3, answer and 1. Compare the Dominican Fathers' translation: "Wherefore the decalogue includes those precepts the knowledge of which man has immediately from God. Such are those which with but slight reflection can be gathered at once from the first general principles . . . for they need no further promulgation after being once imprinted on the natural reason to which they are self-evident; as, for instance, that one should do evil to no man, and other similar principles: . . ." Dominican Fathers, *Summa Theologica*, 1 of 2, Q 100, Art 3, answer. It should be noted here that in this context Aquinas is speaking only of moral truth. Other principles are involved where he discusses divine facts, mathematical knowledge and matters of natural science in terms of self-evident

truth. Ibid., vol. 1, pp. 11-12, Pt 1, Q 2, Art 1. I have not discussed those here. See Morton White, *The Philosophy of the American Revolution* (Oxford: Oxford University Press, 1978), 11-22.

19. Dominican Fathers, *Summa Theologica*, 1:4, Pt 1, Q 1, Art 6, answer; and 1:12, Art 2, contra.

20. E.g., Ibid., 11-12, and P 1, Q 88, Art 3, answer, p. 451.

21. For the Greek text, see Kurt Aland, et al., eds., *The Greek New Testament*, 3d ed. (Munster: United Bible Societies, 1975), 531. Keep in mind that the correspondence is in terms of moral self-evidence only. Paul's words do not parallel the whole range of philosophical meaning that came to be associated with the term self-evident.

22. *Phaneros* — evident, *en* — in, *autos* — self.

23. The Greek here can be either the locative or the instrumental case, either "in the created things themselves is understood, being clearly seen," or "by means of the created things is understood, being clearly seen." Human beings are created things. According to these verses, the knowledge can be "in man" as a created being, or can be communicated to man by means of other created things. Such knowledge is *per se notum* — "through self-noted," or alternatively "noted by means of some object."

24. For a more complete discussion of Romans 1 and 2 and of God's general revelation in history, conscience, and nature see Appendix B. See also John Murray, *The Epistle to the Romans*, vol. 1, F. F. Bruce, gen. ed., *The New International Commentary on the New Testament* (Grand Rapids: Eerdmans, 1965), 26-79 [Hereafter, Murray, *Romans*]; C. E. B. Cranfield, *A Critical and Exegetical Commentary on the Epistle to the Romans*, 2 vols., ed. J. A. Emerton, C. E. B. Cranfield, *The International Critical Commentary on the Holy Scriptures of the Old and New Testaments* (Edinburgh: T. & T. Clark, 1985), 1:103-17, 125-26, 133-35, 155-63; William Hendrikson, *Exposition of Paul's Epistle to the Romans*, vol. 12, *The New Testament Commentary* (Grand Rapids: Baker Book House, 1981), 68-70, 78, 96-97, 99-100; James Denny, *St. Paul's Epistle to the Romans*, in *The Expositor's Greek Testament*, vol. 2, ed. W. Robertson Nicoll (Grand Rapids: Wm. B. Eerdmans, 1980 reprint), 590, 594, 597-98; Henry Alford, *Alford's Greek Testament: An Exegetical and Critical Commentary*, l. 2 (Grand Rapids: Baker Book House, 1980 reprint), 320-22, 332-33; and, W. J. Bradnock, H. K. Moulton, eds., *The Translator's New Testament* (London: British and Foreign Bible Society, 1973), 245-46.

25. Romans 1:16-18.

26. Although the Latin Bible does not employ the term *per se notum* in Romans 1:18-20, its translation of the Greek is worth noting. *"Revelatur enim ira Dei de caelo super omnem impietatem et iniustitiam hominum eorum qui veritatem in iniustitiam detinent. Quia quod notum est Dei manifestum est in illis, Deus enim illis manifestavit. Invisibilia enim ipsius a creatura mundi per ea quae facta sunt intellecta conspicuntur, sempiterna quoque eius virtus et divinitas, ut sint inexcusabiles."* Romans 1:18-20 in *Biblia Sacra: Iuxta Vulgata Versionem*, vol. 2 (Stuttgart: Deutsche Bibelgesellschaft, 1983), 1750.

27. See generally William Masselink, *General Revelation and Common Grace* (Grand Rapids: Wm. B. Eerdman's, 1953).

28. Romans 1:32. In this verse *dikaioma* signifies a judicial verdict based on law.
29. For a critique of contemporary evangelical anti-intellectualism and a system-
    atic treatment of the Bible and reason see Ronald H. Nash, *The Word of God
    and the Mind of Man* (Grand Rapids: Zondervan, 1982). For a helpful survey
    of how anti-intellectualism has held sway in much of American Christianity,
    see Richard Hofstadter, *Anti-Intellectualism in American Life* (New York: Alfred
    A. Knopf, 1970), 55 et seq.
30. Some of the most frequently used word are: *ginosko* — know, recognize, un-
    derstand; *gnosis* — knowledge; *epignosis* — full knowledge, world-view, con-
    scious awareness; *gnome* — purpose, decision, judgment, advice; *gnoridzo* — to
    make known; *eideo, oida, ideo* — to see, recognize, perceive, come to know;
    logikos — reasonable, logical; *logismos* — thoughts, reasonings; *logidzomai* — to
    reason or reckon; *dialogidzomai* — to reason, debate, or analyze; *dokeo* — to
    think; *krino* — to decide or judge; *nomidzo* — to think or to account; *logos* — ac-
    count; *noeo* — understand; *noema* — mind or understanding; *nous* — mind or
    understanding; *phroneo* — to rightly evaluate, to esteem, to conclude prop-
    erly; *phronema* — mindset, mental inclination, way of thinking; *phronimos* —
    wise person. For a scholarly analysis of the Biblical use of these words, see
    Gerhard Kittel and Gerhard Friedrich, eds., *Theological Dictionary of the New
    Testament*, 10 volumes, (Grand Rapids: Eerdmans, 1964). George Wigram's
    and Ralph Winter's *The Word Study New Testament and The Word Study Concor-
    dance*, 2 vols. (Wheaton, Ill.: Tyndale House Publishers, 1978; Pasadena,
    Calif.: William Carey Library, 1978) makes it possible for the English reader
    to locate all the places in the New Testament where these Greek words are
    used and where they are discussed in Kittel's dictionary.
31. This figure was reached by adding the lexical entries of 37 New Testament
    Greek words used in connection with the mind.
32. *Phronein eis to sophronein, ekasto os o theos emerisen metron pisteos.* Romans 12:3.
33. Perry Miller, "The Marrow of Puritan Divinity," in *Essays in American Intellec-
    tual History*, ed. Wilson Smith (Hinsdale, Ill.: Dryden Press, 1975), 13- 28.
34. E.g., 1 Thessalonians 5:21, "Prove all things; hold fast that which is good"
    (KJV). See also Romans 12:2; 2 Corinthians 10:5; Ephesians 4:17.
35. See Louis Berkhof, *Systematic Theology* (Edinburgh: Banner of Truth Trust,
    1958, 1976 printing), 202-10.
36. James I. Packer, "A Christian View of Man," in *The Christian Vision: Man in
    Society*, ed. Lynne Morris (Hillsdale, Mich.: Hillsdale College Press, 1984), 112.
37. Ibid.
38. Ibid.
39. Ibid., 112-13.
40. Ibid., 113.
41. Will Herberg, "Religion and Education in America," in *Religious Perspectives
    in American Culture, Religion in American Life*, ed. James W. Smith and A.
    Leland Johnson, vol. 2 (Princeton: Princeton University Press, 1961), 15.
42. There is significant debate over the force of the term *katecho* in this verse. I
    agree with Murray that it should be translated "hinder" rather than "sup-
    press." Murray, *Romans*, vol. 1, 36-37.

43. For the meaning of the "work of the law" of Romans 2:15, see *TDNT*, 2:637-641, 646, 650-651, s.v. *"Ergon."*
44. Murray, *Romans*, 36-38.
45. E.g., Acts 23:1; 24:16; 2 Corinthians 1:12; 1 Timothy 1:19.
46. 2 Corinthians 3:14-16; Acts 14:15, 15:19, 26:18, 20; 1 Thessalonians 1:9; 1 Timothy 1:6; James 5:19-20, 28; Titus 1:14.
47. See also 1 Corinthians 1:18-25, 2:14; 2 Corinthians 10:5; 1 Timothy 1:5-6; 2 Timothy 3:7-8.
48. John Locke, *An Essay Concerning Human Understanding*, 2 vols., ed. Alexander Campbell Fraser (New York: Dover Publications, 1959), 2:276, bk. 4, chap. 7, sec. 10. [Hereafter, Locke, *Essay*.] Fraser's edition has been severely criticized for its inaccuracies. The best edition is that of Peter H. Nidditch (Oxford: Clarendon Press, 1975). I have used Fraser's because its language is modernized for the ordinary English reader.
49. Locke, *Essay*, vol. 1, xli-li, lviii-lxiv, 37ff., 121-143. See Louis Berkhof, *Systematic Theology* (Edinburgh: Banner of Truth Trust, 1958, 1976 printing), 35.
50. Hooker wrote in *Ecclesiastical Polity* that the "soul of man" is at first "a book . . . wherein nothing is and yet all things may be imprinted; . . ." 120, bk. 1, chap. 6, sec. 1.
51. Morton White, *The Philosophy of the American Revolution* (Oxford: Oxford University Press, 1978), 18 et seq.
52. Locke, *Essay*, 1:44, n. 1, and 1:47.
53. Ibid., 1:32, n. 2.
54. Ibid., 2:268, n. 1.
55. Ibid., 1:29.
56. Ibid., 1:30.
57. Ibid., 1:30, n. 1.
58. Ibid., 2:177, n. 1.
59. Ibid., 1:30, n. 1.
60. Ibid., 2:177, bk. 4, ch. 2, sec. 1, and nn. 1, 2.
61. Ibid., 2:175, bk. 4, ch. 1, sec. 9; and 2:188, bk. 4, chap. 2, sec. 14.
62. Ibid., 2:178, bk. 4, ch. 2, sec. 1.
63. Ibid., 2:211, bk. 4, chap. 3, sec. 19.
64. Ibid.
65. Ibid., 2:212, bk. 4, ch. 3, sec. 22.
66. Ibid., 2:222, bk. 4, chap. 3, sec. 29.
67. Ibid., 2:304, bk. 4, chap. 9, sec. 2.
68. Murray, *Romans*, vol. 1, pp. 37-39. Locke failed to account for the definite article in Romans 1:21, a common mistake.
69. Locke, *Essay*, 2:311, bk. 4, chap. 10, sec. 7; and 2:339, bk. 4, chap. 11, sec. 13.
70. Ibid., 2:383 et seq.
71. White, 15. See also, Locke, *Essay*, 2:211-212, n. 2.
72. Ibid., 2:431, bk. 4, chap. 19, sec. 4; 2:229; bk. 4, chap. 4, sec. 4.
73. Ibid., 2:405-409, bk. 4, chap. 17, secs. 9-16.
74. Ibid., 2:279, bk. 4, chap. 7, sec. 11(3).
75. Ibid.
76. Ibid., 2:407, bk. 4, chap. 17, sec. 14.

77. Ibid.
78. Ibid., 2:409, bk. 4, chap. 17, sec. 17.
79. Ibid., 2:418, n. 3.
80. Ibid., 2:420, bk. 4, chap. 18, sec. 5.
81. Ibid., 2:421, bk. 4, chap. 18, sec. 5.
82. Ibid., 2:426, bk. 4, chap. 18, sec. 10.
83. See, e.g., Will Durant, *The Age of Louis XIV*, vol. 8, *The Story of Civilization* (New York: Simon and Schuster, 1963), 588-589; and Morais, *Deism in Eighteenth Century America*, 57.
84. Hooker, *Ecclesiastical Polity*, 113, bk. 1, chap. 3, sec. 1.
85. Ibid., 124, sec. 4.
86. Ibid., 111-12, 127-28, 131, 133-34, 157, 165, 171-72, 197-99, 202-07.
87. Ibid., 128.
88. Ibid., 131, sec. 9.
89. On Aquinas, Hooker, Suarez, and Locke, see W. von Leyden in Locke, *Law of Nature*, 36.
90. Hooker, *Ecclesiastical Polity*, 132, bk. 1, chap. 8, sec. 10.
91. Ibid., 174-80, bk. 2, chap. 7, secs. 3-10.
92. Ibid., 132, bk. 1, chap. 8, sec. 11.
93. Matthew Tindal, *Christianity as Old as the Creation* (London: n.p., 1730; reprint, New York: Garland Publishing, 1978), 181.
94. Ibid., 182. "Knowledge of God" should be read as a genitive of source, or in modern English — "knowledge from God." Cf. John 1:9, Psalm 4:6 (Vulgate): "*Signatum est super nos lumen vultus tui Domine.*"
95. White, 16.
96. Locke, *Essay*, 2:279, bk. 4, chap. 7, sec. II(2).

CHAPTER 4: "UNALIENABLE RIGHTS" ENDOWED BY THE CREATOR

1. By holding that these rights were "self-evident," or obvious to all men, the colonists were suggesting that one would have to lie to deny that such rights exist, since self-evident truth is known and understood intuitively by all men.
2. See Richard Tuck, *Natural Rights Theories: Their Origin and Development* (Cambridge: Cambridge University Press, 1979), 1-2.
3. The Declaration uses the word "unalienable." The alternative spelling is "inalienable." There is no difference in meaning between the two spellings.
4. Henry Steele Commager, *Jefferson, Nationalism, and the Enlightenment* (New York: George Braziller, 1975), 85.
5. T. Robert Ingram's "What's Wrong With Human Rights" in *The Theology of Christian Resistance*, ed. Gary North (Tyler, Tex.: Geneva Divinity School Press, 1983), 137, asserts: "Attribution of 'inalienable rights' to the endowment of the Creator is not an idea that can be drawn from Scripture or from Christian doctrine, but is a pietism tacked on to the root idea of a state of nature which is postulated as being without law or dependence on God."
6. Compare Ronald H. Nash, "Rights," in *Baker's Dictionary of Christian Ethics*, ed. Carl F. H. Henry (Grand Rapids: Baker Book House, 1973), 589-91. For a contrary view, see Rockne McCarthy, James Skillen and William Harper,

Disestablishment a Second Time: Genuine Pluralism for American Schools (Grand Rapids: Christian University Press, 1982), 20-22. These Christian writers confuse "unalienable rights" with "natural rights" and attribute the rights theory of the Declaration to the ancient Stoics. The Declaration did not rest on a natural rights theory, but an "unalienable rights" theory. Furthermore, they appear unaware that even Puritan theologians such as John Owen, vice chancellor of Oxford under Oliver Cromwell in the 1650s, believed that "natural rights" was a Christian concept: "But that rule is not any free act of the divine will, but a 'supreme,' 'intrinsic,' 'natural' right of Deity, conjoined with wisdom, to which the entire exercise of this justice ought to be reduced. . . . If such a law were not made necessarily, it might be possible that God should lose his natural right and dominion over his creatures, and thus he would not be God. . . . There is also a 'natural right' of government; such is the divine right over the creatures. The right, I say, of God over rational creatures is natural to him; therefore immutable, indispensable, and which cannot by any means be derogated. Thence, too, the debt of our obedience is natural and indispensable, . . . God, from the very nature of the thing, has dominion over us; . . ." in William H. Goold, *The Works of John Owen*, vol. 10 (London: Banner of Truth Trust, 1967), 508, 509, 568. Had the Declaration relied on a natural rights concept, it would not have automatically been outside the Christian intellectual tradition.

7. J. I. Packer, "A Christian View of Man," in *The Christian Vision: Man in Society*, ed. Lynne Morris (Hillsdale, Mich.: Hillsdale College Press, 1984), 111-12.

8. The English reader can study these words by consulting George Wigram, *The Englishman's Hebrew and Chaldee Concordance of the Old Testament: Numerically Coded to Strong's Exhaustive Concordance* (Grand Rapids: Baker Book House, 1980), 776-78, 1062-064; and, R. Laird Harris, Gleason L. Archer and Bruce K. Waltke, *Theological Wordbook of the Old Testament*, 2 vols. (Chicago: Moody Press, 1980), 2:752-55, 2:947-49. [Hereafter, *Theological Wordbook*.]

9. A passive right is a right to expect someone else to act in a certain way toward the holder of the right. I have a "right" to goods I have paid for. The person who received money for the goods has a duty to give them to me. My right is "passive" in that it is fulfilled by the action of another, not by my own action.

10. Deuteronomy 1:17; Exodus 15:25; Isaiah 26:9-10.

11. Exodus 21:1; Deuteronomy 16:18, 17:8-9; Proverbs 1:3; Isaiah 10:1-2, 11:4.

12. Exodus 21:9; Romans 1:26, 27; 1 Corinthians 11:14.

13. Leviticus 24:22; Deuteronomy 1:17; Proverbs 24:23.

14. Isaiah 11:3-4.

15. *Theological Wordbook*, 2:949, sec. 7.

16. On the Greek views of justice and *iustitia distributiva*, see Gerhard Kittel and Gerhard Friedrich, eds., *Theological Dictionary of the New Testament*, trans. Geoffrey W. Bromiley (Grand Rapids: Wm. B. Eerdmans, 1964), s.v. *"Dike"* et seq., by Gottfried Quell and Gottlob Schrenk, 2:174-93, esp., 183-85 and 193.

17. The Biblical model of justice has a three-fold nature. First, justice is the payment due to us for the works of our hands. Justice is proportional to our actions (Ezekiel 7:27). Justice is receiving no more and no less than we de-

serve based on what we have done, whether good or evil (Jeremiah 26:11). In the sense that justice is payment due for a deed done, justice is retributive (Latin *retribuere*, to repay).

Retribution does not mean retaliation or revenge. It is not morally right to hate criminals. Retribution does not mean that the community can satisfy its outrage by heaping abuse on the criminal. Justice is the Lord's, not man's. Since justice belongs to God, there is something sacred about justice. Justice is inseparable from righteousness, making justice a holy thing. When man acts as though there is no divinely given standard of justice, he awakens God's displeasure, and God must vindicate the law of justice man has sought to nullify. So justice is also vindicatory. And the form of vindication is by some "sanction" (from the Latin *sanctus*, meaning sacred). Harris, Archer, and Waltke, *Theological Wordbook*, 2:948, s.v. *"shephet."*

Justice also restores the wrongdoer, the victim, and the community to the condition of peace, harmony, and wholeness that existed before the wrong was committed, ibid., 2:930-931, sec. 2401. So justice is restitutionary. The Hebrew Bible uses the word *shalam* (piel stem: *shillem*), which is translated into English as "restore," "repay," "reward," and "make restitution." The word *shalam* (*shillem*) means to "restore to the covenant of peace." Ibid., sec. 2401c.

In Biblical terms there is a social compact, or "covenant of peace" between all the members of a community whether people know it or not. Justice restores the criminal to the covenant of peace by causing him to make payment for the wrong done. Justice restores the victim by awarding him a proper compensation for the loss or injury suffered. Justice restores the community by bringing its members into right relationship again.

18. This is true because God has posited the law. *TDNT*, 2:176, sec. (2). Therefore, one should not conclude that such a definition is inherently platonistic.

19. "Individual men, as created by God, have inalienable *mishpatim* ('rights')." *Theological Wordbook*, 2:949, sec. 7, s.v. *"Mishpat."*

20. Isaiah 41:21. Also, *Theological Wordbook*, 1:376-377, 2:949.

21. The passive right, active right distinction, introduced by David Lyons and adopted by Richard Tuck, has been roundly criticized by Brian Tierney. I agree with Tierney's conclusions that the notion of active rights occurs centuries earlier in medieval thinking than Tuck suggests. See, Brian Tierney, "Tuck On Rights: Some Medieval Problems," *History of Political Thought*, vol. 4, no. 3 (Winter, 1983), 432-435. [Hereafter, Tierney, "Medieval Rights Problems."]

22. For *exousia* see George V. Wigram, Ralph D. Winter, *The Word Study Concordance* (Wheaton, Ill.: Tyndale House Publishers, 1987; Pasadena, Calif.: William Carey Library, 1978), 269-70; and *TDNT*, 2:560-75. For *dikaion* see *Word Study Concordance*, 155-57; *TDNT*, 4:174-225.

23. See Michael Bertram Crowe, *The Changing Profile of the Natural Law* (The Hague: Martinus Nijhoff, 1977), 33-34.

24. For an excellent survey of the Greek worldview as contrasted with a Biblical worldview, see *TDNT*, 2:284-317, s.v. *"Dunamai"* et seq., by Walter Grund-

man; and *TDNT* 3:65-123, s.v. *"Theos"* et seq., by Hermann Kleinknecht, Gottfried Quell, Ethelbert Stauffer, and Karl Georg Kuhn.
25. *TDNT* 9:251, s.v. *"Phusis"* et seq., by Helmut Koster.
26. Leo Strauss, *Natural Right and History* (Chicago: University of Chicago Press, 1953), 93.
27. *TDNT*, 2:179-80.
28. Strauss, 133.
29. Ibid.
30. Ibid., 134.
31. Ibid., 135.
32. For a review and critique of Villey's work see Brian Tierney, "Villey, Ockham, and the Origin of Individual Rights," in *The Weightier Matters of the Law: Essays on Law and Religion*, ed. John Witte Jr. and Frank S. Alexander (Atlanta: Scholars Press, 1988), 1-31. [Hereafter, Tierney, "Origin of Rights".]
33. Tierney, ibid., 3.
34. See generally Harold J. Berman, *Law and Revolution: The Formation of the Western Legal Tradition* (Cambridge, Mass.: Harvard University Press, 1983).
35. Tuck, 7. Tierney cautions that Tuck's book is "marred by inaccuracies and methodological flaws." Tierney, "Origin of Rights," 1, n. 1.
36. Tuck, 7. "To have a passive right is to have a right to be given or allowed something by someone else, while to have an active right is to have the right to do something oneself." Ibid., 6. For Tierney's criticisms of Tuck's passive right, active right analysis, see Tierney, "Medieval Rights Problems," 432-35.
37. Tuck, 8.
38. Strauss, 147.
39. Tuck, 14.
40. Ibid., 12.
41. Strauss, 144.
42. Ibid.
43. Some think it did not overcome it at all. I disagree.
44. Berman, 2.
45. Not being a medieval expert, I have relied heavily in this section on Richard Tuck's *Natural Rights Theories* (Cambridge, 1979), and Brian Tierney's critiques of Villey and Tuck. All three agree that the western concept of rights arose in the second millennium A.D. Michel Villey traces the modern theory of individual rights to the fourteenth century and the work of William of Ockham. Tuck and Tierney place it earlier. Tierney believes a better starting point is twelfth-century juridical humanism. Tierney also insists that the lack of scholarship on pre-seventeenth-century rights development "leaves open one of the central problems of the modern debate—whether the idea of human rights is something universal, common to all societies or whether it is a distinctive creation of Western culture, which emerged at some specific point in European history." Tierney, "Origin of Individual Rights," 1.
46. Tuck, 13.
47. Ibid.

48. Ibid., 14. For a discussion of how Christian thought influenced secular law, see Berman, pp. 120-64, 204-05, 273-74. Tierney says that "the translation of *meritum* as 'claim' is impossible. Azo really wrote that justice meant giving to each one his desserts. This is far from a claim-right theory." Tierney, "Medieval Rights Problems," 435.
49. Tuck, 15.
50. Ibid., 16.
51. Ibid., 15.
52. Ibid.
53. Ibid., 22.
54. Ibid., 24.
55. Ibid., 27.
56. Tierney insists that Gerson's thought was not original with him as Tuck suggests, but that Gerson was simply "summarizing a way of thinking that had been developing ever since the twelfth century." Tierney, "Medieval Rights Problems," 439. Indeed, Tierney quotes an English canonist's writing in 1186, two centuries earlier than Gerson, making almost identically Gerson's point. Ibid., 438.
57. Tuck, 49.
58. See generally Tuck, chaps. 2, 3, 5, 6, 7.
59. Henry Steele Commager, *Jefferson, Nationalism, and the Enlightenment* (1976), 88.
60. "It was the religion of happiness. . . . Not the answer to the old question, What shall I do to be saved, nor . . . What is man's whole duty to God. No, theirs was a secular religion. What must man do to be happy? What should government do to assure happiness to its citizens?" Ibid., 93.
61. For example, the Dutch Christian writer Bob Goudzwaard, in *Capitalism and Progress: A Diagnosis of Western Society,* trans. Josina Van Nuis Zylstra (Toronto: Wedge Publishing Foundation, 1979; Grand Rapids: William B. Eerdmans, 1979), 54, says: "Finally, we should note that the American Declaration of Independence, formulated by Thomas Jefferson, also bears clear traces of the continental faith in progress. It is fair to describe this Declaration as an attempted synthesis between Christian Puritanism, deism, and the ideas of progress. Deism is present in the express reference to natural rights which are bestowed on all men by a providential God. The progress motif can be detected in the specific mention of each person's fundamental right to the "pursuit of happiness."
62. Virginia Constitution, sec. 1, 12 June 1776, in Richard L. Perry, ed., *Sources of our Liberties: Documentary Origins of Individual Liberties in the United States Constitution and Bill of Rights,* rev. ed. (Chicago: American Bar Foundation, 1978), 311.
63. Sir William Blackstone, *Commentaries on the Laws of England* (1765), ed. St. George Tucker (Philadelphia: William Young Birch and Abraham Small, 1803; reprint, South Hackensack, N.J.: Rothman Reprints, Inc., 1969), vol. 1, chap. 2, p. 40.
64. Ibid.
65. Ibid.
66. Ibid., 41.

67. For *esher* (happy), see Deuteronomy 33:29; 1 Kings 10:8; 2 Chronicles 9:7; Job 5:17; Psalms 1:1; 2:12; 32:1, 2; 33:12; 34:8; 40:4; 41:1; 65:4; 84:4, 5, 12; 89:15; 94:12; 106:3; 112:1; 119:1, 2; 127:5; 128:1, 2; 137:8, 9; 144:15; 146:5; Proverbs 3:13; 8:32, 34; 14:21; 16:20; 20:7; 28:14; 29:18; Ecclesiastes 10:17; Isaiah 30:18; 32:20; 56:2; Daniel 12:12.

For *makarios* (happy) in the Greek Old Testament, see Genesis 30:13; Deuteronomy 33:29; 1 Kings 10:8; 2 Chronicles 9:7; Job 5:17; Psalm 1:1; 2:13; 31:1, 2; 32:12; 33:9; 39:5; 40:2; 64:5; 83:5, 6, 13; 88:16; 93:12; 105:3; 111:1; 118:1, 2; 126:5; 127:1, 2; 136:8, 9; 143:15; 145:5; Proverbs 3:13; 8:32, 34; 20:7; 28:14; Ecclesiastes 10:17; Isaiah 30:18; 31:9; 32:20; 56:2; Daniel 12:12. And *makaridzo* (call happy)—Genesis 30:13; Numbers 24:17; Job 29:10, 11; Psalm 40:3; 71:18; 143:15; Canticles 6:8; Isaiah 3:12; 9:16; Malachi 3:12, 15. For *makaristos* (happy one)—Proverbs 14:21; 16:20; 29:18. For most of the entries above, the Latin vulgate uses *beatus* or happy.

In the Greek New Testament see *makarios* (happy)—Matthew 5:3, 4, 5, 6, 7, 8, 9, 10, 11; 11:6; 13:16; 16:17; 24:46; Luke 1:45; 6:20, 21, 22; 7:23; 10:23; 11:27, 28; 12:37, 38, 43; 14:14, 15; 23:29; John 13:17; 20:29; Acts 20:35; 26:2; Romans 4:7, 8; 14:22; 1 Corinthians 7:40; 1 Timothy 1:11; 6:15; Titus 2:13; James 1:12, 25; 1 Peter 3:14; 4:14; Revelation 1:3; 14:13; 16:15; 19:9; 20:6; 22:7, 14.

68. *TDNT*, 4:364, s.v. "*Makarios*," by Friedrich Hauck and George Bertram.
69. Ibid., 365.
70. Hauck, Ibid., 367.
71. Tuck, chap. 2, 32-57.
72. Ibid., 35.
73. Ibid., 33.
74. Ibid., 33.
75. Ibid., 34.
76. Ibid., 40.
77. Ibid., 40, 41.
78. Ibid., 43, 48.
79. Ibid., 49.
80. For the Greek roots, see *TDNT*, 2:179-85.
81. Tuck, 40.
82. Ibid., 48.
83. Ibid., 44, 75.
84. Ibid., 76.
85. Ibid., 86. Selden was close to the Dominican position when he said "I cannot fancy to myself what the law of nature means, but the law of God." Quoted in Tuck, 92.
86. Ibid., 102.
87. Ibid., 78.
88. That is why T. Robert Ingram's analysis of the rights language in the Virginia Constitution is fatally flawed. He represents the Virginia Bill of Rights as "a repudiation of Christendom," contrary to the belief in rights as founded on Divine law, because the Virginians supposedly wanted to set up a government with "no recognition of God": "(T)he Virginia declaration . . .

is a blind alley search for principles. . . . The direction taken by the Virginia declaration has no other way to go but toward, at the very least, holding God to have no place in temporal government. . . . (C)olonial Virginians . . . were introducing a change, a radical one . . . (of) no recognition of the role of God in government. . . . The Virginia Declaration marks a decisive departure from such often proposed evolutionary ancestors as the Mayflower Compact or documents of the Massachusetts and Connecticut colonies. . . ." T. Robert Ingram, "What's Wrong With Human Rights," in *The Theology of Christian Resistance*, ed. Gary North (Tyler, Tex.: Geneva Divinity School Press, 1983), 134-37, 144. Ingram not only misrepresents the meaning of the terms of the Virginia Constitution, he has missed the founders' point entirely.

89. Perry, *Sources of our Liberties*, 311: "SECTION I. That all men are by nature equally free and independent, and have certain inherent rights, of which, when they enter into a state of society, they cannot, by any compact deprive or divest their posterity; namely the enjoyment of life and liberty, with the means of acquiring and possessing property, and pursuing and obtaining happiness and safety."

90. Tuck, 48.

91. Tierney, "Origin of Rights," 31.

CHAPTER 5: GOVERNMENT BY THE "CONSENT OF THE GOVERNED"

1. See generally, Jerry S. Herbert, ed., *America, Christian or Secular?: Readings in American Christian History and Civil Religion* (Portland, Ore.: Multonomah Press, 1984).

2. See generally, Richard Tuck, *Natural Rights Theories: Their Origin and Development* (Cambridge, Mass.: Cambridge University Press, 1979).

3. "(A)ll men are created equal . . . they are endowed, by their Creator, with certain unalienable rights. . . . (T)o secure these rights, governments are instituted among men, deriving their just powers from the consent of the governed. . . . (W)henever any form of government becomes destructive of these ends, it is the right of the people to alter or to abolish it, and to institute new government, laying its foundation on such principles, and organizing its powers in such form, as to them shall seem most likely to effect their safety and happiness. . . . (G)overnments . . . should not be changed for light and transient causes. . . . But when a long train of abuses and usurpations . . . evinces a design to reduce them under absolute despotism, it is their right, it is their duty, to throw off such government, and to provide new guards for their future security. . . . (T)he history of the present King of Great Britain is a history of repeated injuries and usurpations, all having in direct object the establishment of an absolute tyranny over these states. . . . We . . . the representatives of the United States of America, in General Congress assembled, appealing to the Supreme Judge of the world for the rectitude of our intentions, do, in the name, and by the authority of the good people of these colonies, solemnly publish and declare, that these United Colonies are, and of right ought to be, Free and Independent States.

. . . And for the support of this Declaration, with a firm reliance on the protection of Divine Providence, we mutually pledge to each other our lives, our fortunes, and our sacred honour."

4. On the Christian "just war" theory see Robert A. Morey, *When Is It Right To Fight?* (Minneapolis, Minn.: Bethany House, 1985).

5. See Harold J. Berman, *Law and Revolution: The Formation of the Western Legal Tradition* (Cambridge, Mass.: Harvard University Press, 1983), 2, 19, 50.

6. Cited in Michael Lessnoff, *Social Contract* (Atlantic Highlands, N.J.: Humanities Press, 1986), 12.

7. Ibid., 15-16.

8. Ibid., 17. One should also be aware that the development of the western political concept of "the people" was influenced by the medieval idea of the *populus christianus* (Christian people). In explaining the factors that led to the separation of church and state and other "western" changes in the eleventh and twelfth centuries, Harold Berman notes: "Yet all of this would have been impossible if a preexisting community, the *populus christianus*, had not been formed in Europe between the fifth and eleventh centuries." See Berman, *Law and Revolution*, 51.

9. For a brief account of the historical background of the writing of the Magna Carta see Richard L. Perry, *Sources of Our Liberties: Documentary Origins of Individual Liberties in the United States Constitution and Bill of Rights*, rev. ed. (Chicago: American Bar Foundation, 1978), 1-10.

10. Langton (d. 1228), while a lecturer at the University of Paris in the early thirteenth century, was the first to divide the Bible into chapters. His chapter divisions, with a few modifications, are still used today. See Bruce Metzger, *Manuscripts of the Greek Bible: An Introduction to Greek Paleography* (New York: Oxford University Press, 1981), 41.

11. The Magna Carta was written in the form of a feudal compact between the king and the lower rulers and people. In it the king promised that "the English church shall be free," and that all free men would be protected in all their rights and liberties. See Perry, *Sources of Our Liberties*, 11-12.

12. See Louis B. Wright, *Magna Carta and the Tradition of Liberty* (U.S. Capitol Historical Society and the Supreme Court Historical Society, 1976), 7.

13. Perry, 5.

14. Ibid., 9-10.

15. Wright, 9.

16. Ibid., 43.

17. Ibid., 10.

18. Ibid., 45.

19. Ibid.

20. Berman, 50.

21. An excellent source for Luther's thought is Edward M. Plass, ed., *What Luther Says: An Anthology*, 3 vols. (St. Louis, Mo.: Concordia Publishing House, 1959). See 1:262, sec. 782; 1:294, sec. 1813; 2:600, sec. 1829; 2:601, sec. 1830.

22. See John T. McNeill, ed., *Calvin: Institutes of the Christian Religion*, 2 vols., trans. Ford Lewis Battles; in *The Library of Christian Classics*, vol. 20 (Philadel-

phia: Westminster Press, 1960), 2:1518-1519, bk. 4, chap. 20, sec. 31. [Hereafter, McNeill, *Institutes*.]

23. John Calvin, *Institutes of the Christian Religion*, trans. Henry Beveridge, 2 vols. (Grand Rapids: Wm. B. Eerdmans, 1981 reprint), 2:675, bk. 4, chap. 20, sec. 31.

24. McNeill, *Institutes*, 2:1518-519, bk. 4, chap. 20, sec. 31.

25. Cited by Eerdmans Publishing Co., on cover of John Calvin, *Institutes of the Christian Religion*, 2 vols., trans. Henry Beveridge (Grand Rapids: Wm. B. Eerdmans, 1981).

26. McNeill, *Institutes*, 2:1518-1519, n. 54.

27. For the account of this period, see John T. McNeill, *The History and Character of Calvinism* (London: Oxford University Press, 1954; reprint 1977), 243-54.

28. See Stephen Junius Brutus, *A Defense of Liberty Against Tyrants: A Translation of the Vindiciae Contra Tyrannos*, ed. Harold J. Laski (Gloucester, Mass.: Peter Smith, 1963). [Hereafter, Brutus, *Vindiciae*.]

29. Ibid., 80, 180-81, 190-91.

30. Ibid., 97.

31. Ibid., 97, 119, 122, 126, 174, 196-97.

32. Ibid., 97. Also, "Now that which we speak of all the people universally, ought also to be understood of those who in every kingdom or town do lawfully represent the body of the people, and who ordinarily are . . . officers of the kingdom . . . and not of the king. . . . (T)he officers of the kingdom receive their authority from the people in the general assembly of the states. . . ." Ibid., 126.

33. Ibid., 99.

34. Ibid., 118, 119, 122, 124.

35. Ibid., 118.

36. Ibid., 119.

37. Ibid., 139.

38. Ibid., 140.

39. Ibid.

40. Ibid., 144.

41. Ibid., 145, 151.

42. Ibid., 174.

43. Ibid., 174-75.

44. Ibid., 175.

45. Ibid., 181.

46. Ibid., 199.

47. Ibid., 195-96.

48. Ibid., 196.

49. Ibid., 199.

50. Ibid., 195-96.

51. Ibid., 195-99.

52. Ibid., 213.

53. Ibid., 199-212.

54. See Harold J. Grimm, *The Reformation Era 1500-1650*, 2d ed. (New York: Macmillan Publishing Co., 1973), 382-86.

55. Ibid., 444 et seq.
56. See, Samuel Rawson Gardiner, ed., *The Constitutional Documents of the Puritan Revolution 1625-1660* (Oxford: Clarendon Press, 1979), xvi-xvii.
57. Grimm, 444-58.
58. See Samuel Rutherford, *Lex Rex, or The Law and the Prince* (London: John Field, 1644; reprint, Harrisonburg, Va.: Sprinkle Publications, 1982), 80, Q 19, Arg 10.
59. At first, Parliament commissioned the reforms of the English church to be carried out under a Presbyterian model. However, the Independents gained control of Parliament and finally beheaded Charles I, a deed that horrified the Presbyterians. See, McNeill, *The History and Character of Calvinism*, 324-30; and, Grimm, *The Reformation Era*, 457-62.
60. Rutherford and Jefferson disagreed only in that Rutherford wanted a state-established church and Jefferson was for a disestablished church. Except for that one point, their views on the theory of revolution in *Lex Rex* and the Declaration are identical.
61. Rutherford, *Lex Rex*: "What is warranted by the direction of nature's light is warranted by the law of nature, and consequently by a divine law; for who can deny the law of nature to be a divine law? . . . (The) power of government in general must be from God . . . (Rom. xiii. 1). . . . Now God only by a divine law can lay a band of subjection on the conscience, . . ." (1, Q 1). "The power of making laws is given by God as a property flowing from nature . . . not by any special action or grant, different from creation. . . . This also the Scripture proveth. . . ." (2, Q 2). "God hath immediately by the law of nature appointed that there should be government. . . ." (3, Q 2). "(T)he court of nature, which is God's court. . . ." (5, Q 3). "The community's law is the law of nature—not their arbitrary lust" (35, Q 9). The king's duties are under the "moral law of God" in Scripture (4, Q 3).
62. Ibid.: "(A)ll men are born equally free. . . ." (2, Q 2). "(A)ll are born alike and equal . . . (and cannot) in the compact . . . surrender the native right of every single man . . . because the (compact) is founded on the law of nature. . . . This constitution . . . hath below it the law of nature for its general foundation, and above it, the supervenient institution of God, ordaining that there should be magistrates, . . . Individual persons, in creating a magistrate, doth not properly surrender their right, which can be called a right; . . ." (25, Q 7). "(T)he power of government is immediately from God . . . proceeding from God by the mediation of the consent of a community" (3, Q 2). "God gave authority mediately, by the consent of man" (26, Q 7). For the principle of inalienability in Rutherford see 51, Q 13.
63. See generally ibid., 6-38, Qs 4-9.
64. Ibid., 106, Q 14, assert 3.
65. Ibid.: "The power of creating a man a king is from the people. . . ." (6, Q 4). "(T)he kingly office itself come(s) from God . . . and floweth from the people, . . . God ordained the power" (6, Q 4). "(In) 1 Kings xvi the people made Omri king . . . the people made Solomon king and not Adonijah. . . . God by the people, by Nathan, the prophet, and by the servants of David and the states crying, 'God save king Solomon!' made Solomon king; and

here is a real action of the people. . . . God, by the people's free suffrages
and voices, createth such a man king" (6-7, Q 4). "The prophets were immediately called of God to be prophets, whether the people consented that
they should be prophets or not; therefore God immediately and only sent
the prophets, not the people; but though God extraordinarily designed
some men to be kings and anointed them by his prophets yet were they
never actually installed kings till the people made them kings" (7, Q 4).
"Expressly Scripture saith, that the people made the king, . . ." (7, Q 4).
"(N)o man can be formally a lawful king without the suffrages of the people:
for Saul, after Samuel from the Lord anointed him, remained a private
man, and no king, till all Israel made him king at Hebron; and Solomon,
though by God designed and ordained to be king, yet was never king until
the people made him so, . . ." (9, Q 4).

66. Ibid., 5-6, Q 3; and generally 6-38, Qs 4-9.
67. Ibid., 9, Q 4. "The power that the king hath . . . he hath it from the people
who maketh him king, . . ." (102, Q 22, Arg 2). "Those who make the king,
and so have power to unmake him in the case of tyranny, must be above the
king in power of government; . . ." (98, Q 21, Arg 9).
68. Ibid.: "There is an oath betwixt the king and his people. Laying on, by
reciprocation of bands, mutual civil obligation upon the king to the people,
and the people to the king; 2 Sam. v. 3, . . ." (54, Q 14, Assert 1). "Then
there (is) . . . a covenant betwixt the king and the people" (54, Q 14, Assert
1). "But the contracts of men to give a kingdom to a person, which a hea-
then community may lawfully do, and so by contract dispose of a kingdom,
is not opposite to the immediate hand of God, appointing royalty and monarchy at his own blessed liberty" (16, Q 5).
69. Ibid.: "(W)e hold that the covenant is made betwixt the king and the people,
betwixt mortal men; but they both bind themselves before God to each
other" (56, Q 14, Assert 2). "But the general covenant of nature is pre-
supposed in making a king, where there is no vocal or written covenant. . . .
(T)hose things which are right and just according to the law of God . . . are
understood to rule both king and people, . . . The law of nature will war-
rant a people to repeal their right and plead for it, in a matter which con-
cerneth their heads, lives, and souls" (59, Q 14, Arg 3). "When the people
appointed any to be their king, the voice of nature exponeth their deed, . . .
(F)or that fact—of making a king—is a moral lawful act warranted by the
word of God . . . and the law of nature; and therefore, they having made
such a man their king, they have given him power to be their father, feeder,
healer, and protector; and so must only have made him king conditionally,
so he be a father, a feeder, and tutor. . . ." (59-60, Q 14, Arg 3; 2).
70. Ibid.: "(W)hoever maketh a covenant with the people, promising to govern
them according to God's word, and upon that condition and these terms
receiveth a throne and crown from the people, he is obliged to what he
promiseth, to the people, . . ." (57, Q 14, Assert 4). "(T)he people gave the
crown . . . upon condition that he should perform such and such duties to
them. . . ." (54, Q 14, Assert 1). "Now, if this deed of making a king must be
exponed to be an investing with an absolute, and not a conditional power,

this fact shall be contrary to Scripture and to the law of nature; for if they have given him royal power absolutely, and without any condition, they just have given to him power to be a father, protector, tutor, and to be a tyrant, a murderer, a bloody lion, to waste and destroy the people. . . ." (60, Q 14, Arg 3, sec. 2).

71. Ibid.: "(I)f the conditions be not fulfilled, the party injured is loosed from the contract" (54, Q 14, Assert 2). "The covenant giveth . . . a sort of action at law. . '. . (A) covenant giveth ground of a civil action and claim to a people and the free estates against a king, seduced by wicked counsel to make war against the land, . . ." (54, Q 14, Assert 1). "It is a vain thing to say that the people and the king make a covenant . . . if he be obliged to God only, and not to the people, by a covenant made with the people, . . ." (54, Q 14, Assert 2, answer). "Whoever maketh a promise to another, giveth to that other a sort of right or jurisdiction to challenge the promise. . . . (H)e is insofar only made king . . . as he fulfilleth the condition; . . . (T)he people make a king, as a king, conditionally, for their safety, and not for their destruction, . . ." (57, Q 14).

72. Ibid.: "It must be such a breach of the royal covenant as maketh the king no king, that annulleth the royal covenant, and denudeth the prince of his royal authority and power, that must be interpreted a breach of the oath of God, because it must be such a breach upon supposition whereof the people would not have given the crown, but upon the supposition of his destructiveness to the commonwealth, they would never have given to him the crown" (58, Q 14, answer).

73. Ibid.: "Arbitrary government is not sovereignty" (15, Q 5, answer 1). "If a king sell his subjects by sea or land to other nations,—if he turn a furious Nero, he may be dethroned; . . ." (63, Q 15). "We acknowledge tyranny must only unking a prince" (132, Q 26). "He who receiveth a kingdom conditionally, and may be dethroned if he sell it or put it away to any other, is a fiduciary patron, and hath it only in trust" (72, Q 17). "(I)f he use a tyrannical power against the people for their hurt and destruction, he useth a power that the people never gave him, and against the intention of nature; for they invested a man with power to be their father and defender for their good; and he faileth against the people's intention in usurping an overpower to himself, which they never gave, never had, never could give, for they cannot give what they never had, and power to destroy themselves they never had" (102, Q 22, Arg 2). "If the king should sell his country, and bring in a foreign army, the estates are to convene, to take course for the safety of the kingdom" (97, Q 21, Arg 6).

74. Ibid.: "Now that cannot bear . . . that any one or two acts of tyranny doth denude a man of the royal dignity that God and the people gave him; . . ." (58, Q 14, Obj 1, Ans). "(N)either every abuse of power in a king dethroneth a king, . . ." (199, Q 40, 3, Ans).

75. Ibid.: "Because the estates of the kingdom, who gave him the crown, are above him, and they may take away what they gave him; as the law of nature and God saith, If they had known he would turn tyrant, they would never have given him the sword; and . . . the contract they made with the

king (is) conditional, . . . They gave the power to him only for their good, . . ." (128, Q 26, Arg 1).

76. Ibid.: "Any tyrant standeth in titulo, so long as the people and estates who made him king have not recalled their grant; . . ." (59, Q 14, Ans 1). "The covenant may be materially broken, while the king remaineth king, and the subjects remain subjects; but when it is both materially and formally declared by the states to be broken, the people must be free from their allegiance; . . ." (61, Q 14, Arg 6).

77. Ibid.: "The states may resist a tyrant" (114, Q 24). See generally, 159–84, Questions 31-35.

78. Gary North, ed., *The Theology of Christian Resistance* (Tyler Tex.: Geneva Divinity School Press, 1983), viii. Adrian C. Leiby notes that one British observer in America said "Presbyterianism is really at the bottom of this whole conspiracy, has supplied it with vigor, and will never rest till something is decided upon it." Adrian C. Leiby, *The Revolutionary War in the Hackensack Valley: The Jersey Dutch and the Neutral Ground, 1775-1783*, p. 20, quoted in North, *The Theology of Christian Resistance*, 248. Cf., Robert Bryan, *History, Pseudo-History, Anti-History: How Public-School Textbooks Treat Religion, Policy Studies in Education* (Washington, D.C.: Learn, Inc., 1983?), 11: "(T)here has always been current in Britain the belief that 1776 was the Puritans' revenge for 1662."

79. In John Locke, *The Second Treatise of Government*, ed. Thomas Peardon (New York: Liberal Arts Press, 1956), xi, n. 6, Peardon writes: "It can safely be supposed that Locke was familiar with the celebrated treatise, *Vindiciae Contra Tyrannos*, published anonymously in 1579. . . ." It can also be safely supposed that Locke was familiar with *Lex Rex*. Locke's father was a leading Puritan in Parliament who knew Rutherford. Locke was a student at Westminster just two years after *Lex Rex* was published there, causing a great stir.

80. See Winthrop S. Hudson, "John Locke: Heir of Puritan Political Theorists," in *Calvinism and the Political Order*, ed. George L. Hunt (Philadelphia: Westminster Press, 1965), 108-29.

81. Carl Becker, *The Declaration of Independence: A Study in the History of Political Ideas* (New York: Vintage Books, 1958), 30-37.

82. *Vindiciae*, 175.

83. Ibid., 181, 190, 191.

84. An earlier chapter has already shown that Locke did not put the law of nature in conflict with the moral law of Scripture. See also, Merwyn S. Johnson, *Locke on Freedom: An Incisive Study of the Thought of John Locke* (Austin, Tex.: Best Printing Company, 1978), chap. 2.

85. *Lex Rex*, 54, Q 14.

86. Ibid., 54–62.

87. *Second Treatise*, 56, sec. 99.

88. Ibid., 98, sec. 171.

89. Ibid., 97-99, secs. 171-73; and 112, sec. 199.

90. Ibid., 119-22, secs. 211-21.

91. Ibid., 126, sec. 225.

92. Ibid.

93. Ibid., 124, sec. 221; 126, sec. 226; 130, sec. 231.
94. See, Ibid., 127-39, secs. 227-43.
95. Ibid., 138, sec. 241.
96. *Lex Rex*, 219, Q 43, sec. 7; 92, Q 20; 232, Q 44.
97. Of the importance of the colonial charters, Charles Goodrich wrote: "By the crown (the charters) were viewed as constituting petty corporations . . . which might be annulled or revoked at pleasure. To the colonists, on the other hand, they appeared as sacred and solemn compacts (covenants) between themselves and the king; which could not be altered either by the king or parliament, without a forfeiture on the part of the colonists. . . . They indeed regarded the charters as irrevocable. . . . (B)ut writs were issued against the colonies . . . to surrender these instruments into the royal hands. . . . It was a blow aimed at their dearest rights — an annihilation of that peace and liberty, which had been secured to them by the most sacred and inviolable compact." Charles A. Goodrich, *Lives of the Signers to the Declaration of Independence*, 4th ed. (Boston: Thomas Mather, 1834), 16.
98. "We, therefore, the representatives of the UNITED STATES OF AMERICA, in General Congress assembled, . . ." In Perry, *Sources of our Liberties*, 321.
99. Ibid., 321.
100. John A. Garraty, *The American Nation: A History of the United States to 1877*, 5th ed. (New York: Harper & Row, 1983), p. 84, 88; Mark Noll, Nathan Hatch, and George Marsden, *Search for "Christian" America* (Westchester, Ill.: Crossway Books, 1983), 81.

CHAPTER 6: GOD AS SUPREME JUDGE AND DIVINE PROVIDENCE

1. E.g., Catherine Albanese, *Sons of the Fathers: The Civil Religion of the American Revolution* (Philadelphia: Temple University Press, 1976), 79.
2. Within the various sects of Christianity significant disagreement has arisen about the precise definition of Providence and fallen man's ability to know it outside of Christ. The debate parallels the Catholic and Reformed dispute over general and special revelation, and fallen man's knowledge of general revelation apart from Christ. Even from the Reformed perspective, the worst that can be said of colonial theology's impact on the Declaration is that it was more Catholic and Anglican than Reformed. But Catholicism is still a form of Christianity. It should not be equated with deism. See, G. C. Berkouwer, *General Revelation, Studies in Dogmatics* (Grand Rapids: Wm. B. Eerdmans, 1955, 1983 printing); and, G. C. Berkouwer, *The Providence of God*, trans. Lewis B. Smedes, Studies in Dogmatics (Grand Rapids: Wm. B. Eerdmans, 1952, 1980 printing).
3. John Locke, *The Second Treatise of Government*, ed. Thomas Peardon (New York: Liberal Arts Press, 1956), 14, chap. 3, sec. 21.
4. Samuel Rutherford, *Lex Rex, or The Law and the Prince* (London: John Field, 1644; reprint, Harrisonburg, Va.: Sprinkle Publications, 1983), 219, Q 43, sec. 7; 92, Q 20; 232, Q 44.
5. Gerhard Kittel and Gerhard Friedrich, eds., *Theological Dictionary of the New Testament*, trans. Geoffrey W. Bromiley (Grand Rapids: Wm. B.

Eerdmans, 1964, 1978 printing), 2:174-178; s.v. *"Dike,"* by Gottfried Quell. [Hereafter, *TDNT*.]

6. Ibid., 176.
7. Ibid.
8. Ibid., 177.
9. Ibid., 934, n. 54. But cf., Philip P. Weiner, ed., *Dictionary of the History of Ideas* (New York: Charles Scribner's Sons, 1973), 1:646, s.v. "Deism," by Roger Emerson.
10. *TDNT*, 3:934, s.v. *"Krino."*
11. Ibid., 935.
12. "(T)he colonie of Providence Plantations . . . that they, pursueing, . . . their sober, serious and religious intentions, of godlie edifieing themselves, and one another, in the holie Christian ffaith and worshipp . . . where, by the good Providence of God, from whome the Plantationes have taken their name . . . there may, in due tyme, by the blessing of God upon theire endeavours, bee layd a sure ffoundation of happinesse to all America: . . ." Charter of Rhode Island and Providence Plantations, July 8, 1663, quoted in Richard L. Perry, *Sources of our Liberties*, 169-70.
13. William Ames (1576-1633), *The Marrow of Theology*, trans. John D. Eusden (Boston: Pilgrim Press, 1968), 107.
14. Quoted in John Leith, ed., *Creeds of the Churches: A Reader in Christian Doctrine from the Bible to the Present*, 3d ed. (Atlanta: John Knox Press, 1982), 200.
15. See, Philip Schaff, ed., *The Creeds of Christendom with a History and Critical Notes*, 3 vols., 6th ed., rev. by David S. Schaff (Grand Rapids: Baker Book House, 1983), 3:244-46, chap. 6, *"De Providentia Dei."* (No English translation.)
16. John Calvin, *Calvin: Institutes of the Christian Religion*, ed. John T. McNeill, 2 vols., trans. Ford Lewis Battles, vols. 20-21, *The Library of Christian Classics* (Philadelphia: Westminster Press, 1960), 1:201-202, bk. 1, chap. 16, sec. 4.
17. John Calvin, *Institutes of the Christian Religion*, 2 vols., trans. Henry Beveridge (Grand Rapids: Wm. B. Eerdmans, 1981), 1:171, 172, bk. 1, chap. 16, sec. 1.
18. Ibid., 1:175, bk. 1, chap. 16, sec. 4.
19. Ibid., 1:180, bk. 1, chap. 16, sec. 8.
20. McNeill, *Calvin's Institutes*, 1:198, bk. 1, chap. 16, sec. 2.
21. Ibid., 1:207, bk. 1, chap. 16, sec. 8.
22. McNeill, *Calvin's Institutes*, 1:222, bk. 1, chap. 17, sec. 9.
23. Berkouwer, *The Providence of God*, 10.
24. For the differences cf., Berkouwer, *The Providence of God*, 31-49; Berkouwer, *General Revelation*, 61-83; and Reginald Garrigou-Lagrange, *Providence*, trans. Dom Bede Rose (St. Louis: B. Herder Book Co., 1937), pts. 1-2. On Aquinas's doctrine of providence, see Thomas Aquinas, *Summa Theologica*, 5 vols., trans. Fathers of the English Dominican Province, 1920 rev. ed. (Westminster, Md.: Christian Classics, 1981 reprint), 1:120-25, Pt 1, Q 22, Arts 1-4.
25. See John F. Berens, *Providence & Patriotism in Early America, 1640-1815* (Charlottesville: University Press of Virginia, 1978), 124-28.

26. "(I)t follows logically that references to Providence, the Lord of Hosts, the Governor of the Universe, and other intangible realities ought then to be relegated to the poetic attic in similar fashion" Albanese, 79.
27. Ibid., 79 et seq.
28. Louis Berkhof, *Systematic Theology* (London: Banner of Truth Trust, 1958, 1976 printing), 167. Cf., infra n. 44, Bob Goudzwaard, *Capitalism and Progress*, 20, 204: "Deism indeed maintained the term providence but filled it with a totally different meaning. . . . We can speak of God's providence only insofar as it refers to God's acts before the beginning of world history. . . ." "(D)ivine Providence (was) transformed into the great Cheerleader on the sidelines."
29. John Orr, *English Deism: Its Roots and Its Fruits* (Grand Rapids: Wm. B. Eerdmans, 1934), 14.
30. Ibid., 205.
31. Ibid., 211.
32. Albanese, 120.
33. See Wilbur Fisk Tillett, *Providence, Prayer and Power: Studies in the Philosophy, Psychology and Dynamics of the Christian Religion* (Nashville: Cokesbury Press, 1926), 54-55; and, John Murray, *Calvin on Scripture and Divine Sovereignty* (Grand Rapids: Baker Book House, 1960), 65.
34. See Albert M. Wolters, *Creation Regained: Biblical Basics for a Reformational Worldview* (Grand Rapids: Eerdmans, 1985), 13-17.
35. See Perry, *Sources of Our Liberties*, 60.
36. *TDNT*, 3:1067, s.v. *"Kurios,"* in Gottfried Quell, "The Old Testament Name for God."
37. George V. Wigram, Ralph D. Winter, *The Word Study Concordance* (Pasadena, Calif.: William Carey Library, 1978; Wheaton, Ill.: Tyndale House, 1978), 103, 364, 571, nos. 932, 2316, 3772.
38. Ibid. Matthew uses "kingdom of heaven" 32 times, and "kingdom of God" 4 times.
39. See George Eldon Ladd, *The New Testament and Criticism* (Grand Rapids: William B. Eerdmans, 1967), 122. For heaven as a synonym for God, see *TDNT*, 5:511 et seq., s.v. *"Ouranos."*
40. See Bruce M. Metzger, *Manuscripts of the Greek Bible: An Introduction to Greek Palaeography* (New York: Oxford University Press, 1981), 33-36.
41. Ibid., 36. See also, Jack Finegan, *Encountering New Testament Manuscripts: A Working Introduction to Textual Criticism* (London: S.P.C.K., 1974), 32-33; 102, sec. 119; 103, 113, 115, 125, 126, 131, 136, 140, 149, 154, 163; and, Kurt Aland, Barbara Aland, *The Text of the New Testament: An Introduction to the Critical Editions and to the Theory and Practice of Modern Textual Criticism*, trans. Erroll F. Rhodes (Grand Rapids: William B. Eerdmans, 1987; Leiden: E. J. Brill, 1987), 76.
42. A.H.R.E. Paap, *Nomina Sacra in the Greek Papyri of the First Five Centuries A.D.: The Sources and Some Deductions* (Leiden, 1959), quoted in Metzger, ibid., 37, n. 78.
43. We must remember the feudal elements of British culture with its lords, ladies, knights, and various social strata. The ever-present consciousness of

social status was part of colonial thinking because the colonies were British. Self-effacement, such as ceremoniously bowing in the presence of nobility, was commonplace. The practice of courteous obeisance was extended to God just as it was to men.

44. Bob Goudzwaard, *Capitalism and Progress: A Diagnosis of Western Society*, trans. Josina Van Nuis Zylstra (Toronto: Wedge Publishing Foundation, 1979; Grand Rapids: William B. Eerdmans, 1979), 16-17.
45. Metzger, 5. See also F. G. Kenyon, *The Text of the Greek Bible*, 3d. ed., revised and augmented by A. W. Adams (London: Duckworth, 1975), 13-62, chap. 2.
46. *TDNT*, 4:362, s.v. *"Makarios,"* by Friedrich Hauck.
47. *TDNT*, 5:500, s.v. *"Ouranos,"* by Helmut Traub.
48. This particular kind of mistake is a misuse of "etymology," the history of a word.
49. *New Catholic Encyclopedia*, 1967 ed., s.v. "Natural Law," by B. R. Brown.
50. William Ebenstein, *Great Political Thinkers: Plato to the Present*, 4th ed. (Hinsdale, Ill.: Dryden Press, 1969), 215-16.
51. See *Aristotle in Twenty-Three Volumes*, vol. 2, *Posterior Analytics*, trans. Hugh Tredennick, in *The Loeb Classical Library*, ed. G. P. Goold (Cambridge, Mass.: Harvard University Press, 1976; London: William Heinemann, 1976), 70-71, bk. 1, 76b, 15.
52. *TDNT*, 3:66, n. 9.
53. Ibid., 3:68.
54. Ibid., 3:69.
55. Ibid., 3:75.
56. Ibid., 3:74.
57. Ibid., 3:75.
58. Ibid., 3:75, n. 48; and 4:1012—"(T)he concept of providence becomes a dogma for the Stoics; indeed, it is the heart of their theology."
59. *TDNT*, 4:1009, s.v. *"Pronoeo."*
60. Ibid., 1009-010.
61. Ibid., 4:1012.
62. Ibid., 4:1013.
63. Wisdom of Solomon 14:3, *The Apocrypha of the Old Testament*, RSV, 2d ed., ed. Bruce M. Metzger (New York: Oxford University Press, 1977), 118.
64. "Allusion has already been made to Stoic influence on the apocryphal writers, who even borrowed the phraseology of the pagan school." In *The New Schaff-Herzog Encyclopedia of Religious Knowledge*, ed. Samuel Macauley Jackson (Grand Rapids: Baker Book House, 1950), 9:307, s.v. "Providence," by C. A. Beckwith. And, "Into this terminologically imprecise circle of Jewish ideas, Hellenistic Judaism imports the Stoic concept of pronoia." *TDNT*, 4:1015.
65. Tillett, 17.
66. See generally Tillett, Garrigou-Lagrange, Murray, Berkouwer, 9 *Schaff-Herzogg*, Berkhof, and 4 *TDNT*.
67. Augustine used the Latin *providentia* almost as a direct equivalent of the Greek word *pantakratora*, meaning "all-governing," which was part of the earliest Church creeds. For examples of *pantakratora* see, Leith, *Creeds of the*

Churches, 19, 23, 27, 30, 33. On Augustine and the earlier creeds see J. N. D. Kelly, *Early Christian Creeds*, 3d ed. (London: Longman, 1972), 132-37.

APPENDIX B: THE BIBLE AND "SELF-EVIDENT" TRUTHS

1. Romans 1:18: *Apokaluptetai* (is revealed); *ten aletheian* (the truth).
2. Greek — *to gnoston tou theou*, Romans 1:19. Literally — "the thing known of God." What any man can know about God, all men know.
3. Greek — *phaneron* — evident, manifest, revealed. Romans 1:19. Here the Apostle uses the word meaning "to make evident or visible" as a synonym of "to reveal."
4. Greek — *aoratos* — invisible. Romans 1:20.
5. Greek — *kathorao*. Romans 1:20.
6. Greek — *nooumena*. Romans 1:20.
7. Romans 1:20. God's general revelation of Himself to men is both pre-suppositional and evidential. He makes men know truth directly through conscience and indirectly through observing nature.
8. Romans 1:20.
9. Romans 1:21 — Greek: *Gnontes ton theon*, "knowing *the* God," the real and only God.
10. Greek — *Anapologetous*, Romans 1:20.
11. Romans 1:21-23.
12. Romans 1:24.
13. Greek — *Para phusin* — "against nature" or "beyond nature." Romans 1:26.
14. Romans 1:28. The ordinary word for "know" is *gnosis*. *Epignosis* is an intensive form of the word that denotes a full or whole knowledge. It is a complete awareness. In verse 28 it is used to approximate the idea of "worldview."
15. Romans 1:28.
16. Romans 1:29-31.
17. Greek — *Epignontes dikaioma* — "being fully aware of the just sentence" of God. Romans 1:32.
18. "By nature" — *phusei*, Romans 2:14. "Requirement of the law" — *ergon tou nomou*, Romans 2:15. "Written in their hearts" — *grapton en tais kardiais auton*, Romans 2:15.
19. See for example Acts 14:15-17 and Acts 17:22-31.

BIBLIOGRAPHY

Adams, Charles Francis, ed. *The Works of John Adams*. 10 vols. Boston: Charles C. Little and James Brown, 1850. Text-fiche.

Ahlstrom, Sydney E. *A Religious History of the American People*. New Haven: Yale University Press, 1972.

Aland, Kurt, and Barbara Aland. *The Text of the New Testament: An Introduction to the Critical Editions and to the Theory and Practice of Modern Textual Criticism*. Translated by Erroll F. Rhodes. Grand Rapids: William B. Eerdmans, 1987; Leiden: E.J. Brill, 1987.

Albanese, Catherine L. *Sons of the Fathers: The Civil Religion of the American Revolution*. Philadelphia: Temple University Press, 1976.

Alford, Henry. *Alford's Greek Testament: An Exegetical and Critical Commentary*. Vol. 2. Grand Rapids: Baker Book House, 1980 reprint.

Allison, Andrew M. *Thomas Jefferson: Champion of Liberty, A History of his Life*. Pt. 1 of *The Real Thomas Jefferson*. 2d ed. American Classic Series. Vol. 1. Washington, D.C.: National Center For Constitutional Studies, 1983.

American Heritage Dictionary, 1970 ed.

Ames, William. *Marrow of Theology*. Translated by John D. Eusden. Boston: Pilgrim Press, 1968.

Aquinas, St. Thomas. *Summa Theologiae*. Vols. 1-2. Translated by Thomas Gilby and the Blackfriars. London: Eyre & Spottiswoode, 1964.

_____. *Summa Theologica*. 5 Vols. Translated by the Fathers of the English Dominican Province. 1920 rev. ed. Westminster, Md.: Christian Classics, 1981.

[Aristotle], *Posterior Analytics*. Translated by Hugh Tredennick. In vol. 2, *Aristotle in Twenty-Three Volumes*. In *The Loeb Classical Library*. Edited by G. P. Goold. Cambridge, Mass.: Harvard University Press, 1976; London: William Heinemann, 1976.

Bailyn, Bernard. *The Ideological Origins of the American Revolution*. Cambridge, Mass.: Belknap Press, 1982.

Becker, Carl. *The Declaration of Independence: A Study in the History of Political Ideas*. New York: Vintage Books, 1958.

Berens, John F. *Providence & Patriotism in Early America 1640-1815*. Charlottesville: University Press of Virginia, 1978.

Berkhof, Louis. *Systematic Theology*. Edinburgh: Banner of Truth Trust, 1941.

Berkouwer, G. C. *General Revelation*. Studies in Dogmatics. Grand Rapids: Wm. B. Eerdmans, 1955.

_____. *The Providence of God*. Studies in Dogmatics. Grand Rapids: Wm. B. Eerdmans, 1952.

Berman, Harold J. *Law and Revolution: The Formation of the Western Legal Tradition*. Cambridge, Mass.: Harvard University Press, 1983.

Biblia Sacra: Iuxta Vulgata Versionem. Vol. 2. Stuggart: Deutsche Bibelgesellschaft, 1983.

Black, Virginia. "Did Stoicism Have a Hebrew Origin?" In *Vera Lex: Historical and Philosophical Study of Natural Law and Right*. 2, no. 2. Pleasantville, N.Y.: Natural Law Society, Pace University, 1986.

Blackstone, Sir William. *Commentaries on the Laws of England.* 5 vols. Edited by St. George Tucker. Philadelphia: William Young Birch and Abraham Small, 1803; reprint, South Hackensack, N.J.: Rothman Reprints, 1969.

Boorstin, Daniel J. *America and the Image of Europe: Reflections on American Thought.* Gloucester, Mass.: Peter Smith, 1976.

————. *Hidden History.* New York: Harper & Row, 1987.

Bradford, Alden, ed. *Speeches of the Governors of Massachusetts, From 1765 to 1775; and the Answers of the House of Representatives to the Same; with Their Resolutions and Addresses for that Period.* Boston: Russell and Gardner, 1818. Text-fiche.

Bradnock, W. J., and H. K. Moulton, eds. *The Translator's New Testament.* London: British and Foreign Bible Society, 1973.

Bruce, F. F. *The Letter of Paul to the Romans: An Introduction and Commentary.* 2d ed. vol. 6, *The Tyndale New Testament Commentaries.* Leon Morris, gen. ed. Grand Rapids: William B. Eerdmans, 1985.

Brutus, Junius. *A Defence of Liberty Against Tyrants: A Translation of the "Vindiciae Contra Tyrannos."* With an historical introduction by Harold J. Laski. Gloucester, Mass.: Peter Smith, 1963.

Bryan, Robert. "History, Pseudo-History, Anti-History: How Public School Textbooks Treat Religion." *Policy Studies in Education.* Washington, D.C.: Learn, Inc., 1983.

Calvin, John. *Institutes of the Christian Religion.* 2 vols. Translated by Henry Beveridge. Grand Rapids: Wm. B. Eerdmans, 1981.

Cappon, Lester J., ed. *The Adams-Jefferson Letters.* 2 vols. Chapel Hill: University of North Carolina Press, 1959. Text-fiche.

Carson, Clarence B. *The Rebirth of Liberty: The Founding of the American Republic, 1760-1800.* New Rochelle, N.Y.: Arlington House, 1973.

[Cicero], *Cicero in Twenty-Eight Volumes.* Vol. 16. English translation by Clinton Walker Keyes. *The Loeb Classical Library.* Edited by G. P. Goold. Cambridge, Mass.: Harvard University Press, 1977; London: William Heinemann, 1977.

Commager, Henry Steele. *The American Mind: An Interpretation of American Thought and Character Since the 1880's*. New Haven: Yale University Press, 1950.

_____. *Jefferson, Nationalism, and the Enlightenment*. New York: George Braziller, 1975.

_____. *The Empire of Reason: How Europe Imagined and America Realized the Enlightenment*. New York: Oxford University Press, 1982.

The Confession of Faith; The Larger and Shorter Catechisms, with the Scripture Proofs at Large, Together with the Sum of Saving Knowledge. London: Wickliffe Press of the Protestant Truth Society, 1962.

Conkin, Paul. *Self-Evident Truths*. Bloomington: Indiana University Press, 1974.

Cranfield, C. E. B. *A Critical and Exegetical Commentary on the Epistle to the Romans*. 2 vols. *The International Critical Commentary on the Holy Scriptures of the Old and New Testaments*. Edited by J. A. Emerton and C. E. B. Cranfield. Edinburgh: T. & T. Clark, 1985.

Crowe, Michael Bertram. *The Changing Profile of the Natural Law*. The Hague: Martinus Nijhoff, 1977.

Curti, Merle. *The Growth of American Thought*. New York: Harper & Brothers, 1943.

Denny, James. *St. Paul's Epistle to the Romans*. In Vol. 2, *The Expositor's Greek Testament*. Edited by W. Robertson Nicoll. Grand Rapids: Wm. B. Eerdmans, 1961.

Durant, Will. *The Age of Louis XIV*. Vol. 8, *The Story of Civilization*. New York: Simon and Schuster, 1963.

Ebenstein, William. *Great Political Thinkers: Plato to the Present*. Hinsdale, Ill.: Dryden Press, 1969.

Finegan, Jack. *Encountering New Testament Manuscripts: A Working Introduction to Textual Criticism*. London: S.P.C.K., 1974.

Ford, Paul Leicester, ed. *The Writings of Thomas Jefferson*. 10 vols. New York: G. P. Putnam's Sons, 1892. Text-fiche.

Frisch, Morton J., and Richard G. Stevens, eds. *American Political Thought: The Philosophic Dimension of American Statesmanship.* 2d ed. Itasca, Ill.: F. E. Peacock Publishers, 1983.

Gardiner, Samuel Rawson, ed. *The Constitutional Documents of the Puritan Revolution 1625-1660.* Oxford: Clarendon Press, 1979.

Garraty, John A. *The American Nation: A History of the United States to 1877.* 5th ed. New York: Harper & Row, 1983.

Garrigou-Lagrange, Reginald. *Providence.* Translated by Dom Bede Rose. St. Louis: B. Herder, 1937.

Gay, Peter. *The Enlightenment: An Interpretation, The Rise of Modern Paganism.* New York: Alfred A. Knopf, 1967.

Glare, P. G. W., ed. *Oxford Latin Dictionary.* Oxford: Clarendon Press, 1982.

Goodrich, Charles A. *Lives of the Signers of the Declaration of Independence.* 4th ed. Boston: Thomas Mather, 1834.

Goold, William H., ed. *The Works of John Owen.* Vol. 10. London: Banner of Truth Trust, 1967.

Goudzwaard, Bob. *Capitalism and Progress: A Diagnosis of Western Society.* Translated by Josina Van Nuis Zylstra. Toronto: Wedge Publishing Foundation, 1978; Grand Rapids: William B. Eerdmans, 1978.

Grimm, Harold J. *The Reformation Era 1500-1650.* 2d ed. New York: Macmillan Publishing Co., 1973.

Gummere, Richard M. *The American Colonial Mind & The Classical Tradition.* Cambridge, Mass.: Harvard University Press, 1963.

Harris, R. Laird, Gleason L. Archer, and Bruce K. Waltke. *Theological Wordbook of the Old Testament.* 2 vols. Chicago: Moody Press, 1980.

Harrison, R. K. *Introduction to the Old Testament.* Grand Rapids: Wm. B. Eerdmans, 1969.

Hendrikson, William. *Exposition of Paul's Epistle to the Romans.* Vol. 12, *The New Testament Commentary.* Grand Rapids: Baker Book House, 1981.

Herberg, Will. "Religion and Education in America." In *Religious Perspectives in American Culture*. Vol. 2, *Religion in American Life*. Edited by James Ward Smith and A. Leland Johnson, 11-51. Princeton, N.J.: Princeton University Press, 1961.

Herbert, Jerry S., ed. *America, Christian or Secular?: Readings in American Christian History and Civil Religion*. Portland, Ore.: Multnomah Press, 1984.

Hofstadter, Richard. *Anti-intellectualism in American Life*. New York: Alfred A. Knopf, 1970.

Hooker, Richard. *Of the Laws of Ecclesiastical Polity*. Edited by A. S. McGrade and Brian Vickers. Abridged ed. London: Sidgwick & Jackson, 1975.

Hudson, Winthrop S. *Religion in America: An Historical Account of the Development of American Religious Life*. 3d ed. New York: Charles Scribner's Sons, 1981.

Hunt, George L., ed. *Calvinism and the Political Order*. Philadelphia: Westminster Press, 1965.

Jackson, Samuel Macaulay. *The New Schaff-Herzogg Encyclopedia of Religious Knowledge*. Grand Rapids: Baker Book House, 1950.

Johnson, Merwyn S. *Locke On Freedom: An Incisive Study of the Thought of John Locke*. Austin, Tex.: Best Printing Company, 1978.

Kenyon, F. G. *The Text of the Greek Bible*. 3d ed. Revised and augmented by A. W. Adams. London: Duckworth, 1975.

Kittel, Gerhard, and Gerhard Friedrich, eds. *Theological Dictionary of the New Testament*. 10 Vols. Translated by Geoffrey W. Bromiley. Grand Rapids: Wm. B. Eerdmans, 1974.

Koch, Adrienne. *The American Enlightenment: The Shaping of the American Experiment and a Free Society*. New York: George Braziller, 1965.

Ladd, George Eldon. *The New Testament and Criticism*. Grand Rapids: William B. Eerdmans, 1967.

Leith, John, ed. *Creeds of the Churches: A Reader in Christian Doctrine from the Bible to the Present*. 3d ed. Atlanta: John Knox Press, 1982.

Lessnoff, Michael. *Social Contract*. Atlantic Highlands, N.J.: Humanities Press, 1986.

Locke, John. *An Essay Concerning Human Understanding*. 2 vols. Collated and annotated, with biographical, critical and historical prolegomena by Alexander Campbell Fraser. New York: Dover Publications, 1959.

_____. *An Essay Concerning Human Understanding*. Edited with an introduction, critical apparatus, and glossary by Peter Nidditch. Oxford: Clarendon Press, 1975.

_____. *Essays on the Law of Nature. The Latin Text with a Translation, Introduction, and Notes, Together with Transcripts of Locke's Shorthand in His Journal for 1676*. Edited by W. von Leyden. Oxford: Clarendon Press, 1954.

_____. *"The Reasonableness of Christianity" with "A Discourse on Miracles" and part of "A Third Letter Concerning Toleration."* Edited by I. T. Ramsey. Stanford, Calif.: Stanford University Press, 1958.

_____. *The Second Treatise of Government*. Edited by Thomas Peardon. New York: Liberal Arts Press, 1956.

Lovelace, Richard R. *The American Pietism of Cotton Mather: Origins of American Evangelicalism*. Grand Rapids: Christian University Press, Eerdmans, 1979.

Masselink, William. *General Revelation and Common Grace*. Grand Rapids: Wm. B. Eerdmans, 1953.

Matthews, Richard K. *The Radical Politics of Thomas Jefferson*. Lawrence, Kan.: University Press of Kansas, 1984.

McCarthy, Rockne, James Skillen, and William Harper. *Disestablishment a Second Time: Genuine Pluralism for American Schools*. Grand Rapids: Christian University Press, 1982.

McNeill, John T., ed. *Calvin: Institutes of the Christian Religion*. 2 vols. Translated by Ford Lewis Battles. Vol. 20, The Library of Christian Classics. Philadelphia: Westminster Press, 1960.

_____. *The History and Character of Calvinism*. London: Oxford University Press, 1954.

Metzger, Bruce M. *Manuscripts of the Greek Bible: An Introduction to Greek Paleography*. New York: Oxford University Press, 1981.

Metzger, Bruce, ed. *The Apocrypha of the Old Testament*. RSV, 2d ed. New York: Oxford University Press, 1977.

Miller, Perry. "The Marrow of Puritan Divinity." In *Essays in American Intellectual History*. Edited by Wilson Smith. Hinsdale, Ill.: Dryden Press, 1975.

_____. *The New England Mind: From Colony to Province*. Cambridge: Harvard University Press, 1953.

_____. *The New England Mind: The Seventeenth Century*. Cambridge: Harvard University Press, 1954.

Morais, Herbert M. *Deism in Eighteenth Century America*. New York: Columbia University Press, 1934; London: P. S. King & Son, 1934.

Morey, Robert A. *When Is It Right to Fight?* Minneapolis, Minn.: Bethany House, 1985.

Morison, Samuel Eliot. *The Intellectual Life of Colonial New England*. Ithaca, N.Y.: Cornell University Press, 1956.

Morris, Lynne, ed. *The Christian Vision: Man in Society*. Hillsdale, Mich.: Hillsdale College Press, 1984.

Moulton, John Hope, ed. *A Grammar of New Testament Greek*. Vol. 3, Syntax by Nigel Turner. Edinburgh: T. & T. Clark, 1963.

Murray, John. *Calvin on Scripture and Divine Sovereignty*. Grand Rapids: Baker Book House, 1960.

_____. *The Epistle to the Romans*. 2 vols. *The New International Commentary on the New Testament*. F. F. Bruce, gen. ed. Grand Rapids: Wm. B. Eerdmans, 1959.

Nash, Ronald H. "Rights." In *Baker's Dictionary of Chrisitian Ethics*. Edited by Carl F. H. Henry. Grand Rapids: Baker Book House, 1973.

_____. *The Word of God and the Mind of Man*. Grand Rapids: Zondervan, 1982.

New Catholic Encyclopedia, 1967 ed. s.v. "Natural Law," by B. F. Brown.

Noll, Mark. "The Image of the United States as a Biblical Nation, 1776-1865." In *The Bible in America: Essays in Cultural History*. Edited by Nathan Hatch and Mark Noll, 39-58. New York: Oxford University Press, 1982.

_____. *One Nation Under God? Christian Faith and Political Action in America*. San Francisco: Harper & Row, 1988.

Noll, Mark, Nathan Hatch, and George Marsden. *Search for "Christian" America*. Westchester, Ill.: Crossway Books, 1983.

North, Gary, ed. *The Theology of Christian Resistance*. Vol. 2, *Christianity & Civilization*. Tyler, Tex.: Geneva Divinity School Press, 1983.

Orr, John. *English Deism: Its Roots and Its Fruits*. Grand Rapids: Wm. B. Eerdmans, 1934.

The Oxford English Dictionary, 1933 ed.

Packer, J. I. "A Christian View of Man." In *The Christian Vision: Man in Society*. Edited by Lynne Morris, 101-119. Hillsdale, Mich.: Hillsdale College Press, 1984.

Parrington, Vernon L. *The Colonial Mind 1620-1800*. New York: Harcourt Brace Jovanovich, 1954.

Perry, Lewis. *Intellectual Life in America: A History*. New York: Franklin Watts, 1984.

Perry, Richard L. *Sources of Our Liberties: Documentary Origins of Individual Liberties in the United States Constitution and Bill of Rights*. Rev. ed. Chicago: American Bar Foundation, 1978.

Peterson, Merrill D. *Thomas Jefferson and the New Nation*. London: Oxford University Press, 1970.

Plass, Edward M., ed. *What Luther Says: An Anthology*. 3 vols. St. Louis: Concordia Publishing House, 1959.

Rushdoony, Rousas John. *Foundations of Social Order*. Fairfax, Va.: Thoburn Press, 1978.

Rutherford, Samuel. *Lex Rex or The Law and the Prince*. London: John Field, 1644; reprint, Harrisonburg, Va.: Sprinkle Publications, 1982.

Schaeffer, Francis. *How Shall We Then Live?* Old Tappan, N.J.: Fleming H. Revell, 1976.

Schaff, Philip, ed. *The Creeds of Christendom with a History and Critical Notes*. 3 vols. 6th ed. Revised by David S. Schaff. Grand Rapids: Baker Book House, 1983.

Schlereth, Thomas J. *The Cosmopolitan Ideal in Enlightenment Thought*. Notre Dame: University of Notre Dame Press, 1977.

Singer, C. Gregg. *A Theological Interpretation of American History*. Rev. ed. Phillipsburg, N.J.: Presbyterian and Reformed Publishing Co., 1981.

Sivan, Gabriel. *The Bible and Civilization*. New York: New York Times Book Co., 1973.

Smithline, Arnold. *Natural Religion in American Literature*. New Haven: College & University Press, 1966.

Solberg, Winton U. *Cotton Mather, "The Christian Philosopher," and the Classics*. Reprinted from the *Proceedings of the American Antiquarian Society*, vol. 96, pt. 2, Oct. 1986. Worchester, Mass.: American Antiquarian Society, 1987.

Stephenson, Carl, and Frederick George Marcham. *Sources of English Constitutional History: A Selection of Documents From A.D. 600 to the Interregnum*. Vol. 1. New York: Harper & Row, 1972.

St. John of Damascus. *An Exact Exposition of the Orthodox Faith*. Translated by S. D. F. Salmond. In vol. 9, *The Nicene and Post-Nicene Fathers*. Edited by Philip Schaff and Henry Wace. Grand Rapids: Wm. B. Eerdmans, 1979.

Strauss, Leo. *Natural Right and History*. Chicago: University of Chicago Press, 1953.

Tierney, Brian. "Tuck on Rights: Some Medieval Problems." *History of Political Thought* 4, no. 3 (Winter, 1983): 429-41.

_____. "Villey, Ockham, and the Origin of Individual Rights." In *The Weightier Matters of the Law: Essays on Law and Religion*. Edited by John Witte, Jr. and Frank S. Alexander. Atlanta: Scholars Press, 1988.

Tillett, Wilbur Fisk. *Providence Prayer and Power: Studies in the Philosophy, Psychology and Dynamics of the Christian Religion*. Nashville: Cokesbury Press, 1926.

Tindal, Matthew. *Christianity as Old as the Creation*. London: n.p., 1730; reprint, New York: Garland Publishing, 1978.

Tuck, Richard. *Natural Rights Theories: Their Origin and Development*. Cambridge, England: Cambridge University Press, 1979.

Villey, Michel. "Turns and Movements in the Natural Law Tradition: Answer to Questions." Interview in *Vera Lex: Historical and Philosophical Study of Natural Law and Right*. 6, no. 1. Pleasantville, N.Y.: Natural Law Society, Pace University, 1986.

Weiner, Philip P., ed. *Dictionary of the History of Ideas*. New York: Charles Scribner's Sons, 1973.

White, Morton. *The Philosophy of the American Revolution*. Oxford: Oxford University Press, 1978.

Wigram, George. *The Englishman's Hebrew and Chaldee Concordance of the Old Testament: Numerically Coded to Strong's Exhaustive Concordance*. Grand Rapids: Baker Book House, 1980.

Wigram, George, and Ralph Winter. *The Word Study New Testament and The Word Study Concordance*. 2 vols. Wheaton, Ill.: Tyndale House Publishers, 1978; Pasadena, Calif.: William Carey Library, 1978.

Witherspoon, John. *Lectures on Moral Philosophy*. Edited by Varnum Lansing Collins. Princeton, N.J.: Princeton University Press, 1912. Text-fiche.

Wolters, Albert M. *Creation Regained: Biblical Basics for a Reformational Worldview*. Grand Rapids: William B. Eerdmans, 1985.

Woodbridge, John, Mark Noll, Nathan Hatch. *The Gospel in America*. Grand Rapids: Zondervan, 1979.

Wright, Louis. *Magna Carta and the Tradition of Liberty*. U.S. Capitol Historical Society and the Supreme Court Historical Society, 1976.

Yolton, John W. *Locke: An Introduction*. Oxford: Basil Blackwell, 1985.

ABOUT THE AUTHOR

LAWYER, LINGUIST, HISTORIAN, AND THEOLOGIAN, Gary Amos is uniquely qualified to show how the Bible and Christianity influenced the writing of the Declaration of Independence. Mr. Amos has earned the Juris Doctor degree and also holds a B.A. degree in history, pre-law, and theology. He is a member of the Bar of the Commonwealth of Virginia. Currently he teaches law and government in the College of Law and Government at CBN University in Virginia Beach.

Gary and his wife, Carol Ann, live in Virginia Beach, Virginia with their three children, Derek, Karissa, and Trinity.

The typeface for the text of this book is *Baskerville*. Its creator, John Baskerville (1706-1775), broke with tradition to reflect in his type the rounder, yet more sharply cut lettering of eighteenth-century stone inscriptions and copy books. The type foreshadows modern design in such novel characteristics as the increase in contrast between thick and thin strokes and the shifting of stress from the diagonal to the vertical strokes. Realizing that this new style of letter would be most effective if cleanly printed on smooth paper with genuinely black ink, he built his own presses, developed a method of hot pressing the printed sheet to a smooth, glossy finish, and experimented with special inks. However, Baskerville did not enter into general commercial use in England until 1923.

Substantive Editing:
Michael S. Hyatt

Copy Editing:
Nancy Willis

Cover Design:
Kent Puckett Associates
Atlanta, Georgia

Page Composition:
Xerox Ventura Publisher
Printware 720 IQ Laser Printer

Printing and Binding:
Maple-Vail Book Manufacturing Group
York, Pennsylvania

Dust Jacket Printing:
Weber Graphics, Chicago, Illinois